MR.
SINGLE SHOT'S
GUNSMITHING
IDEA BOOK

MR.
SINGLE SHOT'S
GUNSMITHING
IDEA BOOK

BY FRANK DE HAAS

 TAB BOOKS Inc.

BLUE RIDGE SUMMIT, PA. 17214

FIRST EDITION
FIRST PRINTING

Copyright © 1983 by Frank de Haas
Printed in the United States of America

Library of Congress Cataloging in Publication Data

de Haas, Frank.
Mr. Single Shot's gunsmithing-idea book.
Includes index.
1. Rifles, Single-shot.   2. Gunsmithing.   I. Title.
II. Title: Mister Single Shot's gunsmithing-idea book.
ΓS536.S5D4   1983   683.4″22   82-19441
ISBN 0-8306-0111-2
ISBN 0-8306-1511-3 (pbk.)

Contents

Introduction

The letters *f* and *g* are next to each other on a typewriter and since I am not the best typist, it happened quite frequently while writing this book that instead of typing the word *"gun*smithing" correctly it would show up as *"fun*smithing." That was all right with me because writing this book was more or less a fun project. Also since I quit active gunsmithing some fifteen years ago and resumed it as a hobby, gunsmithing or funsmithing a single-shot rifle is the one and same thing to me. For that matter, working on a single-shot rifle has always been fun from the first firing pin I made from a nail for my newly acquired Stevens Little Scout many years ago to the lock latch I made this morning for my latest .22 single-shot rifle. Anyway, I hope you will enjoy reading this book and that it will make gunsmithing a single-shot a fun thing for you.

There are ever so many people who are familiar with sporting firearms in general but who have little or no knowledge about single-shot rifles or their actions. Many gunsmiths, both amateur and professional, can be included in this group. Somewhere along the line in their gun education, the single-shot rifle book passed them by. The result is that many of these people think of the single-shot as a "simple shot," so simple that it is not worthy of consideration. True, a few single-shot rifles are extremely simple, but not the better ones. If you do not believe this now, you will the first time you disassemble and reassemble the Browning M-78 or the Ruger No. 1.

The complete single-shot rifle gunsmith—that is, a gunsmith who can make one or do any gunsmithing job that might be required on these rifles—must wear many hats. He needs to wear a machinist's hat, a stockmaker's hat, a metal finisher's hat, a small parts maker's hat, and shooter's cap. He also ought to wear a student's cap to enjoy reading and learning about single-shot rifles, a handloader's hat to understand the rudiments of reloading, and an artist's beret if he is to shape a buttstock and forearm that look and feel right. Where can you get all these hats? You can get them in adult night school classes, from gun books and magazines, and from diligent practice of these gunsmithing arts.

While the title suggests that this is a gun-smithing book, it is an idea book for the single-shot rifle gunsmith. In this book you won't find out how to turn down a barrel, or how to crown one, or how to thread it to fit an action. Neither will you find instructions on how to checker a gunstock, install a forearm tip or inlet a forearm. Nor do I have anything on gun bluing, installing scope mounts, or sharpening a drill bit or chisel. These and many more gunsmithing tasks and tricks are more than amply covered in other books and manuals. It has been my experience that most amateur single-shot gunsmiths want *ideas* more than they want detailed instructions on how to carry them out. Where I do give such instructions or describe how I've performed a task, that is not to say that my way is the best way for you. Taking the finger lever for an example, there is not just *one* way to alter it but a dozen or more ways. Just look closely at the rifles and actions in this book and you will see what I mean. Maybe you have your own idea about how a finger lever should be shaped; then by all means go ahead and alter your lever according to your liking.

In the past I have often been accused of promoting the wholesale butchering of single-shot rifles that are of collector value, and that I have caused many collectible single-shots to be altered. This is not entirely true. At one time most single-shot rifles were very common and cheap, and I saw nothing wrong in making an alteration or doing a remodeling job on them. Today it is a different matter with respect to the obsolete single-shots. If, for example you have an original Winchester Model 85, Stevens No. 44 or 44½, Sharps-Borchardt or Remington rolling block in restorable or better condition, it would be a downright shame to remodel or alter it in any way. Restoring a single-shot rifle, however, is another matter.

The point is that there are plenty of single-shot rifles around that are no longer original or that are ruined beyond restoration, and I see no objection in gunsmithing these rifles. I estimate that at least half of all the obsolete single-shot rifles made (which would amount to a quarter million Stevens boy's rifles, half a million Remington rolling blocks, and up to 70,000 Winchester high-walls and low-walls) have been gunsmithed or altered extensively at one time or another. It is the rifles in this category that will not be devalued by re-gunsmithing and updating if that work is properly done. If you have one of these rifles and you want to make it shootable (or *more* shootable), go right ahead and do it, and I hope this book will be of guidance to you. Have the barrel rechambered or rebored, reline the barrel, rebarrel the action, restock the gun, mount a scope on it, bush the firing pin and alter the finger lever, or whatever. I have written Chapters 1, 2, and 3 especially for you. The truth is that I have re-gunsmithed some of my own single shots from time to time. It is a grand pastime and hobby.

Virtually every gunsmithing item in this book (except lathes, milling machines, and the rifle actions themselves) is available from Brownell's Inc., of Montezuma, Iowa. Brownell's have been in business for years supplying the needs of amateur and professional gunsmiths all over the world. They put out a wonderful catalog that is a *must* for all gun tinkerers. The catalog costs two dollars but is worth every penny, listing everything from abrasives to zeroing-in devices, from barrels to wrenches, and from checkering cradles to gun screws. Scopes and mountains, gunstock finishes, bluing supplies, springs, gun and gunsmithing books, and any conceivable type of hand gunsmithing tool—you name it, and if it has to do with gun building, gun fixing, gun refinishing, or gun know-how, it's in that catalog and Brownell's has it in stock. I urge you to get a copy now and save yourself a bunch of time later on.

Much of the material in this book is reprinted from previous articles of mine. Some of this material is reprinted in its original form and the remainder of it revised, enlarged, and combined with related material, all with new and additional illustrations. I wish to thank the editors and publishers of the following magazines for permission to reuse this material: *The American Rifleman, Rifle, Guns & Ammo,* and *Shooting Times*.

Chapter 1

Gunsmithing the Winchester Single-Shot

The Browning-designed Winchester Model 85 falling block single-shot actions are covered thoroughly in Chapter 28 in my book *Single Shot Rifles and Actions*. It covers all the variations of this action, including the high-wall and low-wall models (Fig. 1-1), as well as the flat-spring and coil-spring models, and includes sectional view drawings of these actions and the four different trigger systems used.

Separate Winchester single-shot actions are about impossible to obtain. These rifles in original and very good condition are now valued collector items and priced accordingly, and obtaining one of these actions by purchasing an original high-wall or low-wall rifle is also about out of the question today. Today it is frowned upon to strip an original rifle for the action, unless the rifle is in such poor condition that it cannot be restored. Also, it is considered a breech of ethics to obtain an action in this way, or to remodel or alter an original Winchester single-shot rifle. So how do you go about getting such an action if you are not fortunate enough to already own one?

Well, there were about 140,000 of these rifles made between 1885 and 1920. A lot of them have been lost or destroyed during the intervening years, so there are not that many around today. During these years, and especially during the 1920s and 1930s, a great many of these rifles were remodeled, altered, and converted so that they are no longer original. Serious collectors often refer to these as "butchered" rifles. Often the rifles *were* butchered. Also during this time a great many of these rifles were stripped for their actions and new rifles built on them. The result is that there are many thousands of non-original high-wall and low-wall Winchester rifles around, and these are the ones to look for if you want such an action. You may have to buy a lot of stuff you don't want or need to get the action, but there is nothing you can do about that.

Today, as in the past, it seems like the low-walls are the most common and most easily obtained. This action should be limited to rimfire cartridges like the 5MM Remington, .22 Long Rifle, and the .22 WMR (Fig. 1-2), and to small centerfire cartridges like the .22 Hornet, .22 Jet, .218 Bee,

1

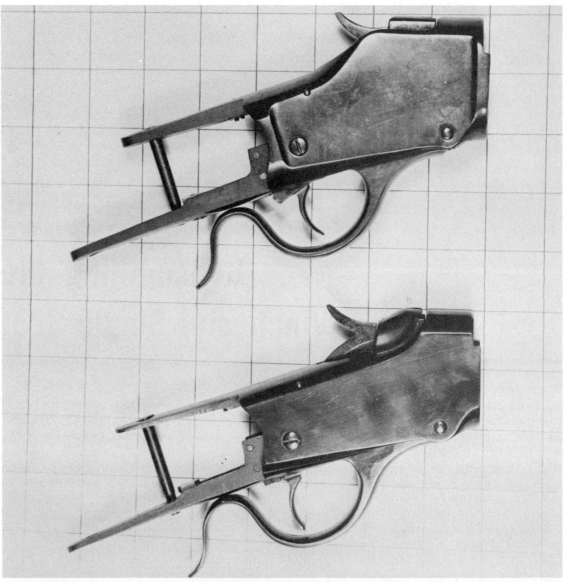

Fig. 1-1. Photographed over a one-inch grid background, the Winchester low-wall action (lower) can be compared to the high-wall action (above).

.25-20, .256 Magnum, and .351 Magnum.

The high-wall is much stronger than the low-wall because the high receiver walls gives more support to the breechblock, and is therefore a much more desirable action on which to build a rifle. This action (Fig. 1-3) is suitable for rebarreling to almost any rimmed cartridge, both commercial and wildcat, and in all calibers from .17 on up to .50. It has long been a favorite action on which to build a custom varmint rifle in calibers like the .22 2R Lovell, .219 Wasp, .219 Improved Zipper (Fig. 1-4), 6MM/.30-30 and .25 Krag. With a suitable extrac-

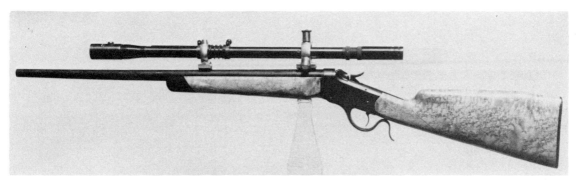

Fig. 1-2. A lightweight small game and varmint rifle built on the Model 85 Winchester low-wall rimfire action. It has a 22″ barrel chambered for the .22 WMR cartridge. The stock and forearm are made of birdseye maple, and the scope is the ⅞″ Litschert of eight power.

tor modification, this action will also handle modern rimless cartridges like the .17 Remington, .222, .20-250, .243, and others.

Most parts of the high-wall and low-wall Winchester actions are interchangable. Spare parts are hard to find; if any parts are needed they may have to be handmade. When making parts a suitably strong steel should be used as required, and if necessary, properly hardened and tempered. Except as will be noted, remodeling and alterations can be done on both actions.

FIRING PIN ALTERATIONS AND BREECHBLOCK BUSHINGS

Most of the Winchester single-shot rifles were originally chambered for low and moderately pres-

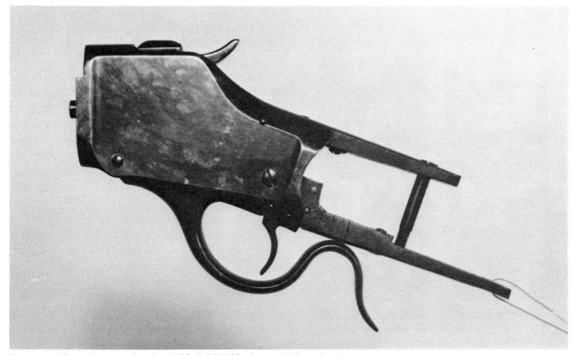

Fig. 1-3. A fine color case-hardened Model 85 Winchester high-wall action.

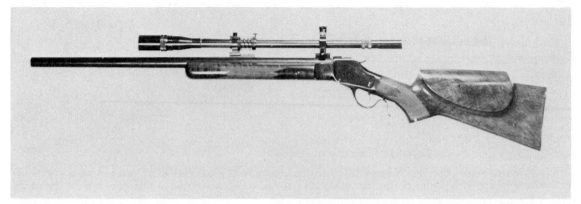

Fig. 1-4. A fine example of a custom varmint rifle built on the Winchester Model 85 high-wall action by the late Harvey Lovell. It is chambered for the Lovell .219 Improved Zipper cartridge, and carries the Unertl 1¼" 10 power target scope.

sured cartridges (Fig. 1-5). Unless the firing pin is properly altered there is a good chance that the high pressure cartridge primer will rupture and let powder gases past the firing pin and into a shooter's face, or even worse, blow the firing pin out of the

breechblock. Also, the poorly fitting pin tip may allow the primer to flow back around the edges of the hole and prevent easy opening of the action.

The original firing pin hole can be closed by welding, but the usual practice is to bush the old firing pin hole with a threaded plug and drill a small hole in this to form the bushing. The firing pin tip is then made smaller to snugly fit this hole.

To install the threaded bushing, drill out the old firing pin hole with a #28 drill and tap 8×40. Tin the threads of the 8×40 scope mounting screw and the threads in the hole, and while the block is still hot, turn the screw in until its end is flush with the main diameter of the firing pin hole. When block has cooled, saw off the screwhead and file level with the breech face. Make up a pilot drill and drill the plug through from the rear of the breechblock. Complete the alteration by filing or turning down the original firing pin tip to fit snugly in the new hole, while free to retract easily.

If the original firing pin tip is badly eroded or broken off, install a new tip. File off the original tip level with the body of the main firing pin and place the main pin in the breechblock along with the retainer screw. Insert a 5/64" drill through the hole in the bushing and drill into the firing pin body far enough to spot the location of the new firing pin tip. Remove the firing pin body from the breechblock and continue to drill the hole until it is about ⅜" deep. The new tip is made from a piece of 5/64" spring or music wire, or from the shank of the drill

Fig. 1-5. The faces of two Winchester high-wall breech-blocks; at left is a block from an early black powder cartridge rifle that has a large diameter firing pin tip hole and that is badly eroded, and on the right is a very late block from a rifle chambered for a smokeless powder cartridge.

used to drill the hole, and sweated in place with soft solder. Then clean off excess solder and fit the pin in the breechblock. Bend the tip if it binds, then file it down until it protrudes no more than .050″ from face of the block when the firing pin is fully depressed. Remove the firing pin and file and polish the tip to a hemispherical shape.

A much stronger bushing (Fig. 1-6) can be made by drilling the main diameter of the firing pin hole clear through the face of the breechblock with a 5/16″ drill. With the breechblock held in a drill press vise, enlarge this hole in the face to 21/64″ and about ¼″ deep. Thread to the bottom with a ⅜″×24 tap. Make the bushing of a ⅜″×24 SAE threaded heat-treated bolt, turning it in the hole very tightly. Saw the bolt off close to the breech face and carefully file smooth. Drill the bushing and fit the firing pin as described above. Drill the hole in the bushing with a new drill so that the hole does not become oversized. The firing pin tip must fit the hole snugly.

If a metal-turning lathe is available, a new bushing can be fitted by boring out the face of the breechblock. This is necessary if the face of the block is badly eroded, which they often are (Fig. 1-7). Bore the face out about 3/16″ deep and large enough to remove the pitted area, up to ⅝″ diameter if necessary. Turn the bushing from drill rod to a tight press-fit in the breechblock. It can be cross-pinned in place or held in place by two small screws along its edge after the bushing is filed flush with the breech face. After the screws are fitted, they too are filed flush with the face. If it is a loose fit, the bushing can be silver-soldered in place, after which it is dressed down flush with the face of the block.

If a .22 rimfire action is to be used for the .22 WMR cartridge, the location of the firing pin need not be changed, but it is advisable to bush the firing pin hole by one of the methods described and make the new firing pin hole 5/64″.

Most low-wall breechblocks which were originally made for the .22 rimfire cartridge, as well as some similar high-wall blocks, have a sloped U loading groove at the top of the face. When an action with this block is used with small centerfire cartridges like the .22 Hornet, .218 Bee, .22 Jet, .256

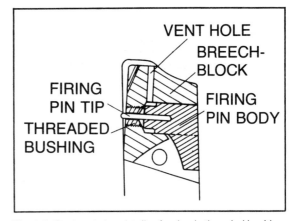

Fig. 1-6. Sectional view details of a simple threaded bushing system. This bushing method can be used with almost any single shot rifle action. See text for full details.

Magnum or .357 Magnum, no concern need be given to its safety even though a bit of the cartridge rim is visible when the action is closed. However, if desired, this groove can be filled with steel weld, or a large diameter bushing can be fitted which will cover the entire cartridge head and thus partly fill this groove.

Drilling a 5/64″ vent hole through the top of the breechblock is suggested if it has not been previously vented. If it does have an old vent hole and if the block has been fitted with a bushing, make sure the vent hole extends into the firing pin hole.

If the firing pin hits too low, the linkage between the finger lever and the breechblock may be worn, or the finger lever bent. New link pins may remedy this; otherwise a new link can be made with holes farther apart. If the finger lever is bent, it should be straightened, or it should be bent to obtain a straight-line linkage as described later on. The firing pin does not have to hit the primer dead center to obtain good ignition, but it should hit fairly close to center.

A SAFETY FIRING PIN

Many years ago, when gunsmith Adolf O. Neidner, Franklin W. Mann, and others began experimenting with high-velocity cartridges, the Winchester high-wall was one of their favorite actions. They considered it as strong as any falling

Fig. 1-7. The faces of three Model 85 Winchester breechblocks. The one on the left is from a low-wall action which has been bushed, but the pitting around the bushing indicates the bushing may have been improperly installed and that it should be redone. On the right is an early breechblock with a badly eroded face which most certainly needs its face restored by the installation of a large diameter bushing. The breechblock in the center has a large diameter bushing installed and its eroded face restored.

block action made at that time. But when working with high-pressured cartridges, they found out that the firing pin was its weak point. No doubt they discovered that a ruptured primer could not only result in gases being blown back along the firing pin, but could blow the entire firing pin out—both conditions being very serious. To correct this design fault, Neidner and Mann developed a gasproof and blowout-proof firing pin for this action which later became known as the Mann-Neidner safety firing pin. It is absolutely the best and safest firing pin system for this action, and I recommend that such a pin be installed in every low-wall and high-wall action that is to be used with a modern centerfire cartridge.

I do not know the exact details and arrangement of the original "Mann-Neidner" firing pin for the Winchester single-shot action, and I doubt whether Neidner always made them alike in the many actions in which he installed them (Fig. 1-8).

There is more than one way to make and install a safety firing pin such as this in these actions; the one you choose, or the method you use, will depend on your gunsmithing skill and the tools and equipment you have. A lathe is necessary to install this firing pin.

In the article "Gunsmithing the Winchester Single-Shot" (*The American Rifleman*, Nov. and Dec. 1965), drawings and instructions are given for two ways to make and install the safety firing pin, and mine is the simple one in the November issue. I learned about this method of installing the safety pin from master single-shot rifle gunsmith. Alferd Loetscher of Sibley, Iowa. My method is not an exact copy of Loetscher's method, but is one which I have worked out after installing a lot of these safety firing pins. My method is quite flexible, and I believe it is the easiest way to make and install such a pin. At any rate, made and installed as shown in Figs. 1-9 and 1-10 and described here, the firing pin

6

Fig. 1-8. Neidner installed a safety firing pin in this high-wall breechblock and it is essentially the same as the one described in the text. This also shows the method Adolph Neidner used to lighten the hammer by cutting out its center. It also shows one of the finger lever alterations he used, and this is a good one.

is not likely to ever puncture a primer, the primer is not likely ever to flow back into the edges of the firing pin hole, no powder gases can escape to the rear past the firing pin stem, the firing pin cannot be blown out under any condition, and dry-firing or snapping the rifle will not harm the firing pin or breechblock.

Before describing this safety firing pin, another matter ought to be considered. As made by Winchester, when the action is closed the toggle linkage between the finger lever and the breechblock moves well past the dead center location. This causes the breechblock to lower slightly on the final closing motion of the finger lever, and to rise slightly again when the action is opened. This is an annoyance as the depressed firing pin can't be entirely freed before this rising of the breechblock on opening the action. To relieve this annoyance and possible breakage of the firing pin tip, the finger lever should be bent so that the pins in the linkage will be in a straight line when the action is fully closed.

To bend the lever, a simple bending jig should be made as shown in Fig. 1-11. Using the finger lever as a guide for locating the pins, drill the two holes for the holding pins, drive in the pins, and then drill the hole for the stop pin as indicated. With the

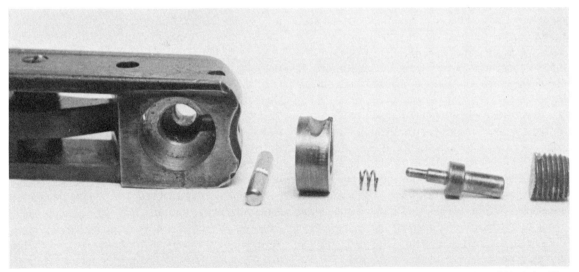

Fig. 1-9. Parts of the Mann-Niedner type safety firing pin as I made them. From left to right: bored-out breechblock, bushing retainer pin, bushing, retractor spring, firing pin and plug. The plug, once turned in tightly, is never removed again.

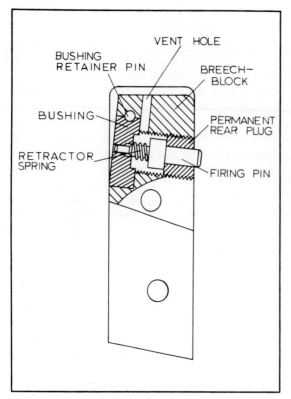

Fig. 1-10. The Mann-Niedner type safety firing pin for either the Winchester low-wall or high-wall breechblocks. See text for further details.

jig held in a vise, heat the finger lever in the spot indicated, and bend the lever until it touches the stop pin. If any other work is to be done with the finger lever such as reshaping its fingerpiece, it should be done now. Afterwards, polish and refit the lever.

Generally, when making the safety firing pin for the flat-mainspring action, nothing more need be done before or after installing the new pin. However, after the new pin has been installed, check the action to see that the hammer, under mainspring tension, rests firmly against the breechblock when the action is fully closed, and that on the initial swing of the finger lever on opening the action that the firing pin retracts before the breechblock moves. If neither takes place, the toe on the hammer against which the mainspring bears should be carefully built up or cut down as required.

When making and installing a safety firing pin in the coil-mainspring action, a new link with a longer spur must be made and the front face of the hammer altered so that the initial downward swing of the finger lever tips the hammer back to allow the firing pin to retract .060″ before the breechblock begins to lower. It is even a good thing to do this with the flat-mainspring action. Make the new link and reshape the front of the hammer about as shown in Fig. 1-12 so that when the action is fully closed and the hammer down, the hammer barely touches the spur on the link, so that on opening the action, the link pushes the hammer back sufficiently to allow the firing pin to retract before any downward movement of the breechblock begins.

The procedure for installing the safety firing pin is described below. A metal-turning lathe is needed, as well as a drill press. The breechblock can usually be worked without first annealing it, but if you find it too hard to cut, then anneal it. If it must be annealed, then it should also be hardened again, and I'd recommend carborizing to be done by a heat-treating firm.

Using a drill press, and holding the breech-block in a drill press vise, drill the original firing pin hole clear through with a 5/16″ drill. Notice that the original firing pin hole is at an angle in the breechblock. Turn the block over and redrill the hole with a 21/64″ drill from the face of the block, taking care that the drill is in line with the original hole. With the block still in the drill press vise, remove the drill and put a ⅜″×24 tap in its place and start the tap into the block by hand. This assures correct alignment of the tap with the hole. After it is well started, remove the block with tap in place to a bench vise and continue to tap the hole clear through the block. Now place the breechblock in a four-jaw lathe chuck with the breech face parallel with face of the chuck and centered with the tapped hole. It need not be precisely square or exactly centered; being off a little bit won't do any harm. Now turn or bore a recess in the face of the block about ¼″ deep and about ⅝″ in diameter. The exact depth and diameter is also not too important here.

Bore the recess very carefully, getting the sides and bottom square and smooth. Now remove

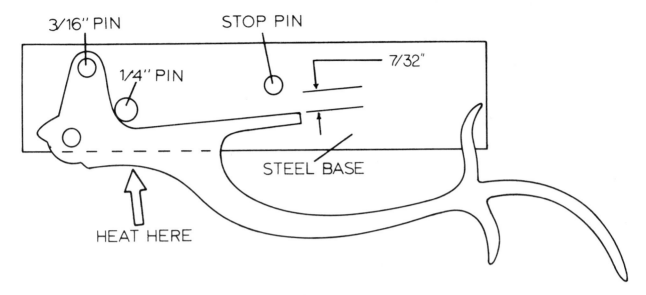

Fig. 1-11. Bending jig for the Winchester single-shot finger lever with lever in place. Make the base of the jig from a piece of ½" thick cold rolled steel and fit the three pins as shown. Hold the jig in a vise, heat the lever with an acetylene torch at the spot indicated, and bend the lever until stopped by the stop pin. This bending is necessary to stop the toggle linkage on dead center rather than well past dead center. See text for further details.

the block from the lathe. Turn one end of a piece of drill rod to fit snugly into the recess. Bevel off the edge of the turned drill rod so it will "bottom" solidly in the recess.

Before removing the drill rod from the chuck, cut a ⅜" recess in the end of the rod about 1/16" deep, as shown in the drawing. Cut this end from the rod leaving it about ⅜" long and place it into the block. With a C-clamp holding the plug bushing in the block, drill a 3/32" hole through top of the block so it goes through the edge of the plug. Fit a steel pin in this hole (drill rod is ideal). Now file the plug level with the face of the breechblock. Take a ⅜"×24 SAE bolt and cut off the end of the threaded part, leaving ¼" of threads. Face this end off square and turn this bolt into the rear of the breechblock very tightly. It need never be removed again. Cut off the bolt shank and file the remaining plug flush with the rear of the block.

Now assemble the breechblock, link, and finger lever in the action and mark the location of the new firing pin hole. The action must be barreled to do this and the marking punches to use are de-

scribed in Chapter 2. When the hole location has been marked and centerpunched deeper, place the breechblock in a drill press vise with the face of the block square with the drill. Using a new 1/16" short shank drill, drill entirely through the block, first through the plug bushing and then through the ⅜" plug through the rear.

Remove the bushing from face of the block and redrill the 1/16" hole in the rear plug with a 3/16" drill for the body of the new firing pin. Also enlarge the 1/16" hole in the bushing from the rear with a ⅛" drill to ⅛" deep.

Make a new firing pin from a piece of 5/16" drill rod making the small tip (1/16") and rear body (3/16") extra long so they can be shortened in the final fitting. Make the base of the firing pin tip ⅛" in diameter. Provide a small coil spring of three to four coils to fit around this base. Make the shoulder on the pin to a width which allows approximately .10" movement in the block. With the firing pin and retractor spring in place in the breechblock, file the tip flush with the breech face. Now shorten the 3/16" body of the firing pin so it protrudes only

.055" from the rear. Remove the firing pin from the block and round the tip to a hemispherical shape and polish. Also slightly bevel the edges of the rear of the pin. Reassemble the firing pin and spring in the block and make final adjustments. Firing pin tip protrusion can be between .050" minimum and .060" maximum, but ideally, with the hammer resting against the rear of the breechblock, the tip should protrude from the front .055".

The final step is to redrill the vent hole to 3/32" diameter from the top of the breechblock into the open space inside ahead of the firing pin shoulder. Also cut off the bottom end of the original firing pin retainer screw and replace it in the breechblock.

Note that earlier I indicated the firing pin tip should be of 5/64" (.078") diameter, while for the safety firing pin I gave the tip size as 1/16". Many gunsmiths recommend the 1/16" pin tip whenever a

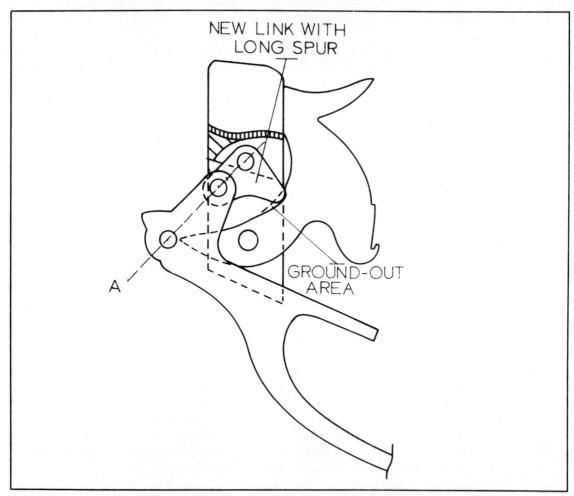

Fig. 1-12. This sectional view drawing shows how the finger lever, toggle linkage, link, and hammer should be when a Model 85 breechblock has a Mann-Niedner firing pin fitted in it. This is a "must" with the coil spring action, and often needed and desirable with the flat spring action. The finger lever is bent (see Fig. 1-11) so as to place the toggle linkage pins in a straight line (dotted line A), a new link made with a longer spur and possible wider spacing of the holes (up to .425"), and the lower face of the hammer ground away for the link spur as shown, so that when the hammer is fully down, the spur just contacts the hammer so that on the first pivotal movement of the link on opening the action, the link will retract the hammer sufficiently to allow the firing pin to retract before the breechblock begins to move down. See text for further details.

single-shot action is used with a modern high-pressure cartridge, but it should be noted that most modern bolt action rifles (including the 1903 Springfield, F.N. 98 Mauser, Model 70 Winchester) have firing pin tips approximately 5/64″ in diameter. While the 1/16″ tip may provide more safety to the shooter than the larger 5/64″ tip, it is not as strong and is more easily broken. The smaller tip is also generally preferred for cartridges using small primers, such as cartridges like the .17 Remington and the .222 series. However, due to the design and construction of the original Winchester single-shot firing pin (which is placed under some torque when it is forcibly retracted by the link), if this pin is made or fitted with the 1/16″ tip, the tip is much more likely to bend and be broken off than if made with the larger 5/64″ tip. No torque is placed upon the safety firing pin, so with it the 1/16th inch tip will stand up. Even so, since the firing pin is easier to make with the 5/64″ tip, I prefer this size even with the safety firing pin.

The important thing with either size is the fit of the tip in the firing pin hole; it must be a snug yet bind-free fit. Equally important is the roundness and smoothness of the end of the tip and the protrusion of the tip from the breech face.

EXTRACTOR ALTERATIONS

The Winchester single-shot action was made mainly with two types of extractors, the narrow hooked type for rimmed centerfire cartridges and the half-circle type for .22 rimfire cartridges. There is not much metal in the upper stem of the extractor and it is not overly strong to extract a tight case from a chamber, but there is little room in the action for a heavier extractor stem. However, the weakest part of the extractor is the hook itself, and this can be made wider and heavier when reworking the extractor. Rebuilding and altering both the hooked and half-circle extractors is not difficult and Fig. 1-13 shows how I do this.

If, for example, an action with a .22 WCF, .25-20, or 2R Lovell extractor is being rebarreled or rechambered for a cartridge of a larger rim size, all that has to be done is to shorten the hook by filing or grinding to nearly the edge of the new chamber and

then finishing and recessing with the chambering reamer. If you feel the hook ought to be strengthened, then rebuild the entire hook as shown in Fig. 1-13.

If the action being rebarreled has an extractor with a hook too short for the cartridge selected, or if the hook is pitted, worn, or if it has been previously welded or worked on, then the hook must be lengthened or rebuilt as shown. Some gunsmiths merely build the end of the hook with steel weld, and this is okay if the welding is skillfully done. But I much prefer to rebuild the hook, replacing the original thin and weak hook with a larger and stronger one by silver-soldering on a piece of steel as shown in Fig. 1-13 and dressing it down as required. You can rebuild and shape the extractor hook first, then cut the slot in the barrel to accept it, or you can cut the slot first and then shape the

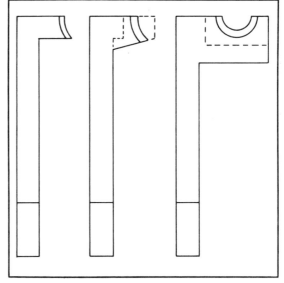

Fig. 1-13. Rimmed extractor alterations: At left is a standard extractor for a small diameter rimmed cartridge like the .22 WCF. When the rifle is rechambered or rebarreled for a larger diameter rimmed cartridge, the hook need only be shortened. If the extractor hook is eroded, broken, or needs to be lengthened for a smaller diameter cartridge, then silver-solder on a piece of metal as shown in dotted lines on the center extractor, and shorten as required. On the right is the rimfire extractor; if it must have the rim recess area renewed, then cut out the damaged section as shown on dotted lines, silver-solder on a new piece of metal, and trim and recut as required. See text for further details.

rebuilt extractor hook to fit the slot, or shape the extractor hook and cut the slot in the barrel at the same time as a single operation. I prefer the latter procedure, although I shape the hook the size I want it first and then cut the slot, doing it as a joint operation. The top edge of the extractor hook should be exactly on the horizontal centerline across the face of the barrel.

The half-circle rimfire extractor calls for special treatment for repair and alteration. The purpose of this type of extractor is to support the cartridge head at this point and to prevent the small rimfire cartridge from slipping past the extractor when loading. In selecting an action for use with the 5MM Remington, .22 Long Rifle, or .22 WMR cartridges, choose one that was originally a .22 rimfire with original half-circle extractor.

Worn, rusted, and pitted half-circle extractors may no longer adequately support the cartridge head. This condition is corrected by cutting out a sizable section from the extractor as shown in Fig. 1-13 and silver-soldering in a new piece. This piece should be thicker and larger than needed, with the excess filed off after it is silver-soldered in place. After the barrel has been fitted and the extractor fitted in the breech face of the barrel so that the breechblock can be easily closed, the center of the new metal inlay is cut out with a round file to the size of the bore, or to allow the entrance of the chambering reamer pilot. With the breechblock removed, but with the extractor held in place by the finger lever pin, the barrel is chambered by hand. In this way the chambering reamer cuts out the extractor to exactly match the chamber and cuts in the rim recess at the same time.

I have used the hook-type extractors in these actions with rimfire cartridges when I had no half-circle extractor available, or when the original half-circle extractor was damaged beyond repair. In this event, merely cut off most of the original extractor top and rebuild it like the regular hook extractor as described previously. Fit the extractor in the usual way and finish it while cutting the chamber. To prevent the small rimfire cartridges from overriding the hook, as well as to prevent the hook from slipping past the rim when extraction

takes place, limit the movement of the extractor to about half its original swing, or to a point where it is impossible to slip a cartridge in the chamber ahead of it. Do this by cutting down the step on the extractor base where it contacts the step on the breechblock as the action is opened, and providing a stop on the forward edge of the extractor stem so it can't swing out too far. This stop can be a strip of metal silver-soldered in place. It will then be necessary to extract the cartridge cases all the way from the chamber with the fingernail. No single-shot rifle fan will object to this, but it's practical only with the low-wall action.

RIMLESS CARTRIDGE EXTRACTORS

Altering the Winchester single-shot extractor to handle a rimless cartridge like the .222 Remington or .243 is not difficult. The extractor must not only move backward and forward on opening and closing the action, but it must also move slightly sideways. This is necessary because, first, the cartridge must chamber without interference from the extractor and also fly free when extracted, and second, when the cartridge is in the chamber and the action is being closed, the extractor must be able to slip over the rim and then snap into the extractor groove. To get this side motion, the top part of the extractor is made narrower and a spring is provided to hold the extractor hook in the cartridge extractor groove.

The original extractor is used in this modification. The stem of the extractor is about .150″ thick and the average depth of the extractor groove in a rimless cartridge is about .032″. To allow sufficient lateral movement, the extractor stem must be tapered, leaving the bottom the original thickness and the top about .115″. To do this, file the metal from the left side of the extractor, removing slightly more metal from the top than the depth of the case extractor groove. The extractor hook is shortened or lengthened as needed, or rebuilt first, and the extractor is fitted to the barrel after the barrel is fitted and chambered. With the top part of extractor against the side of the receiver, the hook end is filed down level with the chamber wall plus a few thousands more so the cartridge can be chambered without touching the hook. The forward edge of the hook is given a bevel and a rim recess if filed on its face to allow the spring-backed extractor to slip over and engage the rim.

A spring is needed to push the extractor hook to the right so it will not slip out of the extractor groove. However, spring tension must only be applied to the extractor when the hook is close to and behind the rim—not when the extractor is in the extended position, for then the extractor must be free to fall to the left so the hook will not interfere with loading or ejection.

There are several ways to provide this spring tension to the extractor. One way is shown in Fig. 1-14. A hole is drilled through the left receiver wall and a round-ended plunger fitted to bear on the extractor as shown. This is under tension of a small leaf spring attached to the side of the receiver.

Another way to provide spring tension to the extractor is shown in Fig. 1-15. Here the spring and plunger are fitted to the extractor stem and concealed within the action. The extractor is filed thinner and tapered as in Fig. 1-14. In about the midway

point of the extractor stem, and near the front edge, drill a #31 hole through the extractor and bevel the right side of the hole with a larger drill. Make a small round-end plunger with a slight flare on the other end for this hole. The rounded end should protrude about .050". About ¼" below this hole, drill and tap another hole for a very small screw.

From a piece of thin clock spring, fashion a leaf spring about ⅛" wide to bear against the plunger. To make room for the spring and screwhead, some metal must be removed from the left side of the finger lever base. Determine where and how much metal to remove by fitting the extractor and finger lever in place and then remove enough metal to

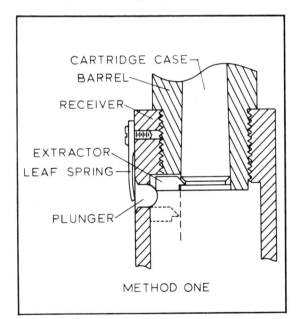

Fig. 1-14. Rimless extractor—Method 1. Top sectional view of a rimless extractor system for the Model 85 Winchester action. Drawing is self-explanatory, but additional details are contained in the text.

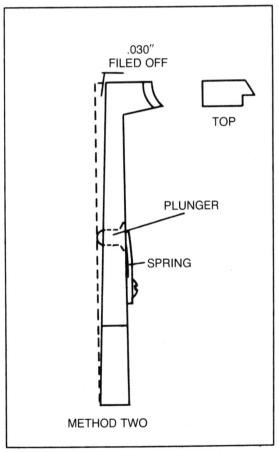

Fig. 1-15. Rimless extractor—Method 2. Details of a simple rimless extractor for the Model 85 Winchester; see text for details.

allow the lever to close without touching the screw or spring.

A small detent must be made inside the receiver wall into which the plunger can fall when the extractor is extended. Assemble the plungered extractor, breechblock, and finger lever into the receiver and operate the action a number of times—or, with the action open, depress the top of the extractor against the side wall and move it back and forth a few times so the plunger will leave a track where it slides. Remove the parts from the receiver and using a round emery burr in a hand grinder, grind out a small hollow at rear end of track to accept the plunger.

A third way to provide spring tension to the extractor is shown in Figs. 1-16 and 1-17. This method is best adapted to the low-wall actions and a few high-wall musket actions with the milled cut and screw hole in the front of the receiver for the

original .22 ejector spring. This method can also be used in other actions as well by providing a screw hole and spring groove without weakening the action.

The cut can be made with a hacksaw blade and the hole drilled and tapped for a 6×48 screw. First file a beveled slot on the left side of the extractor stem in line with the spring slot. The slot on the extractor stem must be beveled from rear to front to the width of the stem as shown in Fig. 1-17. The spring is of .040″ spring wire looped at one end for screw attachment to the receiver. It is bent at right angles to extend into the receiver and should be just long enough to remain under the extractor when it is extended, and its end bent so the extractor is not under tension when action is fully open. The extractor is then free to move against side of the action. As the action is closed and extractor depressed, the spring contacts the beveled slot and

Fig. 1-16. Rimless extractor—Method 3. A simple rimless extractor design for the Model 85 Winchester actions. The wire spring is fastened to the front of the receiver as shown and its end projects rearward to contact a beveled groove on the extractor stem. See text for more details.

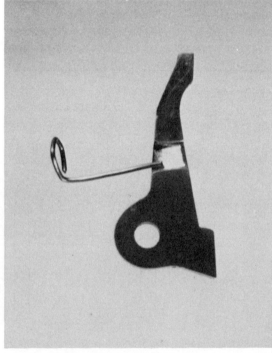

Fig. 1-17. Spring and beveled side of the extractor for the rimless extractor, Method No. 3.

Fig. 1-18. A Neidner remodeled high-wall action, showing lower tang bent for a pistol grip.

pushes the extractor hook to the right so it snaps behind the cartridge rim.

REMODELING THE GRIP

The usual practice in restocking the Winchester single-shot rifle is to make a pistol grip stock for better handling and looks, and to fasten the buttstock to the receiver with a throughbolt. This will improve appearance and accuracy of the rifle.

There are several methods of altering the lower tang for a pistol grip stock. The simplest is to bend the lower tang just behind the tang screw hole (Fig. 1-18). To bend a smooth curve in the tang it is necessary to heat it red-hot. When doing this, first remove the knock-off spring from the tang, but do the bending with the tang screw in place in order to avoid squashing its threaded hole. To bring the comb line further forward, up to ⅜″ of the end of the upper tang can be cut off; the end can be left square or made rounded as desired. Don't shorten the lower tang, and *do* use the wood screw in its end as its use greatly helps secure the stock to the action. This sort of grip is adequately close to the trigger for average-sized hands and the stock fastening is fully adequate for most shooting.

If a closer pistol grip is wanted (one which places the grip closer to the trigger), the lower tang

can be bent beginning just behind the knock-off spring screw hole. When this is done it will be necessary to redrill and tap the tang screw hole, and perhaps make a new tang screw from a ¼″×28 bolt.

The most popular method is to bend the lower tang into a full pistol grip starting at the tang screw hole and then fitting a block between the tangs in place of the tang screw, as shown in Fig. 1-19. The block may be either a ½″ square or round bar. It is silver-soldered to the lower tang, and attached to the upper one by a short ¼″×28 screw through the original tang screw hole. This allows the lower tang to be removed from the action.

A favorite method of mine is shown in Fig. 1-20. Here the bar is positioned farther forward and is welded or silver-soldered to the upper tang. It is located directly over the knock-off screw and is attached to the lower tang by a longer knock-off spring screw tapped into the square bar. After fastening the bar in place, the ends of the tangs are cut off flush with it. The lower tang, to be removed, must have the two ridges on its upper surface filed off. This alteration gives the closest possible pistol grip and simplifies inletting the stock to the action.

The throughbolt hole is drilled lenthwise through the buttstock. Drill the hole as close as possible in the center of the stock, and then use this hole to spot the location of the hole in the tang bar, which is then drilled and tapped. It is best to anchor the threaded throughbolt to the bar with a crosspin,

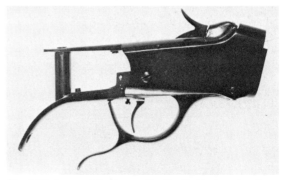

Fig. 1-19. A remodeled low-wall action that is rigged up for a through-stock bolt. On this action the tang bar is silver-soldered to the bent lower tang and fastened to the upper tang by a screw in the original tang screw hole. Note finger lever alteration.

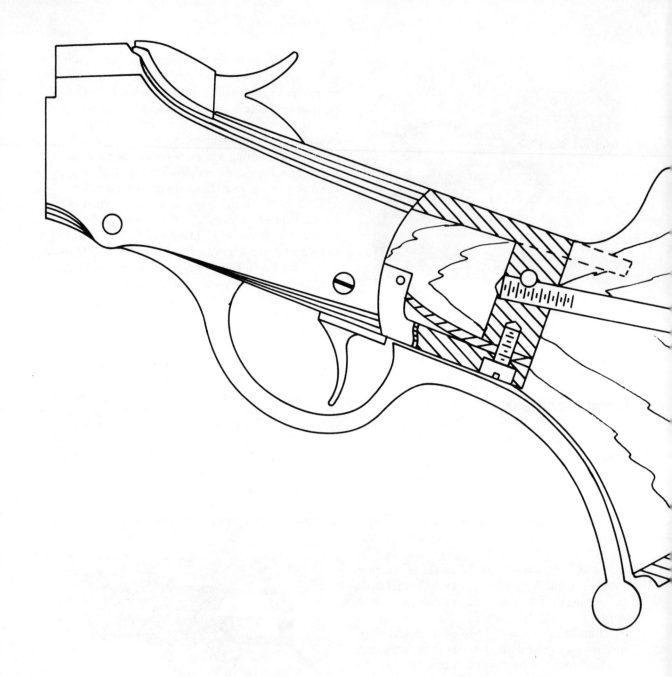

Fig. 1-20. This drawing shows a suggested method of altering the finger lever, altering the tangs for a through-stock bolt

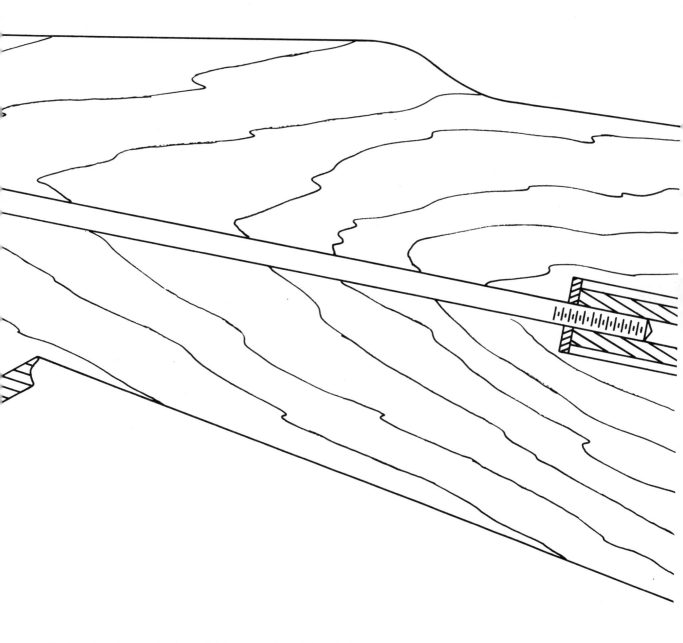

attachment, and suggests shape of pistol grip and comb. See text for details.

and then use a nut or threaded sleeve on the other end to tighten the stock to the action.

The top tang can be shortened, but it never should be bent.

Semi-finished and semi-inletted buttstocks in three styles (original, classic, and custom varmint) are available for the Winchester high-wall action from Reinhart Fajen Inc., (Box 338, Warsaw, Mo. 65355). The same stock will fit the low-wall musket, and can also be used on the flat-side low-walls. Semi-finished replacement duplicates of the original Scheutzen-style are also available from some gunsmiths.

FINGER LEVER CHANGES

The original finger lever (Fig. 1-21) cannot be improved upon if the rifle is to retain the straight grip, or if restocked with a long or normal pistol grip wherein the lower tang is bent behind the tang screw hole. However, if the action is altered for a close and full pistol grip, the finger lever should be altered to avoid a crowded grip. I like to do this by cutting off the original hook from the end of the finger lever, and then welding the sawed-off hook back on (Fig. 1-22). This method gives a slimmer pistol grip and no part of the lever interferes with the gripping of the rifle. Also, much less swinging room is required when opening the action. I also

like this method of altering the finger lever when the action is fitted with set triggers.

Another method is to cut off the original hook and then weld on a piece of strap iron to be bent along the inside curve of the pistol grip as shown in Fig. 1-20. The end of the lever is fitted with a round ball.

Still another way is shown in Fig. 1-23, wherein a loop is made of strap iron and welded on to the altered finger lever and bent to the shape of the bent lower tang. In all cases, considerable filing has to be done to shape the new lever to blend with the original part of the lever. For those who want to make a Schuetzen-type lever, Fig. 1-11 shows an original version of this lever on the finger lever bending jig.

BARRELS

Turned, threaded, and chambered barrels in various calibers are available for the Winchester high-wall action from G. R. Douglas Inc., (5504 Big Tyler Rd., Charleston, West Virginia 25312). These pre-chambered barrels are chambered deeper than necessary so that each barrel can be properly fitted to the individual action, with the breech end faced off as required to obtain correct headspacing. A lathe is almost essential in fitting these barrels. They are available in several standard

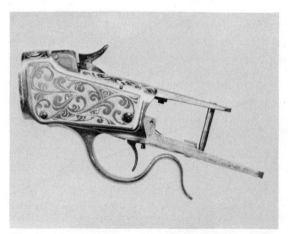

Fig. 1-21. This engraved early version low-wall action with the original S-shaped finger lever is ideal with a straight grip stock.

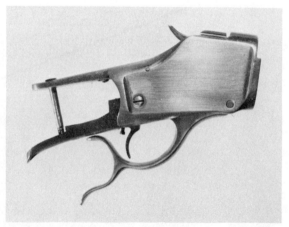

Fig. 1-22. An ideally shaped finger lever for the Winchester high-wall.

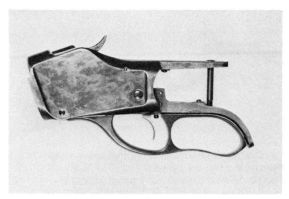

Fig. 1-23. A fine custom reworked high-wall action with a lower tang bent for a pistol grip.

weights and contours, from light sporter to heavy target weights. The No. 4 barrel (26″ long and .650″ at the muzzle) is a good choice for a light rifle; the No. 5 (26″ long and .700″ at the muzzle) is fine for a medium-weight varmint rifle (Fig. 1-24); but my first choice would be the No. 6 for a varmint rifle. This barrel has a straight taper, is 26″ long, and .750″ in diameter at the muzzle.

To be well-proportioned, the high-wall rifle should have a barrel at least 26″ long. A barrel 28″ long (Fig. 1-25 is perhaps the ideal length, and

some single-shot fans prefer the 30″ length. A 24″ barrel looks good on the low-wall, provided it is not too slender or heavy, but a 26″ barrel looks even more classy. Full octagonal and part octagonal barrels are also available and these really add class to these rifles. These barrels are expensive and it takes more time to install them, but many fans don't mind the extra expense. The full and part octagonal barrels should be tapered, as opposed to the low-cost untapered drawn octagon barrels that some firms are selling.

Figure 1-26 gives the specifications of the barrel shank and threads of these actions.

The same procedure is followed in fitting a barrel to these actions for any other single-shot rifle. With the barrel blank between lathe centers, the breech end is turned down and threaded. The barrel should fit the receiver tightly, because in fitting the extractor the barrel may have to be removed and replaced a number of times and the threads should still provide a snug fit when the fitting is done. Make the shank a bit longer than needed at the start, then face it off squarely to the correct length so the breechblock can be raised and lowered in the action with the finger lever while barrel is set up in place.

Fig. 1-24. My own custom long-range varmint rifle built on a Winchester Model 85 Schuetzen double set trigger action. The No. 5 26″ Douglas barrel is .700″ in diameter at the muzzle, chambered for the .25 Krag Short Ackley cartridge, and has a rifling twist of one turn in ten inches. On the barrel is mounted Unertl 1¼″ Varmint scope of ten power. The wood is A Fancy grade from Reinhart Fajen Inc. The buttstock is Fajen's "classic" design and is fitted with a Neidner-type checkered steel buttplate and pistol grip cap. The fine checkering was done by my son and the engraving was done by Neil Hartliep of Fairmont, Minnesota. The rifle as shown weighs ten pounds, and is extremely accurate.

Fig. 1-25. A fine target rifle in .45-70 built on the high-wall action by George Meyer. A Numrich 28″ heavy barrel blank with a 1-in-22 rifling twist was used. The front sight is a Redfield International and the rear sight is the obsolete Vaver micrometer target sight attached to a special base milled to fit on the rear target scope base. The stock and forearm are of fancy French walnut. The rifle weighs about eleven pounds.

Before the barrel shank is faced off, check the face of the breechblock against the square face of the breech end of the barrel and make any corrections necessary. If the block has been bushed or dressed down, it may be entirely true or flat, and in this case the high spots should be leveled out prior to final fitting. There should be .001″ gap between the block and barrel on final fitting. The extractor is fitted after the barrel has been properly fitted, and if an extractor alteration is required, it should be done prior to the fitting of the extractor. Fitting the extractor is painstaking work; for the amateur gunsmith it is best all done with files.

After the barrel has been fitted, it is removed from the receiver and chambered just deep enough to allow the head of the cartridge to be flush with the face of the barrel breech so that the headspace is the space left between the barrel and the breechblock after the barrel is screwed in tight. First rough out the chamber and then use the finishing reamer to

cut the chamber nearly full depth. The extractor is fitted at this point, filing its end so that it is level with the chamber. Now turn the barrel in, and with the extractor in place, final chambering is done *through the receiver*, cutting the rim recess in the extractor at the same time.

FITTING THE MAINSPRING

After the barrel and extractor have been fitted, it is necessary to fit the mainspring, unless the action is of the coil-spring variety. To attach the original mainspring base it is necessary to cut a large dovetail slot in the bottom of the barrel. The original barrel can be used as a guide in locating the exact position of the slot. The hole in the dovetail base must be exactly 3-1/16″ ahead of the inside face of the receiver. An alternate method is to modify the original base by cutting off the dovetail portion, drilling out the threaded hole, and attaching both mainspring and base (which acts only as a

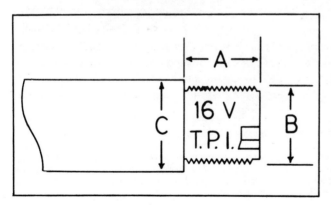

Fig. 1-26. Barrel shank and thread specifications for the Model 85 Winchester actions.

	A	B	C
High-wall*:	.850″	.935″	1.100″
Low-wall:	.845″	.825″	1.00″

*Some high-walls have same thread specifications as low-walls and vise versa.

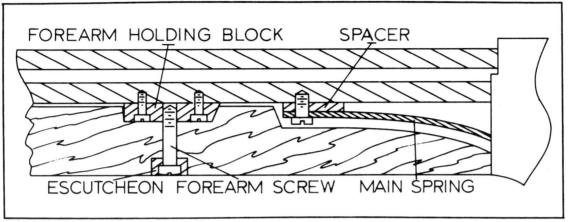

FOREARM HOLDING BLOCK   SPACER

ESCUTCHEON   FOREARM SCREW   MAIN SPRING

Fig. 1-27. Method of attaching forearm and mainspring to the barrel.

spacer now) to the barrel with a 10×32 screw. This method is not recommended for a very slim or large caliber barrel because the tapped hole should be at least 3/16″ deep to hold the screw securely. New replacement mainsprings, both the flat and coil types, for these actions are available from Christy Gun Works (875-57th Street, Sacramento, California 95819).

FOREARM ATTACHMENT

On all the Model 85 Winchester rifles except the muskets, the forearm is attached with a single screw threaded into a stud which is in turn dovetailed into the barrel. This is as good a method to attach a forearm as any, and especially so if you have the original forearm stud and screw and if the forearm is similar in size and length to the original. If the original forearm stud is not available, the forearm can be attached to the barrel by a single 10×32 screw threaded directly into the barrel at about the midpoint of the forearm. If the forearm is much longer and heavier than the original, then two screws can be used, spacing them about 6″ apart. An escutcheon should always be provided in the forearm for the head of the screw.

A preferred forearm attachment method, when the barrel may be sensitive to forearm pressure (such as when a large forearm is used on other than the very heavy barrels) is to attach a forearm mounting block to the barrel with two 8×40 screws and thread the forearm holding screw into it, as shown in Fig. 1-27. Make the block of ⅜″ square stock about 1¼″ long and groove one side to fit the barrel circumference. As shown in Fig. 1-27, slope both ends of the block and carefully inlet the forearm over it. If preferred, a glass bedding compound can be used around the block. After forearm is inletted over the block, remove the forearm and drill a hole for the holding screw from the center of the block recess through the bottom of the forearm.

Use this hole as a guide to spot the hole in the block for the forearm screw, as well as for the escutcheon. After the forearm is fully inletted and attached, the barrel channel can be relieved to clear the barrel which gives a nearly full-floating barrel.

(Author's note: This chapter is largely excerpted and revised from an article which first appeared in the November and December 1965 issues of *The American Rifleman*, and it appears here with permission.)

Chapter 2

Gunsmithing the Rolling Blocks

Hardly any mention is made of rolling block actions and rifles in any of the numerous gunsmithing books that have been published, despite the fact that the rolling block has been around since about 1865. This might be because these actions and rifles were never around in quantity until after World War II, at which time—and all of a sudden—the gun market was flooded with them when thousands upon thousands which Remington originally made for countries like Argentina, Mexico, Cuba, Spain, Egypt, and others began coming back home via the surplus arms importer.

Not that there weren't already a lot of rolling block rifles around in the U.S. before World War II, since they were regularly available from Bannerman at very low prices for many years before, but it was not until about that time—when most of the other better single-shot actions were "used up"— that the amateur gunsmiths became aware of the possibilities of the single-shot action with the rolling block.

While the gunsmithing books have nothing much on remodeling or building sporting arms on these actions, a number of the gun magazines in recent years have published some excellent articles on gunsmithing the rolling block. In this connection, I would like to think that my article on this subject which appeared in the March, 1967, issue of *The American Rifleman* was among those most helpful to the home gunsmith.

In the several years that have gone by since writing that article, I have gathered much more information about rolling block rifles and actions, including more dope on remodeling and rebuilding. In that *Rifleman* article I included only Remington rolling block actions (Fig. 2-1), but as most single-shot fans and amateur gunsmiths know, there are other rolling block actions besides the Remington—including the Whitneys, those made by the Springfield Armory, and several foreign-made copies of the No. 1 Remington. Therefore, I'll try to cover the gunsmithing of the rolling block in detail and from every angle.

ROLLING BLOCK TYPES

In view of the number of different makes, mod-

Fig. 2-1. Here are the four principal Remington rolling block actions shown photographed on 1″ grid background. From top to bottom are: No. 4 rimfire solid-frame action; No. 2 action; No. 1½ Sporting action; and No. 1 Military action.

els, sizes, and calibers of these actions, let's start by dividing them into groups as to size, from the smallest to the largest, listing the cartridges most suitable to be used with the actions in each grouping.

Group 1

☐ Remington No. 4 (solid frame).
☐ Remington No. 4 (takedown).
☐ Crescent (takedown).

The above three actions are suitable for the following cartridges:

.22 BB or CB
.22 Short
.22 Long
.22 Long Rifle
.22 W.R.F.
.22 WMR (No. 4 Rem. Solid Frame only)
.25 Short
.25 Long
.32 Short
.32 Long

(The above are all rimfire cartridges.)

.32 Colt Short Centerfire
.32 Colt Long Centerfire
.32 S&W Short Centerfire
.32 S&W Long Centerfire

Note: I do not consider these actions to be safe enough for the 5MM Rem. Magnum cartridges.

Group 2

☐ Remington No. 2 (late version).

This action (Fig. 2-2) is suitable for any cartridge listed in Group 1, as well as the following:

.25-20
.32-20
.38 S&W
.38 Special
.38-40
.44 Special
.44-40
.45 Auto Rim
.45 Colt

Note: I consider this action as only marginal for use with the .357 Magnum, .41 Magnum, and .44 Magnum cartridges, and for the .25-20 and .32-20 high-velocity loadings.

Group 3

☐ Remington No. 1½ (Fig. 2-3).
☐ Whitney New System*.

These two actions are suitable for any cartridge

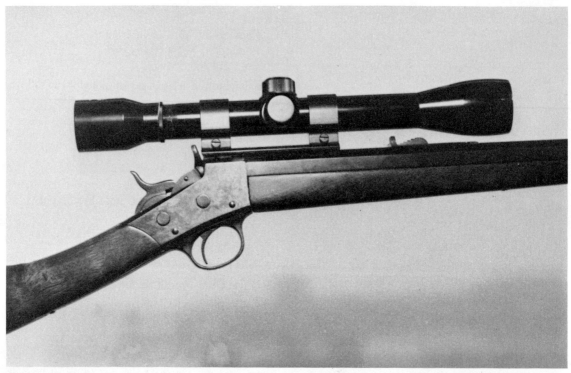

Fig. 2-2. A Remington No. 2 rifle originally in .22 rimfire caliber restored to shooting condition by reboring and rechambering the barrel to .25-20 W.C.F. The scope is mounted with Weaver tip-off rings and a tip-off base for the Marlin Model 39A.

listed in Groups 1 and 2, as well as the following cartridges:

.22 Jet
.22 Hornet
.218 Bee
.219 Zipper*
.22 Savage HP*

.256 Magnum
.25-35*
.30-30
.32 Special
.32-40*
.38-55*
.357 Magnum*

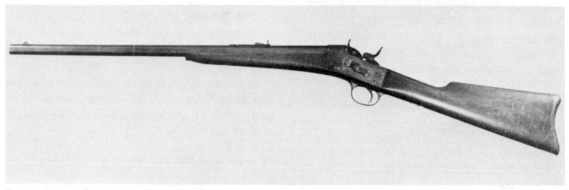

Fig. 2-3. No. 1½ Remington rolling block rifle.

.41 Magnum
.44 Magnum
.410 bore*

Note: While the Whitney New System action is as large as the Remington No. 1½, I consider it generally unsuitable for most of the cartridges in Group 3 except those marked with an asterisk (*).

Group 4

☐ Remington No. 1 Blackpowder Actions*.
☐ Springfield Navy Model 1870.
☐ Springfield Army Model 1871.
☐ Danish Model 1867
☐ Spanish-made No. 1 .43 cal.
☐ Whitney Model 1872.

*This includes the Remington-made No. 1 blackpowder actions made for Mexico, Spain, Egypt, Argentina and others made in various 11MM and .43 calibers, and includes the 7MM actions on which the last patent date is prior to 1901. The above actions are suitable for any of the cartridges listed in Groups 1, 2, and 3, as well as for the following:

.44-100 Remington Creedmoor
.444 Marlin
.45-70
.45-90
.50-70
28 Gauge
20 Gauge

Group 5

☐ Remington No. 1 Smokeless Action (Fig. 2-4) (with 1901 or later patent date)

This action (Fig. 2-4) is suitable for any of the cartridges listed in Groups 1, 2, 3, and 4, and for any of the following cartridges:

.222 Rimmed
.250-3000 Savage
.257 Roberts
7MM (7×57) Mauser
7×57R
.300 Savage
.30-40 Krag
.303 British
8×57 JR
.35 Remington
9.3×74R
.45 ACP

DESCRIPTION OF ACTIONS

The Remington No. 4 (1890-1933) is the smallest of the true Remington rolling block actions (Fig. 2-5). The No. 4 rifles were only made in the .22, .25 and .32 rimfire calibers. It was made in two styles, takedown and solid frame, with the solid frame action comprised of only 17 parts. Beside its small size, it differs from the other Remington rolling block actions in that it has only an upper tang, the receiver is a once-piece forging, and has breechblock and hammer screws instead of pins. This action is 5⅜″ long, 1″ thick, and weighs about one pound. The sidewalls are .240″ thick. The weak part of this action is the breechblock, the weak spot being the thin web of metal in front of its pivot hole. The solid frame action is much more desirable for rebarreling than is the takedown version.

The Crescent rolling block action (circa 1891-1932) is almost a direct copy of the No. 4 Remington except that the front end of the receiver is longer and that it has a different takedown system (Fig. 2-6). Like the Remington No. 4, it is a sound little

Fig. 2-4. A .45-70 sporting rifle built on the Model 1902 No. 1 Remington rolling block action.

Fig. 2-5. A No. 4 Remington action. This one is the solid-frame model which has the barrel threaded into the receiver. There are two take-down versions of the No. 4 in which the barrel is a slip-fit into the receiver and held in place by a cross turn lever or cross thumb screw.

Fig. 2-7. A refinished and color case-hardened No. 2 Remington action, my favorite.

Fig. 2-6. The Crescent rimfire rolling block action. It was used for rimfire cartridges only and is a close copy of the No. 4 Remington.

action and all of the gunsmithing suggestions and instructions given for the No. 4 apply as well to the Crescent.

The Remington No. 2 (1873-1910) action is often referred to as the "medium-sized" Remington rolling block action (Fig. 2-7). It weighs about 1 pound 4 ounces, is about 7½" long, 1" thick, and has sidewalls about .200" thick. It is readily identified by its sloping rear receiver line. It is the only Remington rolling block action in which the trigger is not in direct contact with the hammer. In former years this action was sought after for converting into a

pistol, but the high tax imposed on this practice by the Federal Firearms Act now discourages this practice. I consider this action as the best rolling block action on which to build a light small game rifle in the .22 Long Rifle, .22 WMR or .25-20 caliber. Although others have done it, I do not feel this action should be subjected to, or trusted to breech pressures of the .22 Hornet, .218 Bee, or Magnum handgun cartridges.

The Remington No. 1½ action (1888-1897) is merely a thin-walled version of the much more common Remington No. 1 action—or, in other words, a lighter and sporting version of the No. 1. The No. 1½ action weighs 2 pounds 4 ounces, is 1.140" thick, and has sidewalls about .205" thick. This action requires the same barrel shank diameter as does the smaller No. 2 Remington action. The No. 1½ is a very desirable action, but extremely hard to come by.

The Whitney New System (circa 1880-1888) rolling block action is very similar in size and weight to the No. 1½ Remington, but generally not nearly so well made or finished (Fig. 2-8). Unlike the Remington rolling block actions and the earlier Model 72 Whitney action, the New System Whitney has a round-edges receiver, which leaves less metal in the upper receiver sidewalls and thus weakens it as compared to the No. 1 Remington and Model 72 Whitney. Except for the round-edged receiver and a different extractor, this Whitney rolling block ac-

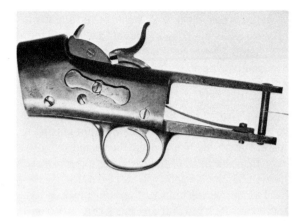

Fig. 2-8. The Whitney New System rolling block action. This action is a very close copy of the Remington No. 1 and it was the last rolling block the firm made before they sold out to Winchester in 1888.

tion is almost a direct copy of the common Remington No. 1.

The Remington No. 1 blackpowder action (circa 1867-1895) is the most common of all the rolling block actions and is represented by the Remington-made actions of .43 Spanish caliber (Fig. 2-9). It's the "large" Remington rolling block action, being 8½" long, 1.1312" thick, and weighing about 2 pounds 10 ounces. The sidewalls are about .290" thick. There are two main versions of this action: the military version with the heavy and very high hammer spur, and the sporter version with its trimmer hammer and breech block spurs. Two main types of extractors were used, the sliding type and the pivotal type, and made only for rimmed cartridges. Most of them were made with large diameter firing pin tips which are generally only suitable for low to moderate pressure cartridges.

The Springfield Model 1870 Navy rolling block action is a No. 1 blackpowder action and almost identical to the Remington above.

The Springfield Model 1871 Army action is also a No. 1, and it differs from the regular Remington No. 1 and the Navy Model 1870 in that it has a slightly different internal mechanism.

The Danish-made Model 1867 and the Spanish-made .43 caliber rolling block actions can also be placed in the Remington No. 1 group of actions; except for their firing pin retractor systems, they are almost direct copies of the No. 1 Remington military rolling block action.

The Whitney Model 72 action (Fig. 2-10) is a "blackpowder" action of the same size as the No. 1 Remington, but greatly unlike it in that it has a much different locking and firing mechanism. This action cannot be remodeled or gunsmithed to any extent. Since these Whitney rifles and actions are quite rare, few will be available for gunsmithing. However, the rebarreling, reboring, relining, and firing pin bushing information given later on can be applied to these rifles.

The Remington Model 1902 No. 1 Smokeless action (1901-1917) is the most modern, strongest, and safest of all the rolling block actions discussed here, and probably the strongest such type action ever made commercially. The most common of this action is the one which was used to make up the 7MM Mauser-calibered military rifles and carbines for Mexico and other Latin American countries. The same actions were also used by Remington for building rifles for France in the 8MM Lebel caliber. Remington also made them in other calibers such as the .30-40 Krag, .303 British, and others. Naturally, this is the most desirable action to use for building a rolling block rifle. This action has a pivotal spring extractor and the 7MM extractor will handle any cartridge of .30-06 head size, but is equally functional with large rimmed cartridges like the .444 Marlin. This action is fitted with the .080" diameter

Fig. 2-9. A refinished and color case-hardened No. 1 Remington blackpowder action.

Fig. 2-10. The Whitney M-72 rolling block action, made by the Whitney Arms Company of New Haven, Conn. Although it is a rolling block action and in the photograph it appears to be a close copy of the Remington No. 1 action (both are the same size), this early Whitney action is entirely different from the Remington system inside in that it has a separate locking cam apart from the hammer.

firing pin tip and therefore the firing pin hole does not have to be bushed. (For more detailed mechanical and structural information on these various actions the reader is referred to the book *Single-Shot Rifles and Actions* for complete details on the Remington No. 4, 2, 1½, and No. 1 actions, the Whitney Model 72 and New System actions, and the Crescent action. The data is complimented with a sectional view drawing of each action, parts photo, and assembly instructions.)

BUSHING THE BREECHBLOCK

Unless the face of the breechblock of the No. 1 smokeless action is badly corroded or the edge of the firing pin hole is eroded, nothing need be done. If there is such damage on the breechblock of this action, or on the block of any of the *other* actions, it is usually necessary to reface the breechblock or bush the firing pin hole. With any of these actions, if the tip of the firing pin is badly rusted, worn, damaged, or broken off, it will be necessary to make an entire firing pin or install a new tip on the old body.

If any of the actions other than the No. 1 smokeless are to be rebarreled or converted to a modern cartridge, the firing pin hole should be bushed and the firing pin tip made smaller or replaced with a smaller one (Fig. 2-11).

If the breechblock face is only pitted slightly it can be carefully filed down a bit with a wide mill file. This should always be done *before* rebarreling the action, and never done this way if the rifle is not to be rebarreled or relined. If there are pits around the firing pin hole, a large diameter bushing should be fitted as shown in Fig. 2-27 rather than trying to file down the face and taking a chance on not getting it square. I generally like to make the bushing slightly larger than the head of the cartridge for which the rifle will be chambered.

To bush a breechblock of a rolling block action, I set up the block in a four-jaw chuck (Fig. 2-12) on a metal-turning lathe, and bore out the bushing recess with a thin, square-faced tool. The recess is bored about 3/16″ deep and large enough to remove all the pitted area, but seldom over ⅝″ in diameter. This recess does not have to be exactly centered or square with the face of the breechblock or original firing pin hole. Next, I turn a steel plug with square end to fit the recess, leaving about .002″ clearance for silver-soldering. I leave the plug about ¼″ long. Flux the recess and the plug, place the squared end

Fig. 2-11. One of the important differences between the older blackpowder Remington rolling block action and the later smokeless action is in the size of the firing pin tip. On the left is a breechblock and firing pin from a .43 caliber action and on the right is a breechblock and firing pin from the M/02 7MM action. When the older action is to be used for any model cartridge that develops pressures over the 30,000 psi level, the firing pin hole should be bushed and the firing pin tip made smaller. Nothing has to be done to the 7MM block unless the edges of the firing pin hole have been damaged by corrosion.

Fig. 2-12. The breechblock set up in a four-jaw lathe chuck and its face bored out for a bushing.

advisable to drill the main firing pin hole to a larger diameter, drilling it all the way through the breechblock, and at the same time holding the breechblock to try to make the drill cut to the intended side of the new hole.

ALTERNATE BUSHING METHOD

Bushing a firing pin hole can also be done by tapping in a screw. Enlarge the old firing pin hole with a #28 drill, and tape with a #8×40 tap. Tin an 8×40 scope mounting screw with soft solder and also tin the threads in the tapped hole. While both the screw and the block are hot, turn in the screw to about 3/16″ depth. When cool, the head of the screw is sawed off and the remainder is filed level with the breech face.

I do *not* advise welding the firing pin hole closed as a "bushing" method, as I have seen too many breechblocks spoiled in this way.

After the breechblock face has been renewed by a plug or the large firing pin hole filled with a screw, the new firing pin hole must be spotted and drilled. Ordinarily it can be drilled out directly from the rear through the main firing pin hole. This requires a special pilot drill (Fig. 2-13) to be made. I use a 3″ piece of drill rod the size of the firing pin hole, or turn down a rod to fit snugly. (The caliber .43 breechblock usually requires a 15/64″ rod.) Chuck the rod in the lathe, center the end, and drill a 5/64″ hole about ¾″ deep. Now break off a 1″ piece from the same drill and carefully sweat (with soft solder) this into the drilled rod, leaving a ¼″ length exposed.

With this pilot drill in a hand drill, and working from the rear of the breechblock with the firing pin hole as the guide, drill through the bushing to form the new firing pin hole in correct position and of correct size.

However, if the centerfire action is to be rebarreled or otherwise converted to rimfire, or the other way around, the new firing pin hole must be spotted from the front and on the breechblock face. For centerfire, make a punch of drill rod to fit inside the case neck, the punch point to just fit the flash hole of an unprimed case and long enough to extend out of the case. The punch is then inserted into an

in the recess and, with a Prest-O-lite or acetylene torch, silver-solder the plug in place. Now carefully file the plug down level with the breechblock face and polish it with emery cloth held flat on a file.

I often employ this method in simply bushing the firing pin hole where no pitted area has to be renewed, or when changing a centerfire block to rimfire, or the other way around. In the latter case, the recess in the breechblock is bored large enough to encompass both old and new firing pin holes. When a change in firing pin hole location is intended, after making the recess for the bushing, it is

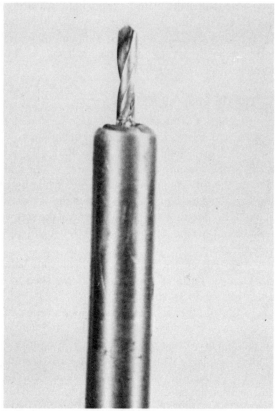

Fig. 2-13. To redrill a smaller firing pin hole in a centerfire rolling block breechblock after the bushing has been fitted, it is best to make a pilot drill as shown here by sweating in a piece of 5/64″ drill in a rod the size of the main firing pin hole.

empty case, both inserted into the chamber, the breechblock closed, and the punch tapped with a cleaning rod through the bore. For spotting a new rimfire hole, make a special punch the same size as the cartridge to be used, *including the rim*. File the head of this punch leaving a small teat on the edge of the rim at the exact location the firing pin should hit a live cartridge. After hardening, insert the punch into the chamber and tap the punch with a cleaning rod to mark the breech face.

After the location of the new hole is marked in either manner, remove the breechblock from the action and deepen the mark with a centerpunch. Now the new hole must be drilled, but special precautions must be taken to get it in line with the main firing pin hole or else the firing pin may bind.

This is best done in the following manner: Find a drill that will just enter the main firing pin hole and chuck it into the drill press. Get a short piece of 4×4 wood and drill a hole a bit more than halfway through this block, stop the drill press, and loosen the chuck, leaving the drill in the block. Now slip the breechblock over the shank of the drill and it is held in correct alignment to drill the new hole for the firing pin tip. Fasten a 5/64″ drill in the drill press, center it carefully in the centerpunch hole, and drill through into the main firing pin hole.

After the new firing pin tip hole has been drilled into a bushed breechblock, and before altering the old firing pin or making a new one, it is a good idea to taper the new hole. With a Swiss round needle file, and working from the rear of the breechblock through the main firing pin hole, carefully taper the hole. This is best done by rotating the file counter-clockwise between the fingers.

Ordinarily, with most bushing jobs, the original firing pin can be used again after the tip is carefully turned or filed down to snugly fit into the new 5/64″ hole. However, if the breechblock has been altered for a new hole location—and especially if the original main firing pin hole has been enlarged—it is necessary to make a new firing pin. Make the body section first, fitting it into the main firing pin hole.

With the body in place in the block, and with a hand drill holding a 5/64″ drill through the front of the breechblock, drill lightly into the firing pin body to spot the location of the new firing pin tip in the body. Now remove the firing pin body and drill into it at least ¼″. This hole is likely to be at the very edge of the pin body, so drill the hole at a slight angle towards the center of the body. Make the tip from a piece of 5/64″ drill rod (or from the shank of a 5/64″ drill) and silver-solder it into the hole. Bend the tip in line with the body and fit it into the breechblock. Bend, file, and polish the completed firing pin so it does not bind in the breechblock; it must be free to move from its own weight. Lastly, the tip must be shortened and rounded, to protrude out .050″ from the breech face (for centerfire; for a .22 rimfire, the tip should be rather flat with rounded edges and should protrude only .035″).

CONVERTING OTHER THAN REBARRELING

If you only have the rolling block action or a rifle on which the barrel cannot be salvaged, then rebarreling is the only course to follow to obtain a shootable rifle on the action. However, if you have a complete rifle, I would consider it unwise to rebarrel it without first considering other alternatives—especially so if it is a sporter model with an octagonal barrel. If the rifle is complete and original, it is probably worth more "as is" than it will be when rebarreled and remodeled. At any rate, it will likely be worth more rebored or relined to put it back into shooting condition than it would be if rebarreled, and by having the rifle rebored or relined it can be left in its original configuration.

There are very few rechambering possibilities with Remington rolling block rifles. I once owned a No. 1½ Remington chambered for the ".44L" centerfire cartridge. Cases to use in this rifle could be made from .30-40 Krag brass and by handloading, the rifle could be used. The groove diameter of the barrel was .429″ and the barrel could easily have been rechambered for either the .44 Magnum or .444 Marlin. As mentioned in the cartridge section of this book, some of these rifles in rimfire calibers could be made shootable with factory or handloaded ammunition by altering the firing pin from rim to centerfire without rechambering, and others by rechambering in addition to the firing pin change. To make a shootable rifle out of some of them it may be necessary to change the firing pin, rebore the barrel, and rechamber.

The rechambering possibilities are very limited, and there are some rechamberings and reborings that are out of the question. There are also some rechamberings that I would advise against. For example, rechambering (or reboring and rechambering) is just about out of the question for the rifles in .43 Spanish, .43 Egyptian, and .50-70 calibers. I also think the 7MM Mauser cartridge is just about the hottest cartridge that should be used with the Model 1902 Remington rolling block action, and that this rifle should *not* be rechambered for either the .284 or .280, and *most definitely not* for the 7MM Magnum. If you have a rolling block rifle in 7MM, and if it does have excessive headspace, then the best way to make a safe shootable rifle of it is to recess the breech face of the barrel so it will chamber the 7×57R cartridge. This recess should be .530″ in diameter and only deep enough to allow the hammer to be fully lowered with a case in the chamber, and which in any case will be slightly less than the thickness of the rim which is normally .057″.

The possibilities for reboring are many. For example, a No. 2 Remington or New System Whitney in .22 rimfire caliber could be rebored and altered to the .25-20 or .38 Special calibers; the No. 1½, No. 1 Remingtons and Model 72 Whitney in .22 rimfire can be rebored and altered to most any larger rimmed centerfire caliber, and the same rifles in .32 rimfire caliber to any larger rimmed centerfire caliber.

The original barrels in most of these old rolling block rifles are quite soft and may not wear well if many jacketed bullets are fired in them, so pick a cartridge which is factory-loaded with lead bullets. If you handload, choose a cartridge that you can handload with cast lead bullets.

The possibilities of relining are also many, although the caliber choice is somewhat limited due to limited caliber choice of liners available. At the present time about the only barrel liners available are in .22 and .45 calibers, and the .22 liners are generally only 26″ or 27″ long. A few gunsmiths will undertake to make liners in other calibers by turning down a regular rifle barrel to liner size, but doing this may not be too practical due to the cost. The best way to restore any rolling block rifle in .22 rimfire caliber with a ruined bore to shooting condition is by relining the barrel. This is especially true for the No. 4 Remington and Crescent rolling blocks in .22 rimfire caliber. These same rifles in .25 or .32 rimfire calibers can also be relined to .22 rimfire caliber, along with the necessary firing pin and extractor changes. The very excellent British-made .22 rimfire Parker-Hale liners are no longer available and the U.S.-made .22 liners like the Federal and Numrich are generally only suitable for the .22 Long Rifle cartridge, and therefore relining may be limited to the .22 rimfires.

Numrich makes .45 caliber liners suitable for

the .45-70 cartridge, and they offer a relining service for this caliber. The Numrich .45 caliber liner is .625″ in diameter and the barrel to be relined with it must be at least .875″ in diameter at the muzzle.

It takes a lot of special equipment to rebore a rifle barrel and only a few shops are equipped to do this. A listing of some of these shops can be found in the trade directory in the back of the *Gun Digest*. Relining a barrel with a straight .22 liner is not too difficult, and most amateur gunsmiths can do it even without a metal-turning lathe. Nowadays, an epoxy glue can be used to anchor the .22 liner in a barrel instead of using soft solder to sweat the liner in place. For information on how the older gunsmiths installed a barrel liner, see James V. Howes' books *The Modern Gunsmith*.

REBARRELING

Figure 2-14 and its accompanying table give the barrel shank and thread specifications for the various rolling block actions discussed here. All are threaded except the No. 4 takedown and the Crescent rifles, and note that the Crescent has a tapered shank. Those that are threaded have square threads except the No. 4 Remington and the Spanish-made .43 caliber actions, which have standard V-type threads.

To fit an unthreaded or unturned shanked barrel to any of these actions, it is necessary to have the breech end of the barrel large enough in diameter so that the shank can be turned down and threaded, and turning down the shank and threading it can only be done on a metal-turning lathe which has a bed long enough to accept the barrel between the lathe centers. I won't give instructions on how to turn and thread a barrel shank here; if you have a lathe and do not know how this is done, then get and study a lathe manual and learn how to do it. Cutting square threads with a lathe is no more difficult than cutting V threads with it. Also, due to space limitations, I must of necessity give only the briefest of instruction on barrel fitting, and therefore anyone attempting the fitting of a barrel to an action should have a gunsmithing book or two which covers all aspects of this work.

Therefore, briefly, the following steps must be

gone through to fit an unthreaded barrel to a rolling block action: Place the barrel in the lathe between lathe centers with the breech end in the tailstock center. Turn the shank down to thread diameter, making it about ⅛″ longer than the final length is expected to be. If you have it, use the shank of the original barrel from the action to take measurements from. Thread the shank, and while doing so, remove the barrel from the lathe as often as necessary to try the shank in the action.

Turn the sub-shank down. Strip the action except for the breechblock and hammer, and with the action closed and while pulling back on the breechblock so that it is in close contact with the fully lowered hammer, carefully measure with a depth micrometer the depth from the front face of the receiver to the face of the breechblock. Face off the breech end of the barrel, leaving the shank the exact length as the depth figure obtained in the preceding step. If you are not sure of yourself or the measurement, then leave the shank a few thousands longer to be trimmed to exact length later on in the lathe or by hand with a file.

Remove the barrel from the lathe, remove the hammer and breechblock from the receiver, and turn the barrel very tightly into the receiver. If there is an index mark on the receiver, mark the barrel accordingly, or index mark both the receiver and barrel, and then scribe a line on the barrel face to indicate where the semicircular breechblock cut has to be made. You can also at this time spot the location of the extractor cut that has to be made.

Remove the barrel from the receiver and with files remove metal for the breechblock cut and make preliminary cuts for the extractor. Finish the barrel fitting by testing the barrel in the receiver as often as necessary so that the breechblock can be put into place, and trim the barrel face as required so that the hammer can be fully lowered on the closed breechblock. Ideally, there should be at least .001″ space between breech face of the barrel and breechblock when the action is closed, but no more than .003″.

Chamber the barrel so that the head of the cartridge is flush with the barrel face. Make the final extractor cuts in the barrel as required for the

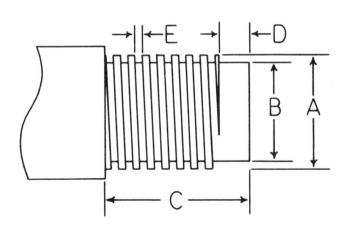

Barrel Shank and Thread Specifications

	(A) Main dia. of shank	(B) Dia. of sub-shank	(C) Shank length	(D) Sub-shank length	Type & number of threads per inch
No. 1 Rem. M/1902					
7MM Action	1.055″	1.00″	1.430″	.430″	12 square
No. 1 Rem.					
Blackpowder Action	.975″	.920″	1.418″	.418″	12 square
No. 1½ Rem.					
Sporting Action	.850″	.800″	1.443″	.500″	12 square
No. 2 Rem. Action	.850″	.805″	1.200″	.400″	12 square
No. 4 Rem. Action					
(Solid Frame Model)	.655″		.665″		16 V
No. 4 Rem. Action					
(Take-down Model)	.675″	.615″	.670″	.219″	No threads

Note: The Whitney M-72 and the New System rolling block actions are threaded almost identically as the No. 1 Remington rolling block action. The Crescent barrel shank is tapered; see separate drawing. The Spanish-made No. 1 rolling block action requires a threaded barrel shank of 1.00″ in diameter, with 14 V threads per inch but otherwise similar to the No. 1 Remington blackpowder action. Barrel shoulder diameter should be at least .050″ larger than thread diameter (A) for adequate shoulder abutment with the receiver. Remington rolling block actions, except No. 4s, have same type and number of threads, and space between threads (E on drawing) is .044″. These specifications were taken from representative barrels but may not be true for all Remington rolling block actions. One may encounter older No. 1 blackpowder actions with same thread size as the M/1902 action, or the M/1902 with the smaller thread size of the older action, etc. Thread sizes and specifications given for the No. 2 Remington action apply to the No. 7 Remington action, and also to the Remington rolling block pistols. The Model 1870 Navy and 1871 Army rolling block actions are threaded the same as the No. 1 blackpowder actions.

Fig. 2-14. Barrel shank and thread specification of Remington rolling block action.

extractor to operate properly. *Note:* With most rolling block actions the barrel cannot be removed or turned all the way in with the breechblock in place, and in most cases the extractor also must be removed. In fitting the barrel, try to make the cuts for the breechblock and extractor; do the trimming and chambering with as few barrel removals as possible because each time the barrel is screwed in tight and removed again, the threads become a bit looser. If the entire barrel has to be turned down, then this can be done after turning down the sub-shank. The muzzle can be trimmed, trued and crowned before or after the turning-down operation. A finish chambering reamer is all that is needed for the barrel chambering, and just a couple of new cartridge cases are required to gauge the headspace when doing the chambering.

BARREL BREECH BUSHINGS

It is possible, and often very practical, to fit a barrel that is too small at its breech end for the rolling block action to which you want to fit it. Such barrels can usually be fitted satisfactorily by employing a bushing on its breech end (Fig. 2-15).

For example, the No. 1 smokeless action requires that the breech end be at least 1.100″ in diameter to provide a sufficient shoulder. If, for instance, you have a barrel that is about 1″ in diameter at the breech and you want to fit it to the No. 1 smokeless action, a section of the breech end can be turned down to a smaller size and a bushing made from a piece of 1⅛″ diameter cold rolled steel and fitted to the barrel, and then the bushing turned and

threaded to fit the action. Or, to save yourself some extra work, time, and perhaps money, the bushing can be best made from the threaded end of the action's original barrel. This applies to all of the actions which have threaded shanks. Since it is almost necessary to use a milling machine to cut the groove in the barrel shank for those actions having sliding extractors, I almost always use the original threaded shanks for barrel bushings for rebarreling these actions.

These bushings can be attached in three ways depending on caliber of the barrel and the length of the bushing. For .22 rimfire calibers, if the bushing is made three inches long or more, the bushing can be attached satisfactorily with soft solder. With a bushing this long, and if the inside of the bushing and the barrel shank are rough, I believe a good epoxy cement would also do.

The bushing can also be threaded on the barrel.

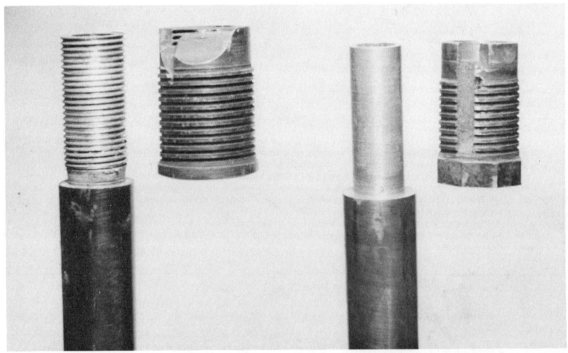

Fig. 2-15. Barrels with a breech end too small for regular fitting can be used in a bushing made from the original barrel shank, for chambering for low-pressured cartridges. On the left is shown a barrel and bushing which are to be threaded and sweated together, and on the right the bushing is bored out to be a slip fit on the turned-down barrel shank and then silver-soldered together. Bushings made from the original barrels also simplify the barrel fitting since extractor and breech block cuts are already made.

With this method the bushing need only be ¼" to ½" longer than the threaded shank, and after boring out the bushing with the lathe, it should then be threaded with the lathe to assure proper alignment. The threads are then cut on the barrel shank with the lathe to be close fit in the bushing. If the thread fit is a bit loose, the threads on the barrel and inside the bushing can be tinned with soft solder and the bushing sweated in place in addition to being threaded in place.

The third method, and the one I most often employ, is to silver-solder the bushing in place. When doing this I make the bushing for the larger actions at least 1.75" long. For the No. 1½ and No. 2 Remington actions (and often with the No. 4 solid frame Remington actions), provided the barrel is large enough in diameter to provide a shoulder, I often use only the original threaded shank portion for the bushing. To prepare the bushing, cut the shank off the original barrel with a hacksaw, chuck the shank in a lathe holding it by the threads, and face the end off square. If the original caliber was a large one, use a boring tool and bore a straight smooth hole entirely through. If the barrel was in a small caliber, start a true centered hole with the boring tool, and then use a drill to remove the bulk of the metal from the hole—or all of the metal, if everything goes right and the drill runs true and smooth.

Next, turn the shank on the barrel with the lathe so the bushing is an easy slip fit on the barrel, with about .001" to .002" clearance between bushing and barrel so that the flux and silver solder can flow freely through the entire joint.

Always make the shank on the new barrel ¼" or so longer than the bushing so that the end of the barrel projecting from the bushing can be faced off afterwards. Bore or drill the hole in the barrel bushing as large as practical without weakening the threaded section of the bushing too much but still allowing the barrel shank to fit inside it to be large enough to put ample amount of metal around the chamber. When making a bushing for the No. 1 smokeless action with the pivotal extractor, a ⅞" hole can be bored through. For the No. 1 blackpowder actions with sliding extractor, the bushing hole can be made up to .700" in diameter. For the No. 1½ and No. 2 action with sliding extractor, 9/16" is adequate for small diameter cartridges. I would advise against using *any* bushing arrangement for the rimless rifle cartridges listed in Group 5. Silver-soldering, if properly done, will not harm or weaken the metal of either the barrel or the bushing, and it is not usually necessary to use an anti-scaling compound in the bore when silver-soldering. However, to be on the safe side, it is good practice to use it.

After the bushing has been installed and the surplus flux cleaned from the shank, the barrel is fitted as described previously.

EXTRACTOR ALTERATIONS

The pivotal extractor in the No. 1 7MM smokeless action does not have to be altered for any of the rimless cartridges listed in Group 5. However, for the large diameter rimmed cartridges, the extractor hook has to be shortened a bit, and for most of the smaller rimmed cartridges it has to be lengthened. To shorten the hook it is just filed down as needed for the cartridge being used. To lengthen the hook it is necessary to add metal to it, and this is best done by silver-soldering on a piece and then trimming down to fit the cartridge.

The extractor hooks of the .43 caliber No. 1 blackpowder actions have to be lengthened slightly when these actions are rebarreled to the .45-70 and .444 Marlin, and lengthened even more for all cartridges with rims smaller than these.

Actions with sliding extractors (like most No. 1½s and all No. 2s) need the extractor hook lengthened or shortened if these actions are adapted for a different cartridge than the original. These rifles are most often encountered in the .32 rimfire caliber, and if these barrels are rebored to a larger caliber the extractor hook need only be shortened and a new rim recess cut with the chambering reamer.

Often, if the extractor hook does not have to be shortened or lengthened (for example, if the rifle barrel is relined to the same caliber), the hook may be in such poor and eroded condition that it should be rebuilt. Do this in the same way as building a longer hook by first filing away most of the eroded hook, silver-soldering on a piece of metal, and then dressing it down to size.

Figure 2-16 shows best how I accomplish the lengthening of these extractor hooks. File part of the original hook away, leaving flat and bright surfaces, shape a piece of steel larger than actually needed to fit close against the cutdown extractor hook, silver-solder it in place, and file the piece of metal down to form a new and longer hook. It is always best to do this extractor alteration work at the same time as or just prior to the chambering operation so that the chamber reamer cuts the cartridge rim recess in the extractor as the chamber is cut.

When remodeling or building a rifle on the small No. 4 Remington or Crescent rolling block actions it is almost always necessary to rebuild the extractor (Fig. 2-17). I find the best way to do this is to file a square notch in the extractor hook to remove all traces of the original cartridge rim recess and silver-solder in a piece of metal fitted closely into this notch, but higher and thicker than needed.

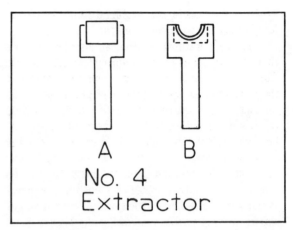

Fig. 2-17. Steps showing how to restore and alter a No. 4 extractor. A shows the original extractor with the center of its hook cut out and fitted with a piece of metal to be silver-soldered in place. B shows the finished extractor.

After silver-soldered in place it is dressed down on top, front, and back to the size of the original extractor. Then, before the barrel is chambered, cut a half-circle notch in it to match the bore, and finish it with the chambering reamer at the same time the chamber is cut.

TRIGGER PULL

Some reasons why the large military rolling block actions are not used more for conversions and rifle building is that many shooters dislike the bulky hammer spur on these actions, the heavy hammer fall, the very stiff mainspring and the stubborn trigger pull, believing that good accuracy is not possible under such conditions. This is not entirely true, for in spite of these faults, these actions are quite suitable for building small-game rifles, big-game rifles, varmint rifles, and even target rifles. With some action alterations and tuning up, these faults can be partly corrected.

The main complaint is the heavy trigger pull. This can be remedied somewhat by doing nothing more than filing the trigger spring thinner. Often with the military actions it takes several pounds of pull on the trigger just for it to bend the trigger spring, and you can test this easily for yourself by having the hammer all the way down and testing the trigger with a trigger pull gauge. Sometimes, just

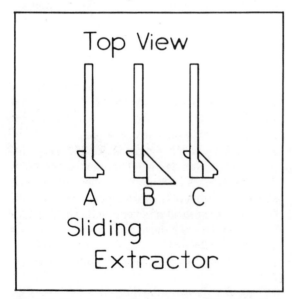

Fig. 2-16. Steps to convert the Remington sliding extractor to handle a cartridge smaller than the original chambering. A is the top view of the original extractor. B shows the original extractor with the hook filed down and a larger piece of metal silver-soldered on to form a longer hook. C shows the completed altered extractor. See text for further details.

by filing the trigger spring thinner, one pound can be taken off of the pull.

Additional improvement can also be obtained by filing the mainspring thinner. This will not only reduce the tension on the sear when the hammer is cocked and make the trigger pull lighter, but it will also make the hammer easier to cock. With modern primers the force of the hammer blow can be cut in half and still fire positively, and in lightening the mainspring to achieve this, the trigger pull will automatically become lighter. With most No. 1 and No. 1½ Remington actions, and with both Whitney actions, file the sides down to give the spring more taper; as much as 1/64″ can be filed away. It is seldom advantageous to thin the mainsprings on the other rolling block actions.

If the mainspring is made thinner (or narrower), the hammer should also be lightened. Two things can be done to reduce the weight of the No. 1 military hammers as shown in Fig. 2-27: thinning and shortening the hammer spur (D) and drilling a hole (E) or holes in its body. Comparing the spur of the No. 1 military action with the spur on the No. 1½ sporting actions shows how much metal can be removed. This leaves the hammer about 20% lighter and much neater. The surplus metal can be ground away, the surface polished, and the spur checkered with a checkering file. The holes or hole should be drilled in the rear part of the hammer body only, where the receiver will cover them. Since the hammer is the locking bolt in these actions, no holes should be drilled in the forward part of the hammer which extends under the breechblock when the hammer is down. On the No. 1, 1½, and No. 2 actions I have found one 7/16″ hole to be sufficient.

If the trigger pull is still too heavy after the above improvements, honing the sear notch with a fine knife-edged hard Arkansas stone may improve it further. The pull should never be made less than four pounds, nor should the depth of the sear notch be reduced.

While at the honing to make the hammer action smoother, it is a good idea to hone the rounded end of the mainspring where it contacts the underside of the hammer (H in Fig. 2-27) and the spot on the hammer where it contacts. In assembling the rifle for the last time, place a small amount of good lubricant on this spot, such as Lubri-Plate. Also put a little dab on the sear notch too.

The flat mainsprings in the Remington No. 1 and No. 1½ rolling block actions often break and quality replacements are not readily available. Using flat spring stock it is possible to make a replacement but this is quite an effort. It is much better to install a coil mainspring system in these actions when a replacement is needed. This is not difficult and you end up with a mainspring that is almost unbreakable and a hammer action that is superior to one powered with a flat spring.

Figures 2-18 and 2-19 show the three parts of the simple coil mainspring system and the parts assembled in the action. The strut is a three inch piece of ⅛″ drill rod smoothly rounded at one end. Bend a curve on the rounded end about as shown. The bending can be done cold and the amount of bend is not critical; it can be bent more or less later on if needed. Take a piece of ¼″ drill rod one inch in length and drill a ⅛″ hole through it lengthwise. Cut the strut collar from one end, square the ends, and silver-solder it over the curved end of the strut rod. The remainder of the drilled rod is used as the strut sleeve.

Square one end of it and chamfer the hole edge. File the other end to a chisel point; file the point straight across and then notch the straight end so that it will center over the threads of the original mainspring screw. This sleeve need not be over ¾″ long. Use a piece of .250″ O.D. heavy tension coil spring about two inches long or slightly longer, depending on the location of the collar on the strut and the length of the sleeve. Using a drill or a ⅛″ round emery point in a Dremel tool, drill or grind a shallow dimple in the U in the upper rear of the hammer. Now you are ready to assemble it.

Remove the breechblock from the action. Remove the broken base of the old mainspring but replace the screw so that its end is flush with the outside surface of the tang. Next, take a piece of light tension spring that will slip over the strut and assemble the strut and sleeve in the action. If, on cocking the hammer, the end of the strut contacts

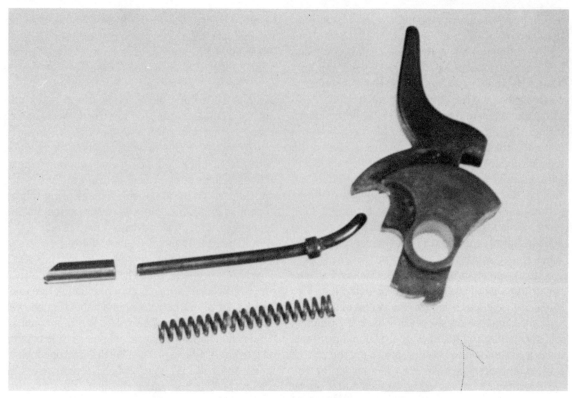

Fig. 2-18. Parts required to install a coil mainspring in a Remington rolling block action.

the mainspring screw, shorten the strut as required. Also check to see that the curved end of the strut is sufficient to allow the hammer to swing freely. Adjust the bend if necessary, then remove the test spring and replace it with the heavy tension spring. After assembling the new mainspring system, replace the breechblock. Now test the hammer pull and fall and if it is too heavy to suit you, shorten the spring.

GRIP CHANGES

The straight-gripped rolling block actions can be readily changed to a pistol grip if the action is to be restocked. On the No. 1 and No. 1½ Remingtons and the Whitney actions, the lower tang can be bent to form a pleasing pistol grip. To do this, first weld the mainspring screw and tang screw holes closed, heat the tang red hot, and bend as desired.

A wedge-shaped steel block (J in Fig. 2-27) must be welded or silver-soldered to the bent tang

as an anchor for the mainspring and tang screws. Figure 2-27 shows the tang bent much like the pistol grip on the Remington or Whitney Creedmoor rifles. (Illustrations of these can be found in *Single-Shot Rifles And Actions*.) If you want to use the original tang screw, you will have to use a 15/64×26 tap. It would therefore be better to make a new one from a ¼×28 bolt. The mainspring screw is also a bastard size (13/64×26), and it can be replaced by a 3/16″ screw instead when the grip is altered and a new hole for it has to be made.

Commercial semi-shaped and inletted butt stocks for the No. 1 Remington are available either in the standard straight-gripped sporter style or modern pistol-gripped and cheekpiece styles from Reinhart Fajen Inc. (Warsaw, Mo. 65355). These stocks can also be used for the No. 1½ Remington and the two Whitney actions.

If additional rigidity is wanted in attaching a new stock to any of the four large Remington and

Fig. 2-19. Coil mainspring assembled in a No. 1 action.

Whitney rolling block actions, a stock throughbolt can be installed. This can be used with the regular tang screw by providing a yoke around the screw into which the stock bolt is screwed (I in Fig. 2-27). Another method is to shorten both tangs ½″ and weld a threaded lug to the bottom of the upper tang for the stock bolt.

Making a pistol grip on the No. 2 action (Fig. 2-20) is easier since the mainspring is attached to the upper tang. A pistol grip on this action is much more pleasing because the frame is not so large as the No. 1 action, leaving the grip less bulky. Heat the lower tang to red hot and bend to the form desired. The lower tang should be shortened about 1″ (or just to the last serial number digit) or the grip will be too long. Drill and countersink a new hole in

the tang ahead of the serial number to accept a flathead wood screw. The original tang screw is discarded and replaced with a wood screw. The two screws will hold the new stock to the action securely.

In restocking the No. 4 Remington and the Crescent rifles, a pistol grip can be shaped on the stock blank as these actions have no lower tang. Replace the original tang screw with a long wood screw. These rifles are often encountered with the tang broken off, or with a poorly repaired broken-off tang. With the No. 4 the problem is not the welding (the steel in this action readily takes steel welding) so much as in correctly positioning and holding the tang in place during the welding operation. The break usually occurs at the tang sight screw hole. I can offer no real solution for aligning and holding the tang during welding; I just hold or wire the tang in place as best I can, tack weld one spot, try it on the stock, bend if necessary, and then make the permanent weld.

The Crescent receiver does not take to steel welding like the No. 4 Remington, and I believe brazing is best used when repair is required.

TIGHTENING THE ACTION

Often Remington No. 1, 1½, and 2 actions are well covered with rust inside as well as outside. Cleaning the rust off may leave the breechblock and hammer pins loose in the receiver and the hammer

Fig. 2-20. I built this small game rifle on the No. 2 Remington action. Originally made for the .32 rimfire cartridge, the action was fitted with .22 rimfire barrel using the original barrel shank as a bushing, with the extractor rebuilt and the breechblock bushed along with a firing pin change, so that the barrel could be chambered for the .22 Long Rifle cartridge. After bending the lower tang, and using a semi-finished stock intended for the Model 98 Mauser action, cutting out the center section, the buttstock and forearm were fitted as shown. The result is a very pleasing and accurate sporting rifle.

and breechblock loose on the pins. Since these parts control the tightness and the solidity with which the action locks on a cartridge, it may be desirable to make and fit new pins. This is especially important when the action is used for cartridges like the .22 Hornet, .219 Zipper, and the rimless rifle cartridges—and especially so if you intend to reload for the rifle.

Fitting new pins requires the holes in the receiver, breechblock and hammer be polished or lapped. Lapping is best. Make the lap (Fig. 2-21) from a 4″ piece of ½″ soft steel rod, turning half of it down to the diameter of the old pins. Drill a 3/16″ hole through the rod at the point where the turned portion ends and with a hacksaw split the turned section to the hole. Spread the halves slightly apart, place the lap in a lathe or drill press chuck, and spread fine lapping compound on the lap. Holding the receiver in the hands with the breechblock and hammer in place, insert the lap into one of the holes.

With the lap turning at a slow speed, move the receiver up and down on the lap so a true hole will result. Continue to lap each hole until it is clean and smooth.

Now carefully turn two pins from drill rod, making them a very tight push fit into the receiver holes. It may then be necessary to lap the holes in the hammer and breechblock separately so they will turn freely—but snugly—on the new pins. If made of drill rod there is no need to heat treat the pins.

SPRINGS FOR THE NO. 4 AND CRESCENT

The Remington No. 4 and the Crescent actions have only two springs each: the mainspring and the combination trigger / breechblock / extractor springs. The mainspring is not hard to make, but the

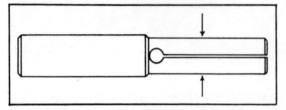

Fig. 2-21. A simple hole lap. Make the laping end (between arrows) the diameter of the hole to be lapped. See text for further details.

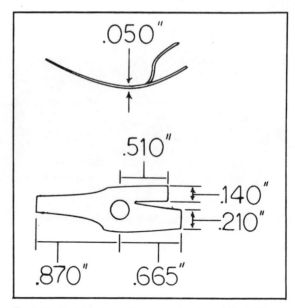

Fig. 2-22. Specifications of the extractor/breechblock/trigger spring for the No. 4 Remington rolling block action.

rather complicated and odd-shaped trigger/breechblock/extractor spring is. Flat annealed spring stock which is easily filed and can be bent cold for making the mainspring is available from Brownell's (Montezuma, Iowa). To make a new mainspring, just file it to the same size as the original spring, bend it to shape, and then harden and draw it. You can find instructions on how to do this in Brownell's catalog and in his book *Gunsmithing Kinks*.

The trigger/breechblock/extractor spring is the one most often broken or missing in the No. 4 and Crescent actions and making a duplicate for either action is difficult. Figure 2-22 shows the exact dimensions and shape of the No. 4 spring, and the Crescent spring is almost identical to it. Rather than attempt to duplicate this spring, I usually try to salvage and use any part of the original broken spring that is still usable and make other arrangements for the broken leaves. Generally, the part of this spring which is broken is the breechblock leaf. In this case the spring is still okay as the trigger and extractor spring and can be used. I then supply the breechblock with a new spring arrangement, making a simple spring and plunger and inserting it in

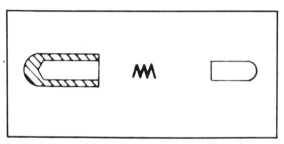

Fig. 2-23. A simple spring plunger assembly that can be made to replace the firing pin retainer pin in the No. 4 breechblock, and which will substitute for the broken leaf on the original extractor/breechblock/trigger spring. See text for details.

place of the firing pin retainer pin. Figure 2-23 shows this spring plunger assembly. Shallow rounded indents should be made inside the receiver wall at the end of the pivotal arc of this plunger and this spring arrangement will function better than the original spring ever did—and it won't break.

If both the breechblock and extractor leaves are broken off the original spring, I retain and use the trigger leaf as before and make a new leaf for the extractor as shown in Fig. 2-24 and use the spring plunger assembly in the breechblock. If the original

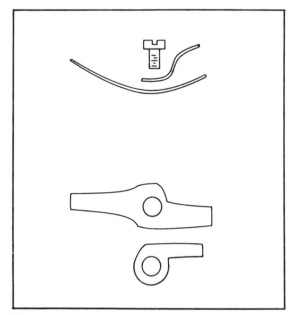

Fig. 2-24. A simple repair on the No. 4 extractor/breechblock/trigger spring when only the breechblock leaf is broken off. See text for details.

spring is missing or entirely unusable, I then make separate leaves for the trigger and extractor from a piece of heavy clock mainspring and use the spring plunger in the breechblock.

SIGHTS

A wide selection of sights are available which can be used on rifles built on rolling block actions. For a hunting rifle, dovetail slots can be filed or milled into the barrel for the installation of common Lyman or Marbles sights, such as bead fronts and open sporting rears. If you want something a little more sophisticated, a low screw-on or sweat-on front sight ramp base can be used to hold the front sight and used with a Williams Guide open rear sight, attached to the barrel about 4″ ahead of the receiver. If you like a receiver sight, then the Lyman or Williams receiver sight made for the Model 70 Winchester rifle can be installed on the large Remington and Whitney actions (Fig. 2-25). When such a sight is used it is necessary to file the top of the receiver ring flat under the slide to allow a lower position of the sight arm. There are several replicas of the old vernier folding tang sights now being made, and although they are expensive, make good sights for these large rifles (Fig. 2-26). With such a sight the Lyman No. 17A front globe target sight can be used. The Parker-Hale tang sights made for the Winchester lever action rifles can be installed and used with good results on the No. 2 and No. 4 rifles, as can receiver sights made for similar flat-side rifles.

Most scopes can be mounted on rifles built on rolling block actions, including varmint and target scopes in target mounts. Unertl target scope mount bases are available to fit just about any barrel size, taper, and shape ever found or put on these rifles. Hunting scopes can be mounted quite low, and such low mounting will not interfere with loading or unloading. On the large rolling block rifles with a round barrel I have used Weaver top detachable mounts with the Weaver No. 53 one-piece base. If the rifle has a octagonal or part octagonal barrel, the Weaver No. 50 base can be used. If you find either base too long to obtain sufficient eye relief, the base can be shortened and a new U-notch filed in the base

Fig. 2-25. A receiver sight made for the Model 70 Winchester is readily adaptable for mounting on a large rolling block action.

for the front mount ring. I have also found the Weaver No. 60 one-piece base made for the .22 Browning auto rifle an excellent one to use on almost any of these rifles. On .22 rimfire rolling blocks, the simple Brownell tip-off base can be used for mounting any of the low-cost scopes with tip-off mounts.

COLOR CASE-HARDENING

The receivers of practically all rolling block actions were originally finished in case-hardened colors. This is a beautiful and durable finish, *but* it is not easy to obtain. Despite what some gunsmithing books have to say about how to obtain this finish on a receiver, it's about impossible for the amateur gunsmith to case-harden a receiver in colors—and indeed, most of the larger professional gun shops can't do it either.

Therefore, if you want to restore the finish on a rolling block rifle or want the action color case-hardened on the rifle you are building on one of these actions, take my advice and don't attempt it yourself. Send the receiver and other parts to be color case-hardened to a professional steel heat treating firm or gun shop that specializes in this type of finish.

Parts to be color case-hardened must be clean and should be highly polished. As with plating or bluing, the higher the polish, the better the color case-hardened finish will be. To help reduce the cost of having an action so finished by a professional shop, as well as to guarantee yourself that the shop won't spoil the receiver by carelessly polishing it, my advice is that you should properly prepare the parts to be color case-hardened before sending them away. In the process of case-hardening, the red hot receiver will be quenched in cold water, and this may cause the sidewalls of the receiver to cave in slightly. To prevent this, you should also send the action so prepared as to avoid this warping.

To prepare the action for color case-hardening, before sending it away to the shop doing the finishing, here are the things you should do:

Cleaning: Before starting any work on the action it is a good practice to clean all the action parts thoroughly after the action has been disassembled. Use a screwdriver to scrape away thick deposits of dirt and grease and then dump the parts in a pail or some other container along with enough water to cover the parts by more than ½", and a half cup of plain household detergent. Place on a stove and let boil for a half hour or so. Drain off the dirty suds water and rinse the parts with *hot* water.

Fig. 2-26. A reproduction of the early vernier tang sight for use on many old single shot rifles is presently available and can be used on the large Remington, Whitney and other rolling block actions. See also pages 160-165.

Removing rust: After the above cleaning, if the action parts are badly rusted, or if there is a lot of rust inside the receiver, use a commercial rust remover to remove the rust. Brownell has a good rust remover; to use it, just follow the directions on the container.

Polishing: I am not going to go into a detailed discussion on polishing, but to obtain any sort of good finish on the outside of the receiver and other action parts, it is absolutely necessary to do considerable polishing, and the amount that has to be done depends entirely on the condition of the action. There is no way to fill up pits and the only way to remove them is to remove enough metal by whatever means necessary until the pits are gone. You can use files and emery cloth, or power-driven sanders and polishing wheels. The problem is that unless you are very skilled with the power polishing rigs, you are apt to come up with a highly polished receiver—but with most of the original square edges rounded off, hole edges dug out, and flat surfaces left wavy.

On most single-shot rifle actions—and this includes all of the rolling blocks under discussion here—it is more important that the two flat sides of the receiver be polished very smooth and absolutely flat and level if the action is to look good after it is finished. The best way I have found to polish the flat receiver sides and have them flat and level afterwards is to hand-polish the receiver on wet-and-dry emery paper rubber cemented on squares of hard-surfaced ceiling tiles. I get about ten sheets of this paper in grits from the coarsest down to #500 grit, cement each one to a ceiling tile, and then *by hand* rub the receiver back and forth across each sheet from coarsest to finest. After the #500 grit rubbing, additional shine can be given to the flat surfaces with a similar rubbing on #600 paper or the finest crocus cloth. The thing to remember is that the better the polishing job, the better will be the final color case-hardened finish or blue.

Shoring: To prevent possible warping and caving in of the receiver sides when the receiver is put through the color case-hardening process, a support or supports should be provided inside the receiver. In other words, the receiver walls must be

shored. No shoring has to be done with the No. 4 Remington and Crescent, but with the rest of the rolling blocks it is usually necessary. With these actions which have the separate removable trigger guard, if this part fits snugly in place in the receiver it can be used as the shoring support, in which case it should be wired in place by two loose loops of stovepipe wire through the front and rear trigger guard screw holes. In addition to the trigger guard, I usually employ two other supports, one in the middle of the receiver between the holes for the hammer and breechblock pins, and one just behind and below the mainspring stop pin. Make these supports from ½″ round bar stock and file or lathe-turn them so they are a very snug fit between the receiver walls. They should be so snug that they have to be tapped in place, but not so long or tight that the receiver walls are spread apart. After the action is case-hardened and returned, you will have to drive these supports out. If, in spite of these short supports, the receiver walls still are drawn together so that the action cannot be properly reassembled, then the walls can be spread apart by using a hex SAE ⅜″ bolt and nut short enough to fit between the walls—use it as a jack to spring the walls apart.

CONVERSION TO LEVER ACTION

Way back in 1875, Frank Freund converted the large Remington rolling block from a thumb-operated action to a lever action. I saw one of the Freund conversions years ago at a gun show in Fremont, Nebraska, and I marveled at the conversion and at Freund's workmanship. The rifle was a fancy No. 1 Sporting Rifle in excellent condition, although if I remember correctly there was a part missing or broken in the action. I could not take the action apart at that time to study it, and all I could do was to work the action a couple of times. On swinging the loop finger lever down and forward, the hammer would be placed in a full-cock position and the breechblock would then swing open. On swinging the lever back, the breechblock would close, leaving the action ready to fire. Everything worked so smoothly and crisply, and the conversion so well executed, that it did not look, feel, or sound like a conversion. Freund was a master gunsmith and his

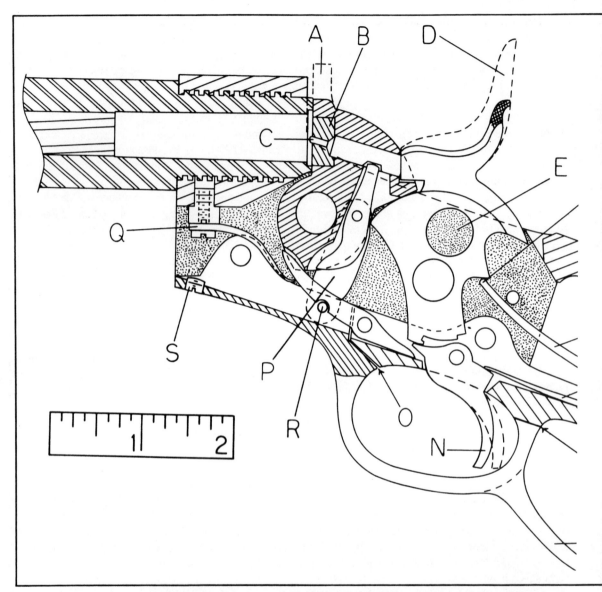

Fig. 2-27. Full-size sectional view drawing of the No. 1 Remington rolling block action which has been converted into a lever action, and illustrating other points that were gunsmithed. (A) In making this action into a lever-operated action, the original spur or thumb-piece on the breechblock is cut off and dressed down as shown. (B) As described in the text, most old rolling block actions should have the breechblock bushed, which means that the original firing pin hole must be made smaller and the firing pin tip made accordingly. Here is shown a rather thick bushing, which is round and silver-soldered in place. This thick bushing could also be anchored in place by one or two small cross pins or by a small screw or two, or it could be made thinner if silver-soldered in place. (C) The bushing, after it is fitted, is drilled for a new firing pin hole with a 1/16″ or 5/64″ drill as explained in the text, and the original firing pin tip turned down to be a snug fit into the hole, or a new firing pin made or a new tip installed in the old firing pin body. The end of the tip must be rounded and smooth, and must protrude no more than .060″ or less than .050″. (D) The hammer spur can be altered to reduce the weight of the hammer and improve its looks. (E) A hole drilled through the hammer at this point will also reduce the weight of the hammer. (F) To lighten the trigger pull, the trigger spring can be filed and polished narrower and/or thinner. (G) The hammer or mainspring can also be filed and polished narrower and/or thinner to reduce the heavy hammer fall, which at the same time will also lighten the trigger pull. (H) The contacting surfaces

44

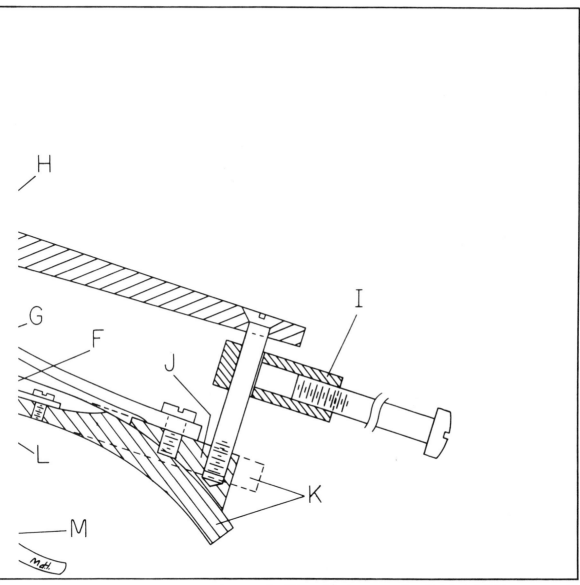

between the end of the mainspring and the hammer should be polished very smooth and lubricated. (I) The accuracy of a rolling block rifle might be improved by adding a through-stock bolt as shown here. A hole must be drilled lengthwise through the stock and a yoke made as shown to anchor on the tang screw. (J) When bending the tang to make a pistol grip, a wedge-shaped block of steel is welded or silver-soldered to the lower tang and this block drilled and tapped to accept the mainspring and tang screws. (K) The locations of the original straight tang and the tang after being bent to form a pistol grip. The original holes for the mainspring and tang screws should be filled with steel weld before the tang is bent. (L) Location for the cut in the rear of the trigger guard bow when the action is converted to a lever action as described in the text. (M) Suggested finger-piece to be welded in place when the action is converted to a lever action. (N) In converting to a lever action, the trigger finger-piece must be curved forward as shown. (O) Location of the cut through the trigger guard when the action is converted into a lever action as explained in the text. (P) Link (or links) which connects the finger lever to the breechblock when the action is converted into a lever operated rifle (see text for full details). (Q) When converted into a lever action, the original lock lever spring is altered and attached as shown so that it performs the same functions as before in the original action. (R) Lower link pin. (S) Plug screw to gain access to the safety lock spring screw.

two favorite rifles to work on were the Sharps sidehammer and the Remington rolling block.

Freund obtained a patent on this conversion (#160, 762) and if any reader is interested in his conversion method, the patent papers are available from the U.S. patent office for 50¢. The patent papers do not show all the details of its construction, but let me assure you that Freund's conversion is not easy to duplicate.

Determining to have a lever-operated Remington rolling block rifle for myself, I worked out a rather simple conversion method and I pass it along here for those hardy amateur gunsmiths willing to undertake almost anything in the conversion line. Figures 2-27 through 2-31 show how I accomplished my conversion.

This conversion is only for the No. 1 Remington rolling block action with the sliding extractor and lever-type firing pin retractor. The conversion was designed and worked out so as to not eliminate the firing pin retractor or safety lever between breechblock and trigger.

Start the conversion by removing the trigger guard from the action and stripping it of all parts. Now, as shown in Fig. 2-27, make accurate saw cuts at L and O to separate the trigger guard into two parts. The front part now becomes the finger lever and the rear part the lower tang. File and polish the sawed surfaces level and smooth. If the original trigger guard has a hole in the front part of its bow for a sling swivel, then after sawing the guard in two this hole should be filled with steel weld and dressed smooth.

Next, drill a ⅛″ hole through the finger lever for the lower link pin (R) 9/64″ below the upper edge and 1″ to the rear (center) of the finger lever pivot screw. If you are unsure about measuring, then it is a good idea to drill a 3/32″ hole first, and later on enlarge it to ⅛″ by filing and/or drilling if a corrected position is needed. With a milling machine or lathe setup with milling attachment and ⅜″ end mill, mill U recesses (Fig. 2-29) on both sides of the finger lever about ⅛″ deep and centered on the pin hole. With the same end mill, and at the same depth, also mill both sides of the breechblock, centering the mill on the firing pin retractor lever pin hole and milling down at a slight forward angle as shown in Fig. 2-29. Also enlarge the retractor pin hole to ⅛″.

Make the two links from a piece of ⅛″ thick strap iron ⅜″ wide. On my conversion I had to space the holes in the links 1.015″ apart, but depending on exact location of the lower link pin hole and on your individual action, you may have to use the trial-and-error method to get the correct hole spacing in the links so the breechblock and finger lever close at the same time. While fitting the links, have the lower tang in place and the buttstock attached, as it is important to have the lower tang correctly positioned the way it will be when the rifle is finally assembled. If you do not like to have the stock in place while you work, then use a piece of rod as a prop or spacer between the ends of the tangs to hold the lower tang in the same position it would be if the stock were in place and the tang screw tightened. You will know what I mean when you get to work on

Fig. 2-28. The "lever action" Remington rolling block sporter which the author built. The 27″ Numrich .44 caliber barrel is chambered for the .444 Marlin cartridge. The sights consist of a Lyman gold bead front sight mounted on a Williams screw-on ramp base, a Lyman No. 16C sporting rear sight mounted on a Lyman screw-on No. 25 rear sight base, and a Lyman No. 66A receiver sight. The original military forearm was shortened and trimmed as shown, and the wood refinished. Rifle weighs about 7.25 pounds as shown.

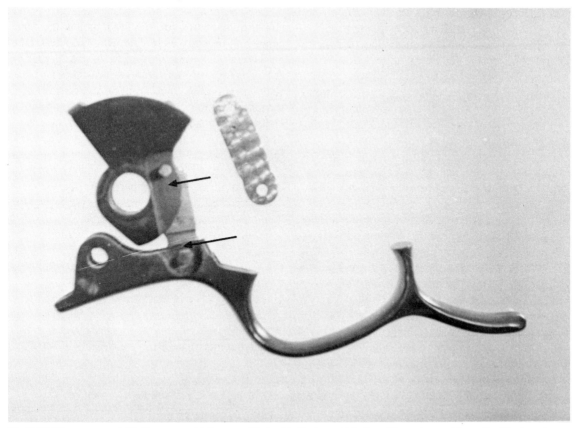

Fig. 2-29. The arrows point to the areas which were milled out in the breechblock and finger lever of the rolling block action to convert it to a lever action. The two links are also shown.

this conversion. You may have to make more than one set of links to come up with the correct hole spacing, and in making the links use a clamp to hold them together so the holes can be drilled through both of them at the same time. Do the same when rounding up the ends of the links.

Replace the firing pin retractor lever pin with a new ⅛″ pin made from drill rod, and make a similar pin for the finger lever. With the receiver stripped, and working with the finger lever, breechblock, and hammer, fit and try *one* link until everything works properly, and then do the same with only the other. If necessary, file down and smooth the sides of the finger lever where it fits inside the receiver, as well as the contact surfaces inside the receiver, so that the finger lever can be pivoted easily.

After the links have been fitted, the lower link

pin must be silver-soldered in place to prevent it from falling out. Since it is also located so that it will contact the lock lever before the action is fully closed, it will be necessary to either cut out the center part of the lower link pin or notch the lock lever.

Anneal the original lock lever spring so that it can be bent cold. If the action has a ramrod stop, use it to mount the safety lever spring. Cut the stop off to ¼″ height and center drill and tap it for a 6×48 scope mounting screw. Assemble the action except for the finger lever and links, and bend the lock lever spring as in Fig. 2-27 (Q) so that when it is screwed to the shortened ramrod stop, it bears heavily against the lock lever. It will be necessary to cut about ¼″ off the thin end of this spring.

After the spring has been properly bent and

Fig. 2-30. Close-up of the lever action rolling block action.

fitted it must be rehardened and tempered. If there is no ramrod stop, then mount the spring directly to the receiver in the same place and bend the spring accordingly. To be able to assemble the action it is helpful to drill out the original lock spring screw hole in the finger lever to accept a ¼ × 28 plug screw (S) as this spring is the last part to put in and the first to take out when assembling the action.

The final step in the conversion is to cut off the thumb piece on the breechblock and weld on a loop, hook, or spur on the finger lever (Fig. 2-30). You may find it necessary to bend the finger piece of the trigger to a more curved shape in order for it to clear the finger lever. It may also be necessary to heat and bend one end of the lock lever after the action is stocked so that the trigger is properly blocked when the breechblock is open.

If you want to make a lever action from a No. 1 Remington that has the pivotal extractor like the Model 1902 action, then use only one link on the right side.

There you have it—a lever-action rolling block (Fig. 2-31). It is no better than the original action was, but it is different. It is still necessary to cock the hammer before the action can be opened, and the action is ready to fire upon closing it, for as of this writing I have not worked out a simple method whereby the hammer is automatically cocked, or put into its *safe* position via the finger lever as the action is opened and closed.

OBTAINING A ROLLING BLOCK ACTION

You may ask, "Where can I obtain a rolling

block action?" The day is past when you could purchase a separate rolling block action for a five dollar bill, or a complete rifle with a usable action for a dollar or two more. As I write this, there are still a couple of dealers who have some of the Remington rolling block actions for sale. However, the usual way most amateur gunsmiths get any one of the rolling block actions is to purchase a complete rifle, and this is certainly the best way to do it. Even though you want only the action, you may have need of the breech end of the barrel for a bushing or to copy when threading a new barrel. As odd as it may seem, a complete rifle can usually be purchased for no more than an action alone.

So, where to find the rifle? I have found that the best places to go to purchase or trade for these rifles are gun collector shows. Another good way to find them is by reading the *Shotgun News,* a paper devoted solely to advertisements of firearms. Their address is: *Shotgun News*, Hastings, Nebraska 68901, and they will send a sample copy on request. And finally, there are also local dealers in firearms who occasionally have one for sale that they have taken in on a trade.

In gun parlance, you want to look for "dogs" or "beaters" which means guns which are no longer shootable, incomplete, or rusted and neglected beyond complete restoration. Since you only want the action, pay no attention to the condition of the bore or to the wood and sights. You also need not pay too much attention to the outside condition of the action unless surface pitting is so deep that it cannot be

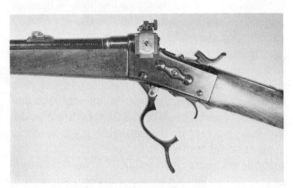

Fig. 2-31. Close-up of the lever action rolling block action opened.

polished out. *Do* check the action carefully to see that no parts are missing, broken or damaged beyond repair, and *don't* buy it unless it is complete and workable—unless you can repair it and make new parts. Some parts for some of the rolling block actions are available, but parts are high-priced. For example, a mainspring for a No. 1 Remington action costs from $4.00 to $5.00. Therefore, before purchasing a beater, make sure the action is usable, and if it needs parts or repairs they should be within your ability to make and restore.

In the past these firms have had rolling block rifles, actions and parts for sale:

Dixie Gun Works, Union City, Tenn, 38261

Sarco Inc., 192 Central Avenue, Stirling, N.J. 07980

Potamic Arms Corporation, Zero Prince St., Alexandria, Va. 22313

Numrich Arms Corporation, West Hurley, N.Y. 12491

Chapter 3

Gunsmithing the Martinis

The little .310 Martini Cadet single-shot rifle (Fig. 3-1) offers excellent possibilities for conversion and remodeling, and its action is an ideal one on which to build a light small game or varmint rifle.

In the 1950s this rifle and separate actions were very common, the rifles often selling for as little as $12.50, and the actions for around $5.00. They were real bargains. Today owners of these rifles and actions are reluctant to sell them, but there are enough of them around so that amateur gunsmiths will rework them for years to come.

As originally imported into the U.S. for sale on the surplus arms market, most of these rifles were in original and very good condition, with excellent bores and the action in excellent mechanical condition. The rifles which had very poor wood or rusty bores were stripped for their actions. The Martini Cadet rifle had a long slender barrel protected by a nearly full-length forearm attached by a crosspin and a swivel band. The barrel will be chambered for the .310-12-120 Cadet cartridge. The action is the famous Martini single-shot with a pivoting breechblock and an under finger lever to operate it

(Fig. 3-2). (This action is described in detail in Chapter 50 in *Single Shot Rifles and Actions*.) It is simple, well-made, and strong. Although considerably smaller than the Peabody-Martini (Martini-Enfield or Martini-Henry) actions, it is fully as strong as its larger brothers. The buttstock is attached with a throughbolt, a good feature. The maker's name will be on the receiver, and may be BSA, W. W. Greener, or Webley & Scott. These rifles are commonly known as the Australian Cadet training rifle insomuch as they were military rifles, used in Australia, and bear the markings of a kangaroo and the words COMMONWEALTH OF AUSTRALIA.

Specifications of the original .310 Cadet barrel are: length 25⅛", shoulder diameter .880", muzzle diameter .630", weight 2¼ pounds, rifling five grooves with one turn in 20", and groove diameter approximately .320".

In its original form and caliber this rifle has little value, except perhaps as a collector item. The .310 Cadet cartridge for which the rifle is chambered is a dead number.

Fig. 3-1. The original British-made Martini Cadet military training rifle chambered for the .310-12-120 Cadet cartridge.

RECHAMBERING THE CADET

For the easiest and quickest conversion, the original barrel can be rechambered for the .32-20 (.32 WCF) or .32 Winchester Special. The .32-20 cartridge is much like the .310 Cadet and very little metal is removed in the rechambering. However, not many shooters desire or have any use for a .32-20 single-shot rifle. Accuracy of the rechambered .32-20 Cadet Martini I had was very poor. Though the bore was perfect, and both factory ammunition and handloads were tried, more than half the bullets keyholed. The rifling twist of the .310 Cadet barrel is the same as that of the American-made .32-20 rifles, so the inaccurate shooting is due to the bore of the .310 Cadet being oversize for the .311 diameter .32-20 bullets.

It is not very practical to rechamber this rifle to the .32 Special cartridge. Although this may make the rifle more useful for some types of hunting, that

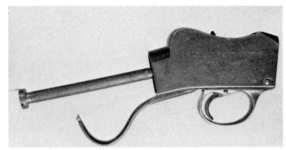

Fig. 3-2. The Martini Cadet action. This action is exactly the same as the BSA No. 12 Martini. It is often referred to as the "small Martini" since it is considerably smaller and lighter than the common British Martini-Enfield action. The Martini Cadet action is about 4.25" long, 1.00" thick, and weighs 1.5 pounds.

cartridge is disproportionately large for the action, and is not convenient for loading and unloading. Accuracy may be poor, and the recoil rather heavy due to the lightness of the rifle. In any event, to rechamber the .310 Cadet Martini rifle to either .32-20 or .32 Special, it is necessary to use a finishing chamber reamer with the barrel removed from the action.

REBORING THE CADET

The commonest conversion done on the original .310 Martini Cadet is reboring and rechambering the barrel for a large caliber revolver cartridge. This little rifle lends itself well to reboring for the .357 Magnum revolver cartridge. This gives the owner a rifle in which he can shoot either the .38 Special or .357 Magnum cartridges with any load that can be safely fired in the heaviest revolver. The rifle so rebored can be used for testing accuracy of revolver loads and bullets, and for some types of hunting. Sometimes the accuracy is very good depending on the smoothness of the rebored barrel, the bullets being used, and the choice of sighting equipment on the rifle.

This rifle can also be rebored for the .41 Magnum and .44 Magnum cartridges. Reboring to the .41 Magnum caliber is okay, but I would advise against the .44 Magnum reboring as this leaves the barrel shank and walls quite thin.

REBARRELING THE CADET

The home gunsmith owning a .310 Martini Cadet rifle is likely to scrap the original barrel, stock and forearm, for it is the action he is interested in. If he is skilled he can build a very fine sporting rifle on it as have many a foreign and American gunsmith done for years (Fig. 3-3). Some years ago, when the .22 Hornet cartridge was very popular, these actions were extensively used in building many of the finest rifles made in this caliber.

This action is known for its very fast and short striker travel and consequently short lock time. It is also known for its strength, and despite its small size I consider it more than equal in strength to the larger Martini-Enfield action. However, being small and having only a small barrel shank, it should be limited to the smaller rimmed cartridges like the .22 Hornet, .218 Bee, .22 Jet, .222 Rimmed, 5.6×50R Magnum, .25-20, .256 Magnum, and wildcat cartridges based on these cases. The action is okay for the standard .219 Zipper, but certainly not for any wildcat cartridge based on this case.

Likewise, it is not an action to use for the .225 Winchester cartridge. Of course, the action is ideal for the 5MM Remington, .22 Long Rifle, and .22 WMR rimfire cartridges.

With a suitable extractor alteration this action can be used with a rimless cartridge. However, I would limit the selection to the .221 Fireball and .222 Remington cartridges only. Bob Snapp of Snapp's Gun Shop (6911 E. Washington, Clare, Michigan 48617) has worked out a good rimless

extractor for this action, and does rimmed and rimless cartridge conversions on the Cadet.

Most amateur gunsmiths who have a small metal-turning lathe with 24″ or more center spacing and who can cut threads with it should be able to fit a barrel to the Martini Cadet action. Figure 3-4 gives the barrel shank and thread specifications. If the original barrel is available, use it as a guide in cutting the new shank and threads. Before the threads are finished, the barrel should be tried in the receiver to assure a tight fit. It is important to have a good snug tight thread fit to start with—tight enough that it takes a barrel vise and wrench to turn the barrel all the way in.

Barrels originally made for the .22 Long Rifle rimfire cartridge can sometimes be used for rebarreling this action for a .22 centerfire cartridge, but many of these barrels are quite soft and accuracy life may not be very long when used with jacketed bullets. In any case, the barrel should have a shoulder diameter of at least .875″, and in handloading, the bullets used should match the groove diameter of the barrel. However, in selecting a barrel for any centerfire cartridge, it's best to purchase a regular chrome-moly blank.

For the .22 Hornet and .218 Bee cartridges the barrel should have a .224″ groove diameter and a 1-in-16 or 1-in-14 rifling twist. For the .219 Zipper, .22 Rimmed, 5.6×50R Magnum, .221 and .222, the groove diameter should be .224″ and the rifling

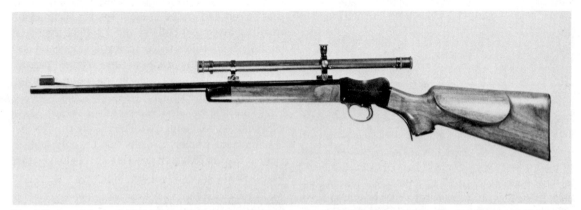

Fig. 3-3. A real lightweight English-styled varmint rifle built on the Martini Cadet action by George Burgers and myself. Chambered for the .218 Bee cartridge, the 23″ barrel was originally used on a Model 54 Winchester rifle. The Fajen aristocrat styled stock and forearm were reshaped along British lines. The scope is an old Lyman A5.

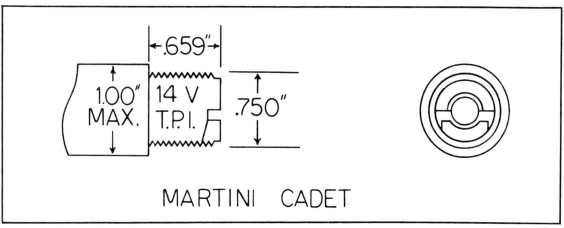

Fig. 3-4. Barrel shank and thread specifications for the Martini Cadet (BSA No. 12) action.

twist 1-in-14. For the .25-20 and .256 Magnum cartridges, get a barrel with a .257″ groove diameter and a 1-in-14 twist.

With the breech end faced off square, and the barrel blank between lathe centers, turn the shank down a bit longer than needed, then turn on the threads. In the ideal fit, the breechblock just snugly closes against the barrel shank after the barrel has been fully screwed in the receiver and set in its final position, but still allows the action to open easily. To do this, place the barrel in the lathe chuck and steady rest and face off the barrel until it can be fully screwed into the assembled action (minus extractor) with the breech closed. The fit between the barrel and the breechblock must be so close that the action closes snugly, for if it isn't fitted this way the finger lever will droop when the action is closed and uncocked.

CHAMBERING THE CADET

Chambering the barrel is done after the barrel has been correctly fitted to the action, but the barrel must be removed for the chambering operation. Chambering a barrel for a small cartridge like the Hornet or Bee can be done by hand if necessary, but is much better done in the lathe. Other than a finishing chamber reamer, no special tools are required.

If chambering must be done by hand, fix the barrel in a padded vise and hold the reamer in a sturdy tap wrench, not a small T-handle tap holder. Use plenty of thread cutting oil on the reamer and clean out the chips frequently. To cut the chamber, apply steady pressure with the palm of one hand on the center of the tap wrench and with the other hand revolve the handles. Make nearly a full turn each time. Apply pressure carefully in line with the bore to avoid cutting an oversized or off-center chamber. Caution should be exercised when the reamer starts to cut the rim recess. After cutting a little more than half the rim recess depth, the chamber should be cleaned and a new cartridge case tried in it.

Continue reaming and checking, and when the case head is flush with the breech face, or about .001″ to .002″ below, the chamber is cut deep enough and the headspace is correct. If possible, try several brands of cases in checking the final chamber to see that all will chamber freely. Polish the reamed chamber with #500 wet-and-dry paper revolved on a split dowel. If the chamber reamer has no integral throat cutter, the throat must be cut with a special reamer.

FITTING THE CADET EXTRACTOR

The next operation is fitting the extractor into the breech end of the barrel. Actually, the final chambering to obtain the correct headspace and chamber polishing could be done after the extractor is fitted so that the rim recess in the extractor hooks can be cut into them with the chambering reamer. The only tool needed to fit the double-pronged extractor is a small 6″ flat mill file. Although one of the extractor prongs could be removed, there is no reason this should be done, as fitting one prong would be as difficult as fitting both. With the barrel fully set up in the receiver and the extractor in place in the action, marks with a bent scribe where the extractor cuts are to be made. Remove the barrel and place it breech end up in a padded vise. Using the original barrel as a guide, as well as the extractor and the scribe marks, start filing the necessary cuts. After the cuts are made as close as possible by trying the loose extractor for fit, reset the barrel in the receiver and try the extractor while it is in the action. If the breechblock will not close over the extractor, or the extractor binds on opening the action, remove the barrel and make the necessary corrections. Use a spotting compound on the extractor while it is in the action to spot the high spots where metal may have to be removed. After the cuts are correct, polish the filed surfaces with emery cloth, and also smooth up the edges of the cuts, especially the chamber edges.

CADET EXTRACTOR ALTERATIONS

There is little alteration required on the .310 Martini extractor to fit it to most centerfire cartridges that are suited for this action. When the rifle is chambered for the .218 Bee cartridge (Fig. 3-5), all that is required is to file the extractor lips a bit thinner to match the rim recess of the thicker rim of the Bee cartridge case. When the rifle is chambered for the Hornet cartridge, the prongs can be bent together slightly so the Hornet case will just pass between them, and the lips filed thinner. If desired, rather than filing the rim recess deeper on the extractor lips, the extractor cuts in the barrel can be made deeper, or, as mentioned previously, the lips can be made thinner with the chambering reamer on the final chambering operation. In this case the extractor is hand-held in place while the reamer is turned.

If the rifle is chambered for the .22 Jet, .222 Rimmed, 5.6×50R Magnum, .219 Zipper, .256 Magnum or .357 Magnum cartridge, the extractor hooks are merely filed shorter so they will fit the case head correctly. After shortening, hold the extractor in place in the cuts in the barrel breech and use the chambering reamer to cut the rim recesses.

For the .22 rimfires (.22 Long Rifle, .22 WMR, or 5MM Remington), the hooks must be made longer. I also favor doing this when rebarreling for the .22 Hornet. Do this by filing the extractor lips square, fit a similar sized piece of steel between them, and silver-solder it in place. Now cut out the center section to fit the rimfire cartridge. To get a perfect rim recess cut in the extractor lips, use the chambering reamer as mentioned before.

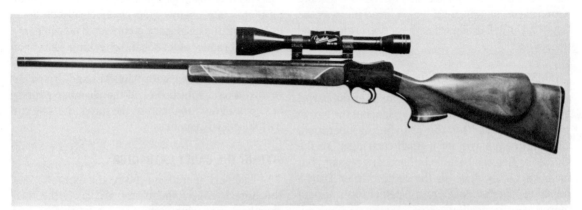

Fig. 3-5. I built this fine lightweight varmint rifle on the Martini Cadet action and chambered the Wilson Arms Company 26″ barrel for the .218 Bee cartridge. The semi-finished stock and forearm with rosewood fittings were made by Reinhart Fajen Inc. The Weatherby 3—9× variable scope is mounted in Weaver top detachable mounts on the Weaver No. 60 one-piece base.

BUSHING THE CADET FIRING PIN HOLE

When the .310 Martini Cadet rifle is rechambered, rebored, or the action rebarreled to a hotter centerfire cartridge, it is necessary to bush the original firing pin hole in the breechblock and make the firing pin tip smaller. If the centerfire action is to be converted for a rimfire cartridge, the original firing pin hole must be closed and a new hole made for the rimfire firing pin. The opposite is necessary when the rimfire No. 12 BSA or similar Martini rimfire action is to be used in making up a centerfire rifle.

If the original centerfire firing pin hole is not suitably bushed when used with a modern cartridge, the usual result when firing these cartridges is that the primer flows back into the firing pin hole, preventing the breechblock from being opened easily, if at all. With a correctly fitted and bushed firing pin tip, there is a little chance of the primer rupturing and no chance of locking the action shut.

Bushing is easily done on the Martini. Drill out the original firing pin hole with a #31 drill and tap it 6×48, the same as for the small scope mounting screws. If you like to use a larger diameter screw, then drill the original hole with a #28 drill and tap 8×40, which is the next larger scope mounting screw. Although the Martini Cadet breechblocks are case-hardened, I have not often found it necessary to anneal them for this operation. However, once in a while a breechblock is encountered that cannot be readily drilled and tapped, and with such blocks it is necessary to anneal the front end, or just the face of it. If this part *only* is annealed, there is no chance of the block warping and it won't have to be rehardened again. The drilling and tapping should be done through the rear of the breechblock so the tapped hole will be aligned with the main firing pin striker hole.

The bushing is made from a 6×48 (or 8×40) heat-treated scope mounting screw with a 1/16″ or 5/64″ accurately-centered hole drilled through it lengthwise. Or the hole can be drilled through it with a pilot drill setup as described in Chapters 1 and 2. Tin the tapped hole and the bushing screw threads with soft solder and while the breechblock is still hot, turn the screw in flush with the inside of the main firing pin hole. After the block has been allowed to cool, the head of the screw is sawed off and the remainder of the screw filed flush with the breech face.

The bushing hole is then tapered slightly with a needle file from the inside. Finally the face of the breechblock is polished with fine emery cloth held under a flat file.

The original firing pin tip is now turned down to fit the hole in the bushing. This is done in a lathe or, if necessary, it can be done in a drill press by holding a file on it until it is reduced the correct amount. An alternate method, and one that must be used when the original tip has been broken off, is to fit a new tip on the firing pin body. To do this, file off the broken part so the end is level, then assemble the firing pin in the breechblock complete with the mainspring. Drill into the firing pin body through the hole in the bushing—about 1/2″ deep if the tip is to be sweated in place, or 1/4″ deep if it is to be silver-soldered in. Disassemble the breechblock again and, using a piece of drill rod for the new firing pin tip (or a section of the drill shank), solder in place. Reassemble again under spring tension, and carefully file it to a protrusion of about .055″ from the breech face. Take the pin out again and file and polish the tip smooth and hemispherical.

When the action is changed from centerfire to rimfire, fill in the old firing pin hole in the same way but with a solid screw. To locate the new firing pin hole a special marker is required, as described in Chapter 2. Insert the marker in the chamber with the marker point to the bottom, close the breech, insert a cleaning rod in the muzzle, and lightly tap the marker. In drilling, make sure the new hole is parallel with the main firing pin hole. Now you must fit a new tip on the main firing pin as described before, making it 5/64″ diameter instead of 1/16″ for a stronger pin.

In changing the No. 12 BSA Martini action from rimfire to centerfire, the old firing pin tip hole need not of necessity be filled. Locate the new hole as described in Chapter 2.

CADET TRIGGER WORK

On most of these small Martini actions I have

found the trigger quite satisfactory, having a smooth pull of about 5 pounds. A long pull is not objectionable if it is smooth. A rough or creepy trigger pull can be made smooth by honing the sear notch and trigger tip with a medium hard Arkansas stone. It is very important to preserve the original sear angle, and to leave the sear and trigger tip edges square and sharp.

To shorten the pull requires that the sear engagement be reduced. As there is considerable pressure on the sear from the very stiff mainspring, the sear engagement should not be reduced below .025". The best way to reduce the engagement is with a stop below the sear notch to regulate tip engagement. If the cocking lever is soft enough, drill a 5/64" hole just below the notch and drive in a tight-fitting pin; this is then filed down to allow the desired engagement. If the cocking lever is extremely hard, sweat a small piece of metal slightly below the sear notch and file this down as required. In any event, the sear engagement must never be so fine that there is a chance it may fail to hold when the action is closed smartly, and the trigger pull must never be reduced below 3 pounds.

To fit a trigger stop, drill and tap a hole in the rear of the trigger guard bow for a small plug screw. I have used a #29 drill to make the hole, tapped it with an 8×32 tap (for a tight fit do not tap clear through), and installed an 8×32 Allen set screw for the stop.

The cocking indicator projecting from the top right side of the breechblock can be removed if desired. There seems to be no particular objection to it, nor any practical advantage in having it. If the indicator is removed, the narrow cut in the breechblock can be filled with a piece of flat steel sweated in place.

I feel that there is no real need for a safety device on the Martini rifle. If the shooter desires to carry the rifle with a cartridge in the chamber, he can do so with perfect safety by simply leaving the action open. The breechblock normally remains open in such a position that the cartridge cannot fall out, and yet it is instantly closed for a quick shot. However, if a safety device is wanted, illustrations and instructions for making a crossbolt safety can be found on page 31 in the Feb. 1968 issue of *The American Rifleman*. It also shows a splendid remodeled and restocked Martini Cadet rifle by Hal Hartley.

CADET FINGER LEVER CHANGES

The original Martini Cadet rifle has the finger lever shaped into a sort of pistol grip, with the end of the lever fitting into a spring-loaded catch in the buttstock. I have seen a number of these rifles with the finger lever apparently bent, notable because the shank of the lever does not touch the receiver. This is also a sign that the locking cams are not fully engaged under the breechblock. With the lever so bent, a friction catch is needed to keep the finger lever from opening easily and to hold the action closed and cocked. If the lever is altered so the shank touches the receiver, no catch is needed, and will then allow full engagement of the locking cams.

After the new stock has been fitted and the pistol grip shaped, the finger lever should be bent to fit the inside grip curve. The lever can be bent cold, but this usually results in an uneven surface and possibly minute surface cracks in the old case-hardened finish. I suggest that the portion of the lever to be bent first be heated to red, then quickly straightened and rebent to approximately the correct grip curve. Now allow the lever to cool slowly. Do the final bending cold, as the heating has now annealed the surface so it will not crack. If only the bent portion is heated, this will not affect the hardness of the locking cams. The usual method is to bend the finger lever to fit the grip closely and then leave about ½" projecting below the grip cap. The end is rounded off or a small steel ball welded on.

Another method is to bend the end of the lever forward into a semi-finger loop. This lever can also be altered in other various ways; an excellent example is shown in Fig. 3-6.

CADET STOCK WORK

If your Martini has only been rechambered or rebored, you may wish to use the original stock and forearm. The stocks I have seen are often considerably battered and could stand complete refinishing. Most dents can be raised. Scrape and sand the stock

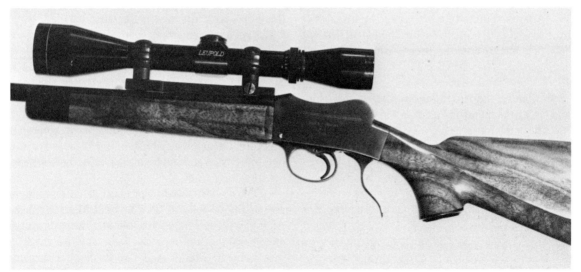

Fig. 3-6. Gunsmith H. L. Grisel worked out this finger lever design for the Martini Cadet action.

and forearm to remove most of the oil-soaked finish. Now wet the wood, place a thick wet cloth over the dents, and steam them out with an electric iron. Finish sanding and apply a new finish. The forearm may be shortened to about 10″ or left the original length.

If the action has been rebarreled, it is worthy of a new stock and forearm. Reinhart Fajen Inc. (Warsaw, Mo. 65355), makes a very nice stock and forearm to fit this action. The semi-inletted and shaped stock intended for the Model 12 Winchester shotgun is almost made to order for the small Martini. There is already a hole through the stock for the stock screw. The enlarged hole in the rear of the butt must be deepened a bit and the end of the grip fitted into the recess in the Martini receiver before it can be attached. After attachment it can be shaped as desired and the comb cut down. To get the comb height correct, the sights should be on the rifle. Trim the comb until the eye naturally aligns with the sights when the rifle is brought to the shoulder.

Shape the pistol grip as close to the receiver as practical and still leave a pleasing curved grip. Up to 5/16″ of the recessed rear end of the receiver can be cut off if desired to bring the grip that much further forward. Remove the finger lever from the receiver when shaping the grip as the lever will later be bent to the grip curve.

Another stock that can be used for the small Martini is the one intended for the British Lee-Enfield rifle. The matching forearm can also be used by cutting off the rear part which has the action inletting cuts.

A sporting forearm should be 10″ long or slightly more, depending on the barrel length, type of scope that will be used, and the type of shooting that will be done with the rifle. With a new target or varmint weight barrel and a target scope, a rather long semi-full forearm may be desirable—say 14″ long and about 2″ wide. With a shorter small game scope and with a shorter and lighter barrel, the forearm should have some taper towards the tip and be no more than 10″ or 12″ long. With one of the low-power and long eye-relief scopes mounted on the barrel, a slim 10″ forearm enhances the rifle's looks. The forearm should always match the buttstock as to size.

The simplest way to attach the forearm to the barrel is with a single screw tapped directly into the barrel. Use an 8×40 screw in the smaller forearms, and a 10×32 screw in the longer and heavier ones. The screw should be centered in the forearm and a brass escutcheon provided for its head. The butt of the forearm should be carefully fitted into the front of the receiver with a short tenon to aid the single screw attachment.

A better method for attaching the forearm to the barrel is to fit a small block to the barrel first and have the forearm screw threaded into this block. This method is described and illustrated in Chapter 1.

Sand the stock and forearm before polishing and bluing the metal as this makes it easier to get a level fit of the forearm and stock to the receiver. A good finish, and then checkering, adds a distinctive touch.

CADET SIGHT SELECTION

If open sights are wanted on the small Martini rifle, there is no better choice than the Williams Guide rear open sight and a front bead or post sight of your choice mounted on the Williams Shorty ramp base. The open rear sight should be mounted on the barrel about 4—5 inches ahead of the receiver. If you want a receiver sight instead of the open rear, then pick a Lyman, Redfield, or Williams receiver sight made for a flat receivered rifle (such as the Lyman No. 66A).

The Martini action, which can only be loaded and unloaded from the very top, requires a rather high scope mounting if the scope has to be mounted over the action. I have found the most suitable scope for the Martini is the target-type (Fig. 3-7) with the two-piece target scope mounts. I believe this is the best scope when the rifle is chambered for cartridges like the .22 Long Rifle, .22 WMR, .22 Hornet, .218 Bee and .222 Rimmed, where the rifle will be used for target and varmint shooting. Any of the popular target scopes will work splendidly on

this rifle, especially the smaller ones like the Unertl 1″ Target scope and the Unertl 1¼″ Varmint scope, If the rifle is also to be used for small game hunting I can't think of a better scope choice than the Unertl Small Game scope. If the barrel is straight tapered, use the same scope bases as listed for the Model 52 Winchester target rifle.

If you want to mount a hunting-type scope on this rifle, I'd suggest the use of the Weaver No. 60 one-piece base and the high Weaver quick detachable mounting rings.

The modern low-power long eye-relief scopes are also ideal for use on the small Martini rifles. Although these scopes are low in power, they are quite ideal for hunting small game at close ranges. The Leupold M8-2X and the Bushnell Phantom scopes are good.

OTHER SMALL MARTINIS

It should be pointed out that there are a number of so-called "small" Martini actions and rifles. A lot of the general information given in this chapter can be applied to some of the other small Martinis, but specifically the information is for the .310 Martini Cadet action and rifle and the BSA No. 12 action, which is the same as the Cadet. In addition, this information also applies to the BSA No. 13, 15, 12/15, and Centurian actions, all of which are basically identical to the No. 12 action. Remember that these are the actions in which the entire mechanism can be slipped out of the receiver as a unit, and that the breechblock and finger lever pivot pins are not fitted through the receiver walls.

Fig. 3-7. A medium-lightweight varmint rifle built on the Martini Cadet action. The 26″ barrel is chambered for the .22 K-Hornet cartridge and mounted on it is a 10× Davis Spotshot target scope.

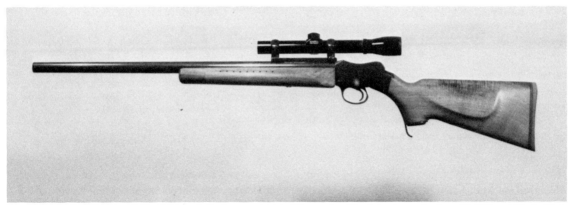

Fig. 3-8. I used a BSA No. 15 Martini target rifle to remodel into this sporter. The barrel was shortened to 24" and fitted with a Redfield Jr. base made for the Remington Model 760 rifle and the Weaver D-6 scope mounted with high ⅞" rings. The forearm was shortened and made thinner. The buttstock was also trimmed to make the grip smaller and wood trimmed from around the cheekpiece to give it a clean-cut outline.

Generally, all the small Martini actions in which the breechblock and finger lever are pivoted on pins or screws through the receiver walls (and there are many of them) are not as strong or as safe as those constructed like the Martini Cadet and No. 12 BSA. Therefore, the caliber suggestions listed herein for the Martini Cadet and its counterparts, *do not* apply to these other small Martini actions or rifles, regardless of their make.

The latest influx of imported surplus Martini rifles were BSA No. 12/15 and 15 .22 rimfire target rifles. For the most part these late arrivals were a sorry lot, although in most cases the bores were in excellent shape. These target rifles have actions almost identical to the common BSA No. 12 except that they have receivers with thicker sidewalls and thumb screws for quick disassembly of the firing mechanism or removal of the barrel. The exteriors of these rifles showed much neglect and abuse and the action parts considerable wear. This wear was usually in the areas of the locking shoulders of the breechblock and/or in the locking arms on the finger lever with the result that the action did not close tightly, producing excessive headspace. Almost everything is salvagable, however.

Here is what can be done: First check the serial number on the internal frame and compare it with the one on the receiver. If they do not match you may have a headspace problem no matter

whether the locking areas are worn or not. If the locking areas are worn—and this is readily detectable at a glance—this condition should be corrected first. I would suggest using nickel steel welding rod for this, building up the worn surfaces and then carefully dressing the built-up surfaces down so that the action closes tightly.

If the locking areas don't seem to be worn, and if the breechblock is loose when the action is uncocked and held upside down, or if the action can be closed with more than a .005" shim between the breechblock and the barrel, then this also indicates excessive headspace. To correct this condition, merely use steel shim stock between the rear of the internal mechanism frame and the receiver. Use a thickness that will bring the internal mechanism forward enough so that the action closes tightly. Cut the shim stock to the size of the rear of the internal frame and just lay it in place as the action is assembled. If the bore and chamber are in excellent shape, the rifle can be remodeled into a very good small game rifle as I did with the one shown in Fig. 3-8. I shortened the barrel to 24" and crowned it. I also shortened and slimmed up the forearm. On the buttstock I installed a Pachmyer rubber buttpad, cleaned up the outline of the cheekpiece, thinned the pistol grip, and installed a Neidner grip cap, and notched it for the finger lever. In the finger lever groove at the lower end of the pistol grip I glass-bedded in a magnet to help hold the finger lever

Fig. 3-9. The British Martini-Enfield military rifle in .577/.450 caliber.

closed. Fitted with a scope in a Redfield Jr. mount made for the Remington Model 760 rifle, polished and blued and the wood finished with Lin-Speed, the old Martini target rifle was transformed into a very neat small game rifle.

With another of these old Martini rifles I found that it was impossible to remove the stock bolt and remove the buttstock. I wanted to save the stock, and I solved the problem of its removal by drilling into the top of the grip and through the stock bolt with a ⅜″ drill to separate the bolt at that point. That done, the stock was pulled off the receiver, the stud unscrewed from the receiver, the head end of the bolt driven from the stock, and the hole in the top of the grip filled with a plug made from a piece of wood salvaged from the forearm.

The No. 12 and 12/15 BSA Martini actions are entirely suitable for rebarreling to some centerfire cartridges such as the .22 Hornet, 218 Bee, .256 Magnum, and .357 Magnum, and to any of the .222 family. Of course, the firing pin has to be changed and a rimless extractor used with the rimless cartridges; these jobs have been described earlier in this chapter.

THE MARTINI-ENFIELD

The "Martini-Enfield" is the large Martini action on which the British built a great many rifles and carbines in the .577/.450 caliber (Fig. 3-9). The same action, but with a Henry rifled barrel, is known as the Martini-Henry rifle or carbine. After the big blackpowder .577/.450 cartridge became obsolete, many of these rifles and carbines were converted to handle the .303 British cartridge. Later on some were even converted to the .22 Long Rifle rimfire caliber for gallery practice. Others

were also converted into smoothbore guns for special police use. A great many of all of the above guns were imported into the United States during the 1950s and '60s and sold on the surplus arms market. At this writing, however, they have disappeared from this market and now generally are available only from individual owners and not from surplus arms dealers.

This big British Martini military action is quite easy to identify by its size and numerous markings. The action is about 5″ long, 1.270″ thick, and weighs about 2 pounds 10 ounces. It is marked on both sides of the receiver with various proof marks, numbers, letters, etc., but its most prominent marking is the large crown with the letters V R under it. The date stamped in the same area is the date (year) of manufacture. If the rifle was converted from the original caliber to another one, additional marks were stamped on the receiver, leaving it well marked up. With all of these actions, most of the individual parts were also marked with numbers and proof marks.

During the years when there were a lot of these rifles available, some of the surplus arms dealers also offered separate Martini-Enfield actions for sale (Fig. 3-10). No doubt a lot of these actions were obtained by stripping the rifles and carbines which had ruined bores and wood. As long as these actions were complete and in reasonably sound condition, they were okay on which to build a rifle. However, at the same time these good British-made large Martini military actions were being sold, a great many similar Martini actions were being sold which were of very doubtful quality. In this last instance I am speaking about the Martini actions which have no British markings, and/or which have had the receiver sides sanded to make it appear that the British markings have been removed. These unmarked Martini actions may not be British-made, and indeed it is most likely they are not. Therefore, use *only* the well marked British-made actions for rifle building.

The American-made Peabody-Martini action is essentially the same as the Martini-Enfield and it can be included in the discussion on gunsmithing it. However, these actions are practically non-existent, as Peabody-Martini rifles are so scarce that they should not be stripped for the action lest a valuable collector item be destroyed.

MARTINI-ENFIELD ACTION STRENGTH

I am keenly aware that opinions differ as to the strength of the large British military Martini action, and I am well aware that a lot of these actions have in the past been used to build rifles in some of the hot wildcat calibers. I know that a sound Martini-Enfield action properly barreled and bushed is adequate for the .303 British cartridge, which is normally factory-loaded to a breech pressure of 45,000 psi. This being the case, this action is then suitable for most commercial rimmed cartridges which do not develop (or are not handloaded to develop) over 45,000 psi. This would include such

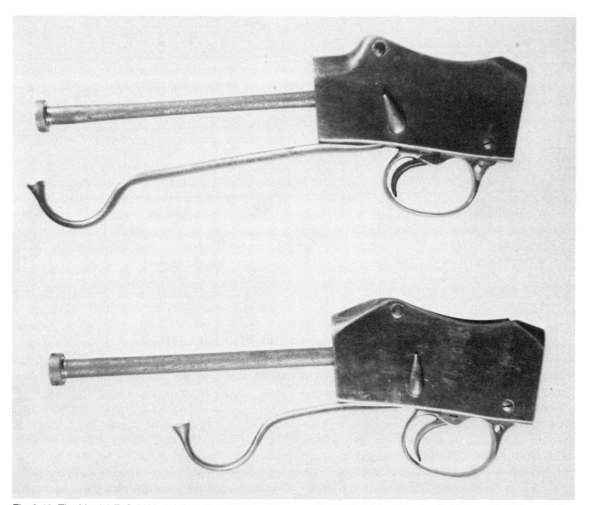

Fig. 3-10. The Martini-Enfield Mark I (long lever) action above, and the Mark II (short lever) action below. The action weighs about 2.5 pounds, is about 5″ long (receiver), and about 1.270″ thick.

common calibers as the .22 Hornet, .218 Bee, .22 Jet, .219 Zipper, .25-20, .256 Magnum, .25-35, .30-30, .30-40, .303 British, .32 Special, .357 Magnum, .38-55, .348, .44 Magnum, .444 Marlin and .45-70. If not loaded too hot it would also be okay for the .222 Rimmed and 5.6×50R Magnum cartridges. It would also be suitable for some "improved" cartridges based on the above listed cases, and for some wildcat cartridges, *provided* sensible loads are used in them. However, I would draw the line when it comes to cartridges like the .219 Improved Zipper, .22-.303, .25-.303, 6MM Krag and .25 Krag which are most often loaded much beyond the 45,000 psi limit. I also would not recommend any large Martini action for the .225 Winchester and the .220 Swift.

Although larger in size than the .310 Martini Cadet action, the Martini-Enfield action is actually no stronger or safer than the smaller Martini Cadet. The larger action has a larger barrel shank diameter and more chamber access room so that it can be used for larger cartridges than can the Martini Cadet, but since it is no stronger than the Martini Cadet, I feel that it should not be used with any cartridge developing much over 45,000 psi breech pressure. If the Martini-Enfield action is made up in the .45-70 caliber (and provided the barrel fitting, chambering, and bushing the breechblock has been properly done), heavy loads as recommended for the Model 86 Winchester can be used.

BUSHING THE ENFIELD BREECHBLOCK

Just as it is necessary to bush the firing pin hole in the Cadet Martini action, so is it necessary to do the same with the Martini-Enfield when used with any of the cartridges named above. The only exception is if the action has already been converted to handle the .303 British cartridge. The instructions given for the bushing of the Martini Cadet action in this chapter also apply to the Martini-Enfield action. However, with the larger Martini action there is an alternate method, the one employed by the British when they converted this action from .577/.450 to .303 caliber. To duplicate it, a female dovetail slot is cut across the face of the breechblock, centered over the firing pin hole, a male

dovetail wedge is made to fill the slot, the original firing pin tip is turned down to .078", a 5/64" firing pin hole is drilled in the wedge, and a small hole is drilled and tapped in the face of the breechblock intersecting the edge of the wedge for a screw to hold the wedge in place. The dovetail slot can be cut with a regular sight slot cutter and the wedge filler filed from a piece of good steel. There is no need to have the retainer screw as the British used. The front end of the breechblock will have to be annealed before the slot can be milled, but I see no need to do any reharding afterwards.

THE .577/.450 MARTINI

Newly manufactured .577/.450 cases with Boxer primer pockets are available from Brass Extrusion Laboratories, Ltd. (800 W. Maple Lane, Bensenville, Il. 60106). Regular .45-70 (.458") bullets can be used. The .577/.450 barrel has a bore diameter of .450", a groove diameter of .464", with seven lands pitched one turn in 22 inches. The .577/.450 chamber is too large to be rechambered for any other practical .45 caliber cartridge, and setting the barrel back sufficiently so that it could be rechambered for the .45-70 cartridge is also out of the question since the barrel is not large enough in diameter at the breech to allow this to be properly done. The original chamber could be bored out and a sleeve fitted and chambered for the .45-70 cartridge, but doing this is not very practical. Therefore, if you have a shootable .577/.450 and want to shoot it, you will be limited to using only .577/.450 ammunition and cases (Fig. 3-11).

REBARRELING THE ENFIELD

Figure 3-12 gives the barrel shank and thread specifications of the Martini-Enfield action. The procedure for fitting a barrel to this action is the same as for the Martini Cadet given earlier in this chapter. The procedure for altering the extractor is also the same. As is the case with the Martini Cadet, the chambering has to be done with the barrel unscrewed from the receiver. Therefore, in threading the barrel, cut the threads to fit the receiver very snugly so that in the process of fitting the barrel (which also includes chambering,

Fig. 3-11. The .577/.450 Martini cartridge.

headspacing, and extractor fitting), the threads will still be a close fit when the fitting has been completed.

The barrel blank should be at least 1.10″ in diameter at the breech to be suitable for this action. For moderate pressured cartridges, a smaller diameter blank can be used by employing a bushing on the breech end threaded or silver-soldered on. If you have the original Martini barrel, the breech end of it can be used for the bushing, thus doing away with the need of threading the shank and cutting the extractor cuts. For complete details on this see Chapter 2.

ENFIELD REMODELING

The military issue British-Martini-Enfield rifle and carbine in either the original .577/.450 or later .303 calibers can be remodeled into very nice sporting arms for hunting. The barrel of the rifle should be shortened to about 26″ and the forearm cut off to about 8″ or 10″ long, and refastened to the barrel with a screw. The forearm should be well tapered, the end rounded and shaped with a schnable, or fitted with a horn tip as similar British-made Martini sporters. New hunting sights such as the Williams Guide sights are ideal on such a rifle. The heavy and wide buttplate can be made thinner and

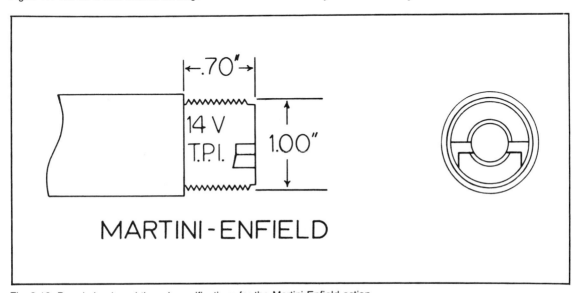

Fig. 3-12. Barrel shank and thread specifications for the Martini-Enfield action.

narrower, especially so near the toe end, and the buttstock trimmed accordingly.

Then the stock and forearm need to be refinished, and the metal parts blued if necessary. To really make it more British in appearance, the grip areas of the wood should be checkered and sling swivels fitted, one under the buttstock and one under the barrel about 4″ ahead of the forearm tip. For this I like to use detachable swivel studs, and for the front one silver-solder the stud head to a curved oblong plate and soft solder this to the barrel. The military Martini carbine can be remodeled in the same way as the rifle, but in this case the barrel does not need shortening.

The finger lever on the Martini-Enfield action is very long and heavy—unnecessarily so. The method I prefer to alter the finger lever is to cut off the lever about 1½″ back of its pivot hole, anneal and straighten out the loop in the part that was cut

off, and then using only enough of the thinner end as required for the grip of the new stock and welding this part back on the base of the finger lever. In other words, the heavy middle section of the finger lever stem is discarded. After the finger lever is welded it is bent cold to conform with the inside curve of the pistol grip (Fig. 3-13).

Reinhart Fajen Inc. makes a nice varmint style stock and forearm for the Martini-Enfield as shown on my own varmint rifle based on this action (Fig. 3-14). The Fajen stock can be used as is, or it can be reshaped and trimmed down to a more classic pattern, and there is plenty of wood to allow this to be done. The "rolled over" top edge of the cheekpiece can be trimmed off, the entire cheekpiece made smaller and thinner, and the pistol grip made slimmer. The end of the pistol grip can be shaped oval to accept a regular pistol grip cap. If desired, up to about ⅜″ can be sawed off the hollow rear end of the

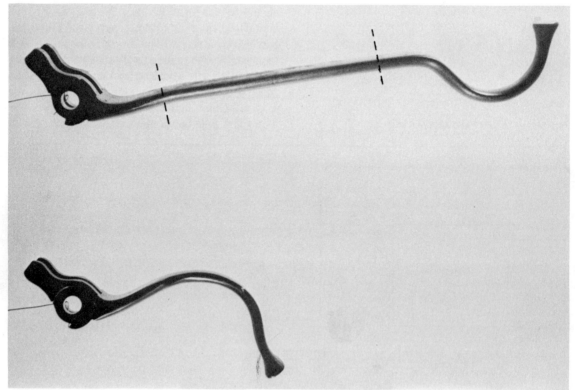

Fig. 3-13. When remodeling the Martini-Enfield finger lever it is suggested that the heavy center section between the dotted lines be cut out, the rear curved and straightened and welded on to the base section, and then curved to fit the pistol grip as shown below.

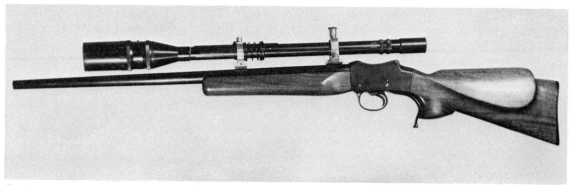

Fig. 3-14. A heavy varmint rifle I built on the British Martini-Enfield action with a semi-finished Fajen stock and forearm and a Wilson .219 Zipper barrel.

receiver, allowing the pistol grip to be placed that much further forward and closer to the trigger. To make the grip as trim as possible, file the rounded metal wall on top of the hollow tang thinner, for whatever metal is removed here will allow the grip to be made that much thinner.

The Fajen forearm made for this rifle is more than ample in size to be slimmed and shortened to any size and shape of forearm you may desire. Attach it the same way as outlined in Chapter 1. Sight selection, scope mounting, and trigger pull changes are the same as those covered earlier in this chapter.

I once made up a custom rifle on the Martini-Enfield action and chambered it for a rimless cartridge (Fig. 3-15). There are few rimless cartridges that I can recommend for use with this action, and those cartridges usually can be duplicated with a rimmed one; therefore I will dispense with instructions on how to modify the extractor for rimless cases. This action is best for only rimmed cartridges. Once I used this action to build a rifle in .22 Long Rifle caliber, but here again I was using an action just not suited for such a small cartridge, and all sorts of difficulties were encountered, the worst of which was altering and fitting the extractor.

I also once made a 12 gauge shotgun (Fig. 3-16) on this action and I soon discovered that the action was just too short and too small in places for this shotshell. While I did finish the job and came up with a shootable shotgun, I'd advise it not be done. Using the Martini-Enfield to make a 20 gauge shotgun would be feasible.

ENFIELD BREECHBLOCK ADJUSTMENT

(The following information and instructions

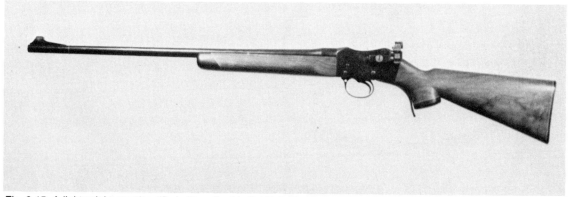

Fig. 3-15. A lightweight sporting rifle built on the Martini-Enfield action.

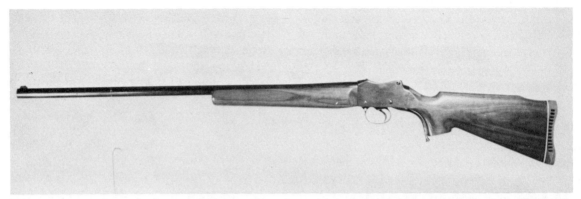

Fig. 3-16. A shotgun built on the Martini-Enfield action. This action is okay in size for the .20 gauge shell, but too small for the 12 gauge.

also applies to the Martini Cadet action.) In the normal Martini-Enfield action, after the action has been opened and the finger lever released, the action of the mainspring automatically swings the breechblock up to a point where the sear notch contacts the trigger. For easy and convenient loading, the breechblock should stop at a point where the groove in its top is slightly below the chamber

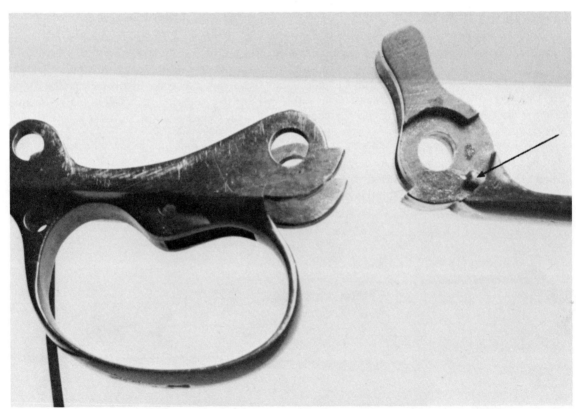

Fig. 3-17. Arrow points to the spring-backed plunger in a hole drilled into the Martini finger lever to provide tension to hold the lever closed. The trigger guard is notched at the spot at the end of the plunger's travel when the action is closed.

so that a cartridge can slide over the breechblock directly into the chamber. In using this variety of cartridges from the .22 Hornet on up, the action can be readily adjusted so the breechblock will return to, and remain in, a position suited to the cartridge the rifle is chambered for. If the .577/.450 action is rebarreled for the .45-70 or similar large diameter cartridge, no adjustment may be needed. But if the same action is used for a smaller diameter cartridge like the .219 Zipper or still smaller cartridges, adjustments should be made to make the breechblock stop at a higher level.

To make the breechblock stop at a higher level, the sear tip of the trigger is shortened. Better still, metal can be removed from the rear inside of the striker where it contacts the upper arm of the cocking lever. Only a small amount of metal removed will cause a considerable change in the stopping position of the breechblock. Even honing the sear will cause a change in where the breechblock stops, so remove metal cautiously to avoid overdo-ing it. In the event the breechblock stops too high, then correct for this condition by welding on some additional metal to the rear of the upper arm of the cocking lever.

If, after you have finished remodeling or building a rifle on the big Martini action, you find that the finger lever droops when the striker is down, this can be remedied by installing a small spring and plunger in the base of the finger lever (Fig. 3-17). Drill a ⅛″ hole about ½″ deep into one side of the base and fit it with a spring and round-ended hardened plunger. Assemble the action and work the lever a number of times so that a track is left on the trigger guard by the plunger. Then file in a shallow notch with a round needle file at the rear end of the track so that the plunger will slip into it when the action is closed. This will end the drooping finger lever. It would be a good idea to harden the surface on the trigger guard where the plunger rides and this can be done by using a case-hardening compound, heating and quenching the area involved.

Chapter 4

Gunsmithing the FBW Falling Block Actions

Single-shot rifle builders, it gives me much pleasure to introduce to you a friend, Falling Block Works, Inc. (Box 22, Troy, Michigan 48084). Since 1973 this small firm has been manufacturing falling block actions of good quality and of immense strength for you to build rifles on. At the time of this writing their catalog listed five different FBW actions and from all appearances it seems likely that they will not soon go out of the action-making business. I have built rifles on four of these and thus know a little bit about them.

THE FBW ACTIONS

Now let me introduce the five FBW actions. From the smallest to the largest they are: FBW Model K, FBW Model S, FBW Models J and H, and the FBW Model L Express. Except for size, all five are essentially alike. Briefly described, they are exposed hammer, manually cocked, falling block actions operated by an under finger lever which doubles as the trigger guard. They are all-steel actions made of precision investment castings with one-piece receivers. All feature throughbolt buttstock attachment, double torsion mainspring, trigger in direct contact with the hammer, half-cock safety notch, vented firing pin, and a plain extractor. All, except the Model H, have blowback and gasproof firing pins. The receiver and all the other important parts are heat-treated for maximum strength. The actions are quite well finished on the outside, ready to barrel and stock. These actions are of rather simple design with the hammers pivoted in the receiver rather than in the breechblock. Except for the Model S, the actions were designed primarily for rimmed cartridges. I can recommend them.

Model K

Action weight:	24 oz.
Action thickness:	1.05″
Sidewall thickness:	.150″
Barrel shank:	.750×16V thread, .990″ long

This is the Falling Block Works small action

Fig. 4-1. The FBW Model K single-shot action. This is a small but very strong falling block action best suited for the smaller rimmed centerfire cartridges such as the .22 Hornet and .256 Magnum.

designed especially for the smaller center-fire cartridges (Fig. 4-1). Cartridges ideal for this action are the .22 Hornet, .218 Bee, .222 Rimmed, .22 Jet, 5.6×50R Magnum, .25-20, .256 Magnum, and any of the K, improved, or wildcat versions of these cartridges. This action is also okay for the .357 Magnum and the .44 Magnum.

I believe it would also be suitable for car-

tridges in the order of the .219 Zipper, .25-35, and .30-30, but I would consider it only marginal for wildcat and improved cartridges based on these cases such as the .219 Wasp, .219 Improved Zipper and .25-35 Improved. The same goes for the .225. The reason why I believe this small action is marginal for the last few cartridges mentioned is that the barrel shank is quite small and unless the barrel shank is fitted very closely in the receiver, the chamber in that area may swell.

Although I have not done it, I feel sure the extractor of this action can be altered and modified similar to that described for the Model J so that it would handle rimless cartridges such as the .221, .222, .222 Magnum, .223, and the .30 Carbine. This action is ideal on which to build a featherweight varmint rifle (Fig. 4-2).

FBW Model S

Action weight:	37 oz.
Action thickness:	1.27″
Side-wall thickness:	.135″
Barrel shank:	Diameter—1″×14V thread, Length—1.495″

This medium-sized action (Fig. 4-3) was introduced in 1980 and in my opinion is the best one Falling Block Works has so far come up with. Its mechanical design and construction is essentially the same as the other FBW single-shot actions, the difference being mostly in the shape of the receiver

Fig. 4-2. The light varmint rifle that I built on the FBW Model K action. It is fitted with a 24″ Federal sporter barrel in .222 Rimmed caliber. The 10× Universal scope is mounted in a Redfield Jr. mount. Although it weighs only 6.5 pounds the rifle is extremely accurate. The walnut stock is fitted with a horn buttplate and pistol grip cap.

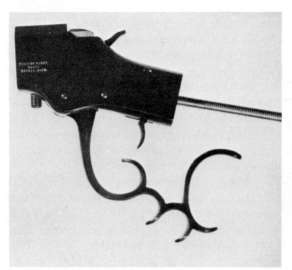

Fig. 4-3. The Model S action is shown here fitted with the Schuetzen-styled finger lever.

and in the extractor. FBW describes this action as being suitable for all rimmed and rimless cartridges up to the .458 Magnum.

The receiver of the FBW Model S action has somewhat lower sidewalls than do the others. This is good as it allows freer access to the chamber. The top of the breechblock slants down toward the rear, not too unlike the block of the Stevens No. 44½.

The extractor of the Model S action is designed and made to handle either rimmed or rimless cartridges, a first for FBW. The extractor is centerhung in the base of the finger lever. From that point upwards it dog-legs to the left, then up to the side of the chamber and then to the right into the chamber. A spring-backed plunger is positioned in the first dog-leg bend, exerting side pressure to the extractor to the right. On opening the action, as the extractor tips back, the slightly angled slot in the receiver in which the extractor moves forces the extractor hook to the left and out of the way of the cartridge. It is a very good arrangement for rimless cartridges. As with all FBW actions, the extractors have a blank hook so that it can be altered and adapted for all sizes of cartridges. The extractor should function with rimmed cartridges just as well as with rimless ones, retaining the side tension arrangement so the hook will snap over the case

rim. However, I think it might be best when making the rifle for a rimmed cartridge to remove the spring and plunger so that the extractor functions just the same as the usual rimmed extractor.

The Model S action has another new feature that reminds one of the Stevens No. 44½, and that is a set screw in the bottom front of the receiver and into the threaded barrel shank hole. It is a socket head set screw, and it can be used to tighten the barrel if you want to make the rifle a take-down or use it with interchangable barrels. In addition, there is a ⅜" hole in the front of the receiver; using the set screw to tighten a ⅜" rod in it, you have a forearm hanger.

Another feature that may interest many rifle builders is that FBW makes six different styles of finger levers for this action. The S-shaped lever is standard but at extra charge you can get a grip lever as shown in Fig. 4-4, two styles of loop levers for straight or pistol grip, and two styles of Schuetzen levers (Fig. 4-3). Another extra for this action is an adaptor to mount a tang sight on. This adaptor is secured to the receiver by the stock bolt. I should mention here that the Model S action also has a greater extractor movement than do the other four FBW actions.

So whether you want to build a light-weight sporter (Fig. 4-5) or any weight sporter, varmint,

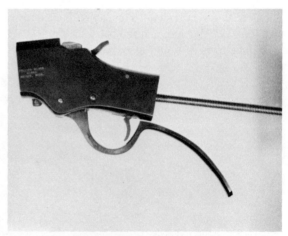

Fig. 4-4. The FBW Model S action. This action is shown with the grip finger lever, although the S-shaped lever is standard. Four other finger lever styles are available for this action, including two Schuetzen styles and two loop styles.

70

Fig. 4-5. My eight-pound varmint/deer rifle in .243 caliber was built on the FBW Model S action. It is fitted with a 25″ Shilen sporter barrel and a Fajen stock and forearm. The 6× scope is mounted in Weaver top detachable rings on a Weaver No. 50 one-piece base.

big game, target or Schuetzen rifle (Fig. 4-6), I can recommend this action.

FBW Models H and J

	Model H	Model J
Action weight:	41 oz.	34 oz.
Action thickness:	1.375″	1.312″
Sidewall thickness:	.187″	.160″
Barrel shank:	1.0′×14V	1.0×14V
	thread	thread
	.990″ long	.990″ long

These two FBW actions (Figs. 4-7 and 4-8) are the Falling Block Works standard or medium-sized actions. As the specifications indicate, the two are nearly alike. They differ slightly in their internal mechanism and outward appearance and shape but otherwise they can be classed as one. Either action may be chosen for the following rimmed cartridges: .219, .225, 5.6×57R, 6.5×57R, 7×57R, .30-40, .32-40, .348, .38-55, .444 Marlin, and .45-70.

They are also ideal for any of the many improved and wildcat cartridges based on these cases, such as those based on the .30-30 and .30-40 cases

Fig. 4-6. My Schuetzen-styled target rifle is built on the Model S action with the Schuetzen finger lever. The half-octagon barrel is tapered from 1.20″ across the flats at the breech to .800″ at the round muzzle and is topped with a Lyman Jr. TargetSpot scope. A novel feature of the buttstock is the integral wood prong, made so to avoid the necessity of purchasing or making a pronged butt plate. This rifle is chambered for the .30-30 cartridge, and it has proven extremely accurate. Weight without scope is ten pounds.

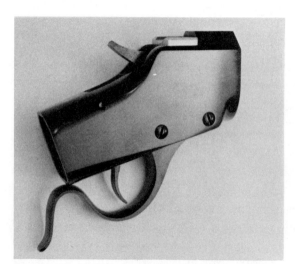

Fig. 4-7. The FBW Model J action. This is the standard or medium-sized FBW action suitable for most rimmed and rimless cartridges from .22 Hornet to .45-70 and from .222 to .30-06. Like all of the other FBW falling block actions, the Model J is of simple design and construction, with the major parts made by the investment casting process of the best steel, and heat treated.

(Fig. 4-9). These would include such popular wildcats as the .22/.30-30, 6MM/.30-30, 6MM Krag, .25 Krag, and .35 Krag. With a rimless extractor alteration, the Model J action is suitable for any of the standard rimless cartridges ranging from the .22-250 to the .35 Whelen. These two actions are suitable for building light to medium weight sporting rifles (Fig. 4-10), medium to heavy weight varmint rifles, and medium to heavy weight target rifles.

FBW Model L Express

Action weight:	44 oz.
Action thickness:	1.47″
Sidewall thickness:	.175″
Barrel shank:	1.125″×12V thread .990″ long

As the name implies and weight suggests, this is Falling Block Works magnum action suitable for the largest and most powerful rimmed cartridges (Fig. 4-11). If you want to build a single-shot rifle in the .45-125 Sharps caliber using the full length .45 RCBS Basic case, or for one of the British express rimmed cartridges, this is the action to use. It is a big action all over with a large diameter barrel shank for large diameter cartridges. There is no stronger or safer falling block action than this one. Designed primarily for rimmed cartridges, the extractor can nevertheless be modified to extract a rimless or belted cartridge. As shown in Fig. 4-12, I used this action to build a sporting rifle in the .375 H & H Magnum caliber.

I would *not* recommend this action be barreled and chambered for the Browning .50 caliber machine gun cartridge. This action is best suited for building a ten-pound American or British styled big game sporting rifle, or a heavier target rifle.

BARRELS AND BREECHING

The FBW Model K is a small action and therefore best suited for the lighter weight barrels. Good barrel size and contour choices for this action are the Nos. 1, 2, 3, and 4 Shilen barrels which range from the 20″ ultra-lightweight No. 1 to the standard weight 24″ No. 4 sporter. Since this action is just over one inch in thickness, the shoulder of the barrel fitted to it should be turned to around .875″.

The No. 3 Shilen light sporter barrel would be a minimum size choice for the FBW Model S, H, or J actions, although for a seven to eight pound sporting

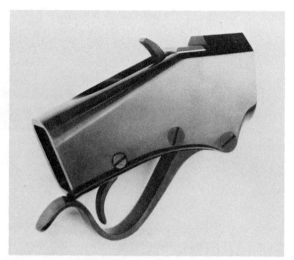

Fig. 4-8. The FBW Model H action. Slightly heavier and thicker than the Model J, it is suited for the same range of rimmed cartridges as the Model J.

Fig. 4-9. My .30-40 Improved caliber rifle built on the FBW Model H action. The scope is mounted in Weaver top detachable mounts. With a 27″ medium heavy sporter barrel the rifle weighs 9.5 pounds.

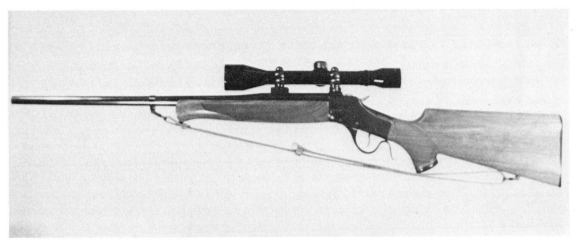

Fig. 4-10. A .257 Roberts sporting rifle that I built on the FBW Model J action. It is fitted with a 24″ standard weight sporter barrel and a stock and forearm of American walnut. The scope is mounted in Buehler rings on Buehler blank bases machined to fit the barrel. With sling, the rifle weighs eight pounds.

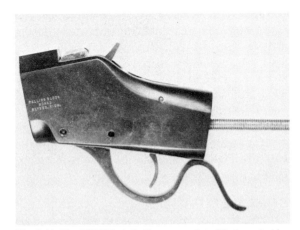

Fig. 4-11. The FBW Model L Express action. It is threaded for an inch and an eighth barrel shank and is the action to choose for building a rifle in one of the larger calibers.

rifle I would suggest the No. 4 Shilen barrel. For a slightly heavier sporter or medium weight varmint rifle, the No. 5 Shilen 26″ barrel would be ideal.

The big FBW Model L action requires a barrel shank diameter of 1.125″ and that means in order to have sufficient shoulder abutment against the receiver, the shoulder must have a diameter of at least 1.200″, although a diameter of 1.250″ would be better. The No. 5 Shilen 26″ medium sporter barrel would be the minimum size choice for this action, although I believe the No. 6 would be better. The ideal sporter barrel for this action is the Federal Firearms 26″ heavy sporter barrel which has a shoulder diameter of 1.250″.

All of the FBW actions are made with the breechblock at a 90 degree angle to the bore and

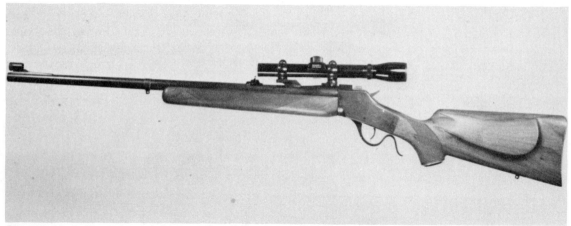

Fig. 4-12. I built this .375 H & H sporter on the Model L action. This shows the rifle with the unaltered finger lever.

this makes breeching quite easy. I recommend that in fitting and breeching a barrel to any of these actions that the breeching space—that is, the space or gap between the breech face of the barrel and face of the breechblock when the barrel is tightly set up in the receiver—be held to a maximum of .001". I prefer an even closer fit than that—say of no more than .0005". When this close fit is achieved, you simply remove the barrel and chamber it to a depth so that an unfired cartridge case head is flush with the breech face.

I usually prefer to do the chambering operation in a lathe setup, especially if it is for a bottlenecked cartridge. I quit the lathe setup when the chamber is about .010" to .015" short of correct depth, then do the final work with the barrel held in a vise and turning the chambering reamer by hand with a tap wrench. If the chamber is for a rimless cartridge, I chamber full depth or to within a couple of thousands or so before making the extractor cut and fitting the extractor, and then set the barrel into the receiver and finish the chamber. When chambering for a rimmed cartridge, I stop short, then make the extractor cut and fit the extractor. Then, with the barrel fully tightened in the receiver, I finish the chamber by hand, cutting in the rim recess in the extractor at the same time.

If you have read the first three chapters in this book you will already have noted that my chambering technique varies depending on the rifle, barrel,

caliber, condition of reamer, etc. Every gunsmith who does any chambering gradually develops his own methods and those methods may well be different from mine. Anyway, chambering a barrel is a reaming operation, a very critical one, so take it slow and easy, use plenty of cutting oil and clean the chips out of the reamer and chamber often. When you get near the final depth, be extra careful. Then, when checking the chamber for depth, just be sure it is clean of oil and chips as either can upset your calculations. Use headspace gauges if you can afford them; I have always preferred to use new, unfired cartridge cases.

If you have purchased a chambering reamer you already know how expensive they are, but you may not know how hard and brittle they are. Handle and use them with care. Drop one on a cement floor and it is likely to break in two. Crowd it in a chamber and it may chip or break. Don't back up a reamer while chambering. If it gets stuck in the chamber, I find it best to loosen it with a steel cleaning rod through the bore, lightly rapping on the reamer with it. Never remove a reamer from a chamber with the barrel in a lathe setup until the lathe is at a dead stop.

FITTING THE EXTRACTOR

The next job after the barrel has been fitted and breeched is fitting the extractor. If the cartridge selected is a rimmed one, the chamber should not

74

be cut to its full depth before the extractor fitting job as the final deepening of the chamber and head-spacing is best done after the extractor has been fitted so that the rim recess can be cut into the extractor hook as the chamber is finished. This applies to all of the FBW action models. However, if the chambering is for a rimless cartridge, the chamber can be finished before fitting the extractor.

The following paragraphs are instructions for extractor fitting with a rimmed cartridge. The FBW Models H, J, and K actions have extractors much alike, and all of them intersect the chamber at the lower left quarter. The first thing to do is file smooth the front and rear of the extractor hook and its left side. Then, with the barrel tightly set up in the receiver and using a narrow steel rule held against the left side of the extractor cut in the receiver, scribe a vertical line on the face of the barrel; this line will represent the left side of the extractor cut that has to be made in the barrel. At the same time, make a horizontal line across the center of the breech face. You can also scribe in the right side line of the extractor cut. This can be done with the rule or by holding the extractor in place in the receiver and against the barrel breech. Now remove the barrel from the receiver.

Perhaps the best way to cut the extractor slot or cut into the barrel face is with a milling attachment in a lathe setup, using a small diameter end mill to do the cutting. Try for a close fit. The cut should not be higher than the center horizontal line.

Now remove the barrel from the lathe and polish the extractor cut. Replace the barrel in the receiver and tighten it to its original position. Fit the extractor so that the breechblock closes over it as easily with it in place as without it. This may require some filing and polishing. When you have achieved this fit, carefully file or grind the right side of the extractor hook level with the chamber (or lacking a few thousands to be finished off, to chamber level) with the chambering reamer. Your final step is to finish up the job with the finish chambering reamer, cutting in the rim recess in the extractor at the same time.

With the extractor so fitted in the Model H and J actions, the extractor is supported at the left by a wall of steel left there when the extractor cut was made. This is what you want. However, in fitting the extractor in the Model K action, the barrel shank is so small that very little left side support wall is left. This is okay. Instead of milling in the extractor cut in the Model K, the cut can be made by filing it in. Rather than being a cut or slot as it is in the Model H and J actions, it is a notch in the Model K.

As for the FBW Model S or L action, its extractor hook extends into the chamber from the left almost exactly like that of the high-wall Winchester, and fitting this extractor is done in the same way. For this information, see Chapter 1.

Now for the rimless extractor installation and modification for the FBW actions. I will first describe how I made this alteration in the Model J action. After the chamber was completely finished, the scribe marks made, and the barrel removed from the receiver and set up in the lathe-mill attachment, I used a 3/16″ end mill and carefully milled out the extractor cut to a depth of .185″. For the extractor to function properly with a rimless cartridge its hook has to have room to swing sideways—and with the .257 case, move about .035″. Thus I made an extra pass with the mill on the left side of the extractor cut to widen it to about .225″. The cut can be narrower than this, but in this event enough has to be filed off one side of the extractor hook to achieve the .035 extractor swing.

After the cut was made and finished, smoothed with files and emery paper, I reset the barrel into the receiver for the last time. I then fitted the extractor, first filing its hook so that the breechblock would close with the extractor in place. I then carefully hand-filed the concave on the right side of the extractor hook so that with the extractor in place and swung to the left a case could be inserted into the chamber (Fig. 4-13). At this point I used a ½″ end mill on my lathe to cut the rim recess into the face of the extractor (with the extractor out of the action, of course). This has to be .050″ deep or slightly more. Lastly, I used a small half-round file to bevel the front edge of the concave so that the extractor would engage in the extractor groove in the cartridge case.

Fig. 4-13. A close-up view of the open breech of the Model J action with a cartridge in the chamber.

Figure 4-14 shows how I supplied spring tension to the extractor so that the hook can snap over the cartridge rim as the action is closed and to hold the hook in the extractor groove as the action is opened. It is merely a thin piece of metal bent and filed as shown and held in place by a 1/16″ crosspin on which is also the coil spring (Fig. 4-15). The rear end of the lever is slightly beveled and just long enough to push the extractor hook to the right for most of its short travel, moving off when the extractor is tipped back to allow the extractor hook to relax and move to the left so it won't interfere with loading and ejection.

An extractor alteration as just described might also work in the FBW Model H action. With some changes in the above dimensions it would work in the Model K action with the .222 family of cartridges. Making the rimless extractor alteration for

the FBW Model L action when chambered for a belted magnum cartridge is rather easy. The dog-legged extractor in this action is a bit difficult to fit and requires considerable filing. Adapting it for a rimless or belted cartridge is only a little more difficult than fitting it for a rimmed cartridge. Here is how I did it: Step one is to file the entire outside surface of the extractor to remove all evidence of a casting so that it is bright all over, then polish it with emery paper. File the top of the extractor hook down level with the horizontal centerline of the bore or firing pin. File the underside of the hook to make it narrower. I made mine about 3/16″ in width and tapered a bit towards the end. With the completely chambered barrel set up tight in the receiver, I put the extractor in place and with a scribe marked the breech for the extractor hook slot.

Next, the barrel is removed and the slot filed or milled out. I try to get this slot correct the first time so that when I again set up the barrel in the receiver, I won't have to repeat this operation again. With the barrel in place I now do the final fitting of the extractor. When it is free to pivot in and out of the extractor cut, I shorten the hook so that it projects the depth of the extractor groove into the chamber, or approximately .030″. I finish by making the rim recess cut, making it from .005″ to .010″ deeper than the cartridge rim. After this I file a 45 degree concave bevel on the front end of the hook just short of leaving the end sharp.

The next step in the extractor alteration for the rimless or belted case is to provide lateral movement for its hook end and to provide spring tension to keep the hook to the right. This is easily accomplished. By the time the extractor is filed and polished smooth and the hook fitted, it may already have all the lateral movement that is needed for the hook to move over the cartridge rim and engage in the extractor groove. If not, all that is required is to file some metal from the top left side of the extractor until the hook can pass over the cartridge rim without restriction. Now install the small spring and plunger in the base of the finger lever. Figure 4-16 shows the approximate location for this hole. I used a 3/32″ drill for this and drilled almost all the way through. A medium tension spring and a

¼" long plunger completed the alteration. To achieve the spring-tensioned lateral movement needed, I also had to file some metal from the bottom left side of the extractor stem. Assembling the action with the plunger in place is not too difficult. Follow this procedure: Cock the hammer, insert the extractor in its place, partly insert the assembled breechblock and finger lever in place, insert the spring and plunger, and using a darning needle or similar tool depress the plunger and shove the finger lever home and insert the finger lever screw. The only other additional work I did to make the extractor perform perfectly was to file a bit of metal from the sharp edge below the face of the breechblock so the block could open a bit further and file away some metal from the angled surface of

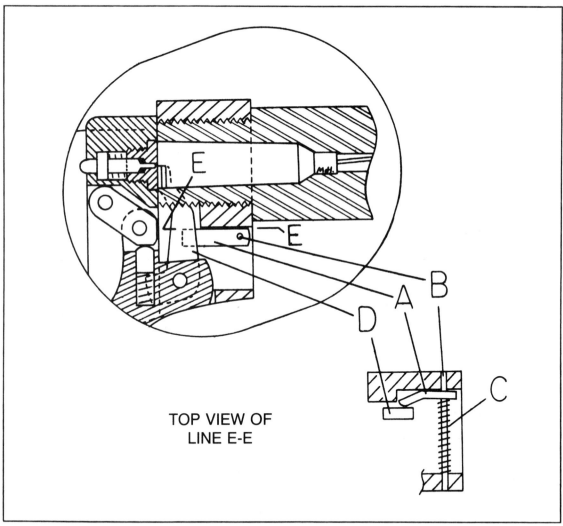

TOP VIEW OF
LINE E-E

Fig. 4-14. Sectional drawing of the Falling Block Works Model J action showing my modified extractor for rimless cartridges. The inset is a top sectional view of the action and extractor parts below Line E-E. It shows (A) the extractor lever, (B) the extractor lever pin, (C) the extractor lever spring and (D) the extractor. The extractor is shown in its forward (action closed position, with the extractor lever holding tension against the extractor so it rides in the extraction groove of a rimless case. As the action is opened and the extractor is tipped back, carrying the case, the extractor clears the end of the extractor lever, relieving the tension and allowing a case to be easily withdrawn or inserted into the chamber.

Fig. 4-15. Front of the Model J action showing the pin, spring, and lever installed to provide lateral tension to the extractor for modification to a rimless cartridge.

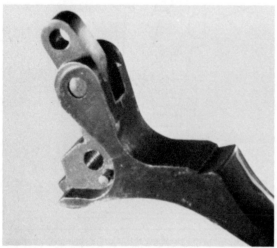

Fig. 4-16. This close-up photo shows the location of the spring-backed plunger in the Model L finger lever base to provide lateral tension to the extractor when altering it to handle a rimless or belted cartridge.

the upper front of the breech face so that the extractor can tip back a bit further.

Getting the Model L action to open a bit further is also a good idea for other FBW models, especially the Model H.

Installing the extractor in FBW Model L and S actions is not unlike the installation in a Winchester high-wall as described in Chapter 1. For the most part, the extractor fitting procedures described in Chapter 2 and elsewhere in this book are almost entirely that of fitting the extractor by hand with files as the main tools. Below however, is the procedure to follow in the fitting of the extractor in the FBW Model S action using a milling machine (in my case, a Jet 626 bench mill) to make the barrel cuts and shape the extractor.

The extractor furnished with this action is a rough, unfinished blank (Fig. 4-17) with its lip or hook left much wider and longer than necessary. The entire extractor should be filed and polished smooth but this should not be done until the extractor cuts have been made in the barrel and the barrel fitted and chambered. The sequence of operations should be as follows:

Thread the barrel. Fit and breech the barrel.

Chamber the barrel. This is best done by removing the barrel from the action. If the chambering is for a rimless cartridge, the chambering can be completed to the proper headspace depth. However, if the chambering is for a rimmed cartridge, then the chamber should not be cut full depth at this stage; cut to a depth to where the rim recess is started and stop.

Replace the barrel in the action and tighten it to final position. Use a square-ended steel rule and scribe a horizontal line centered across the barrel breech. It would also be wise to mark the barrel and receiver with an index mark; use a narrow and sharp chisel for this and stamp the index mark on the upper edge of the barrel breech and receiver ring end. Also at this time tighten and loosen the takedown set screw a few times so that it leaves a mark on the barrel threads. Remove the barrel and set it up for milling, using the line across the breech face to square it up, and with a ⅜″ end mill cut a flat, thread-deep, at the setscrew location.

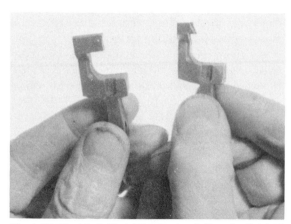

Fig. 4-17. The blank Model S extractor (left) and a finished one for a .30-06 head sized cartridge at the right. All of the shaping was done with a ½" diameter end mill in a milling machine although it could have been done by hand.

Without removing the barrel from this setup, use a 3/16" Woodruff keyway cutter and make the slot in the left side of the barrel breech for the extractor (Fig. 4-18). For either a rimless or rimmed cartridge make this slot .100" deep, which is the approximate thickness of the extractor hook. For a rimless chambering, cut the slot so that ⅛" of its width is below the centerline of the barrel breech. For a rimmed chamber, make the cut below the centerline with the upper edge of the slot on the centerline. The finished slot is 3/16" wide and parallel with the center line.

In the same setup, but with the barrel turned 90 degrees and using a ¼" end mill, cut away metal from the lower left of the barrel to make room for the extractor stem. Use the extractor as a visual guide in determining how far back this cut has to be. For a rimmed chamber, make this side cut the depth of the thickness of the extractor stem (which is about .175") measured from the top of the threads. When chambering for a rimmed cartridge, the spring and plunger in the extractor are not used.

However, when the chambering is for a rimless, semi-rimless, or belted cartridge, the muzzle of the barrel should be tipped up a few degrees so that in milling away this side metal the cut is deeper at the front than at the rear. The angle should match that of the angle of the right side of the extractor stem slot in the receiver. The reason for the angled

cut is to provide sideways movement to the extractor. It is difficult to give measurements for this side cut, but if you carefully examine the extractor in the action, you will see the reason for the angled cut and about how deep it has to be. The side cut for the rimless chambering can be a bit deeper and larger than needed with no harm done.

Replace the barrel and finish the extractor fitting job. File or machine the hook of the rimless extractor so that it is flush with the chamber when the hook is tipped to the left, cut in the rim recess about .003" or so deeper than the thickness of the cartridge rim, and then bevel the forward edge of the hook to a 45 degree angle. The edge between the bevel and the rim recess should not be made sharp. The shortening of the hook, cutting the rim

Fig. 4-18. Machining the extractor cut in a barrel for the FBW Model S action with a Jet 626 milling machine. A 3/16" Woodruff Keyway cutter is used to machine the horizontal cut in the breech face and a ¼" end mill used to remove the metal from the side for the extractor stem as shown here.

recess, and the bevel can be done with a ¼″ diameter end mill (Fig. 4-19) for all .30-06 head sized chamberings. Finishing the rimmed extractor requires only that the end of the hook be shortened to chamber level and then, while it is in place, finished with the chambering reamer as the chamber is cut to final depth to correct headspace. After fitting, the extractor should be filed and polished smooth, tested, and final fitting done if any is needed.

BREECH ACCESS

All of the FBW falling block action models except the Model S have very high sidewalls, and I think needlessly so. The very high walls are fine in that they provide optimum support to the breechblock, but they do interfere with the loading and unloading of the rifle. (I like Ruger's idea on their No. 1 and 3 rifles of having one sidewall lower than the other as this provides ready access to the breech for loading.) This is especially noticeable if

Fig. 4-19. Shaping the Model S extractor hook in a milling machine setup using an end mill.

there is a scope mounted on the rifle and nowadays most single-shot rifle shooters want scopes on their rifles. Therefore, on all the FBW models, and especially so on the little Model K and the large Model L, lowering one wall up to ⅜″ sure makes loading and unloading a lot more convenient (Fig. 4-20). I fail to see that doing this will weaken the action to any adverse extent. If the rifle is scope sighted and if it is to be used for hunting, then I certainly recommend the lowering of one wall. Another advantage gained in so doing is that you also have greater access to the hammer. You can use a milling machine to cut down the wall or you can cut it down the hard way by drilling, sawing, and filing. Not only can the hammer be thumbed better with the sidewall lowered, but if a little metal is removed from the receiver in the area of the hammer spur when the hammer is cocked, an auxiliary hammer spur can be attached to the hammer to make the rifle even more handy to operate. Perhaps a better idea would be to heat and bend the hammer spur to the side of the lowered wall, or weld on a wing to the spur.

MODIFYING TRIGGER GUARD AND FINGER LEVER

The Classic S-style finger lever as found on a number of both old and new single-shot rifle actions is hard to beat. This type finger lever, with the lever doubling as the trigger guard, was the standard style used on the long-obsolete Winchester Model 85 and on the Stevens No. 44 and 44½ single-shot rifles, and this lever is now also standard on the new Browning M-78, Ruger No. 3, and on all but one Falling Block Works actions. On the older rifles which were made with straight-gripped stocks, as well as the new No. 3 Ruger, I like the S-shaped finger lever as well as any I have ever used.

This lever is also quite acceptable on rifles having a pistol grip stock, provided the pistol grip is not a full or close-up one. The ideal pistol grip with such a lever is best typified by the rather long "semi" grips as found on the Winchester M-85 and Stevens No. 44 and 44½s when they were made with a pistol grip stock, and now on the new Browning M-78. I am not at all fond of these long "semi" pistol grips, and on my single-shot rifles I

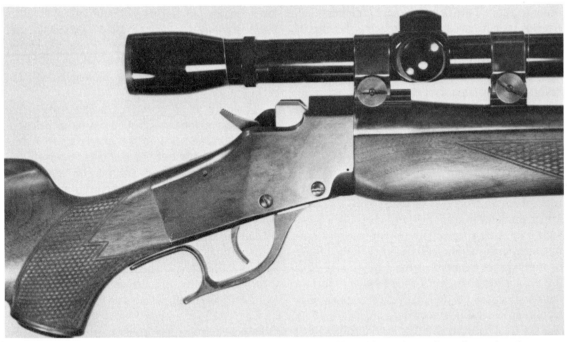

Fig. 4-20. A close-up view of the stocked FBW Model L action. The lowered right side receiver wall permits much easier access for loading and unloading and better access to the hammer. The altered finger lever provides more finger room and greatly reduces the chances of bruised fingers from firing the heavy-recoiling rifle.

like a full pistol grip—one that is well-placed in relation to the trigger, usable and "grippable," and one that is no longer or larger in circumference than necessary. The perfect example of such a grip is on the Ruger No. 1. But with such a grip the S-shaped lever is far from ideal. It just does not fit in.

When I received my FBW Model J action, I was most anxious to get a shooting rifle built on it as quickly as possible and therefore I made no major changes on the action itself. I made the stock for it with a rather full pistol grip and placed it as far forward as its S-shaped finger lever would allow and not cramp my fingers while gripping and triggering the rifle.

Despite this, on firing the rifle I found that the S-hook on the lever still caused a cramped hold on the grip. In particular, the inverted U-loop that formed the S-hook was too narrow for my middle finger, even though my fingers are rather slim. At any rate, something about the grip and lever was not to my liking, and I proposed to correct this condition by installing a separate trigger guard and altering the finger lever to fit only partway around this guard.

The FBW actions are ideal for making this change. All models have solid bottoms, with more than ample metal in front of and behind the trigger opening to which a separate trigger guard can be attached, and the finger lever is such that it can be altered in just about any way you might want it. In checking my Model J action, I could see that a separate trigger guard of any one of various types and sizes could be fastened to the bottom of the receiver in several ways. It was obvious that perhaps the best procedure was to obtain a trigger guard made for a double-barreled shotgun, and attach it the same way it is attached to the shotgun. This is usually done by drilling and tapping a hole in the bottom of the receiver about ¼-inch ahead of the trigger opening to accept the threaded stud on the front of the guard and then inletting the tang of the guard into the bottom curve of the pistol grip and using a wood screw to hold it. I had such a guard on hand but found that the guard bow was too long; in order to get it in the best position in relation to the trigger, I would have had to alter it and relocate the threaded stud or use some other method to attach the front of the guard to the receiver. Instead, I decided to use a simple slip-in hook-on method for both the front and rear of the guard.

I altered the double shotgun trigger guard (similar ones made of steel are available from Richland Arms Corporation, Blissfield, Michigan) as needed. I started by cutting off most of the tang and about a half inch from the stud end. Then I heated the front end of the bow to red hot and reshaped it with a brass hammer over a piece of 1-inch diameter iron bar held in a vise. Figure 4-21 shows the final shape. With the internal parts removed from the action, I filed a notch in the bottom of the receiver in front of the trigger hole (Fig. 4-22). I made this notch just wide enough so that the flat head of an 8-penny nail (yes, a common nail) would slip into it. The stem of the nail under its head was filled smooth; with a No. 27 drill I drilled a hole in the front end of the recurved trigger guard. I cut most of the point end of the nail off, leaving about a ¾-inch stem on the head, and inserted this into the hole. The inside of the bottom of the receiver was quite rough, and using a ⅝-inch wide flat file through the rear of the receiver, I filed the surface smooth and a little bit thinner. Next I put some

silver solder flux on the nail stem, put the nail in place, slipped the guard in place, pulled the nail down snug against the receiver, carefully removed the guard, and then silver-soldered the nail in place. The end of the nail protruding in the guard was cut off.

Using a piece of ¼-inch square cold rolled stock about ½-inch long, I filed this to fit the curve on the shortened tang of the guard; before silver-soldering it in place, I notched one corner of it so that it would engage over the receiver edge. I also filed a slight 45-degree bevel on the bottom rear edge of the receiver the width of the guard at that point. Then I silver-soldered this piece in place and filed the notch so that the hook thus formed, plus the nail head stud up front, would draw the guard tightly against the receiver when it was slipped in place (Fig. 4-23). Lastly, I filed away much of the excess metal from the hook, rounded up the end of the tang, filed the nail head thinner to allow the hammer to be fully cocked, and polished the guard. With the guard in place, I then used small carving chisels to notch the stock which would actually hold the guard in place.

Now the finger lever had to be altered. Removing everything from the lever, I heated the rear part (where it turns down to form the S-curve) to red hot and bent it to about the same curve in the

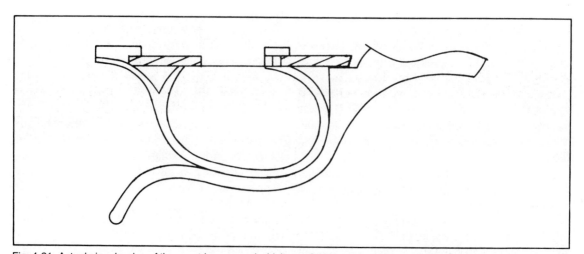

Fig. 4-21. Actual-size drawing of the new trigger guard which was fashioned from one originally made for a double barreled shotgun. The original trigger guard was shortened at both ends, the front end rebent, and a stud and hook silver-soldered in place to hold it to the receiver.

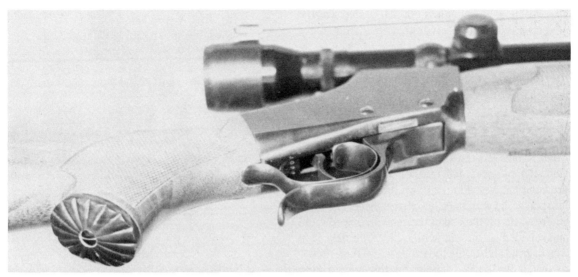

Fig. 4-22. Underside of the Model J action with the remodeled trigger guard and finger lever.

opposite direction. The finger levers of the FBW actions are made of a very tough steel, and it cannot be bent cold. It also takes more than a six-bit hacksaw blade to saw it in two. I then cut the lever off as indicated in Fig. 4-21 and filed metal from the rear of the finger lever base so it would swing past the front of the new guard. This done, I filed the inside of the cut-off piece of the finger lever flat where it would contact the guard and heated and bent it as necessary to fit the guard.

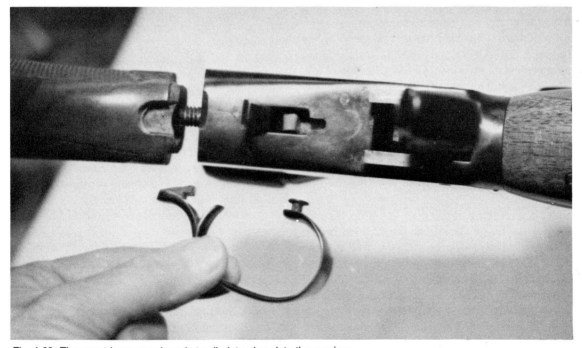

Fig. 4-23. The new trigger guard ready to slip into place into the receiver.

Welding the finger lever back together was the next step. With the receiver held upside-down in a vise, and with the finger lever base in place on its screw, I put a strip of .03-inch thick metal between the receiver and the rear part of the base to hold the lever base from closing fully.

I then clamped the reshaped lever to the new trigger guard, got everything aligned right, and "tacked" the two pieces of the finger lever together. Then I removed the tacked-together finger lever from the receiver and finished welding it. After dressing the welded area down, the lever was put into place, and with the stock also in place, I decided where to cut off the end of the S-hook, sawed it off, and rounded up the end with a file. The next step was to grind and/or file the inside of the finger lever to match the curved surface of the new trigger guard. I did this with an elliptical rotary file held in a drill press, with the lever bolted to a piece of 2×4 so I could manage the filing (Fig. 4-24). With the drill press running at low speed and the press adjusted and locked to bring the file even with the lever, the inside of the lever was easily dished out so that the lever would closely fit against the trigger guard. The last step was polishing and bluing the reshaped finger lever and new trigger guard.

Although it involved considerable work, I like this new finger lever and separate trigger guard arrangement on my Model J FBW rifle (Fig. 4-25). The lever is still more than ample in length to easily open and close the action; yet being shorter, it does not need so much swinging room below the rifle. When swung open it still has a nice surface for "thumping" with the palm if this is needed to extract a stubborn case, and there is nothing on the pistol grip to cramp the fingers when shooting the rifle (Fig. 4-26).

The preceding instructions and procedure for altering the trigger guard and finger lever on the FBW Model J actions can be applied as well as to the FBW Model H action, and to a lesser extent to the Model K and L actions. However, with the Model H action you may much prefer to leave the finger lever as is, or just weld on a short spur to make it similar to the altered lever on my Model L action shown. If you want to make the trigger guard and finger lever

Fig. 4-24. With the reshaped finger lever bolted to a piece of 2×4, and it resting on a drill press table, an elliptical rotary file dishes out the inside curve to match the curved surface of the new trigger guard.

alteration on the Model K action, you will have to use a smaller trigger guard than I used on the Model J action. The small sized S-shaped finger lever on the Model K action is perfectly okay for a shooter with a small hand such as a youngster, but for the adult hand it is just too cramped. If you cannot find a small trigger guard to use for the alteration on this small action perhaps you should consider another style of alteration, for example, like the one I did on the Browning M-78 rifle as shown and described in Chapter 8.

As for the big FBW Model L Express action, if it is on a rifle chambered for a heavy recoiling cartridge, the S-shaped finger lever is a finger buster, and it would not make much difference even if the stock was made with a straight grip (Fig. 4-27). As for the trigger guard and finger lever alteration method I used on the Model J action, I doubt if the

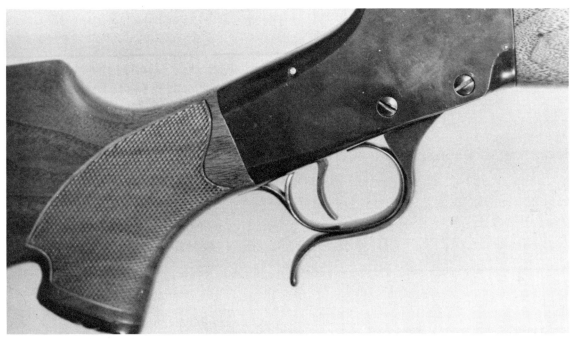

Fig. 4-25. Close-up of the trigger guard and finger lever remodeling on the Model J action showing action closed.

spring-plunger arrangement to hold the finger lever closed is strong enough to hold the altered lever against the trigger guard when the rifle is fired. Therefore, I would suggest making the alteration as shown in Fig. 4-28 and described below.

I did it in this manner and Fig. 4-20 also shows the result. I heated the S part of the lever to red hot and straightened it out. Then I sawed 1.5″ off its straightened end. Then taking a ⅛ × ½″ piece of strap iron about 2½″ long and bending it to a loose

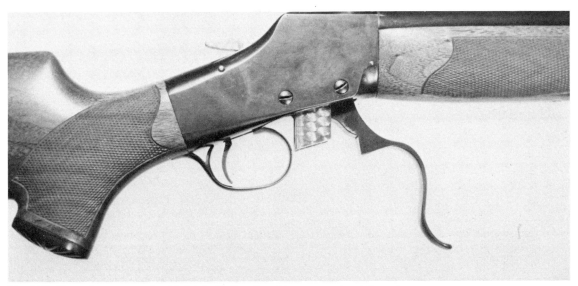

Fig. 4-26. The action open on the Model J with the altered trigger guard and finger lever.

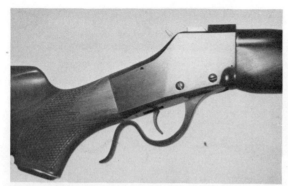

Fig. 4-27. This S-shaped lever on the Model L rifle in .375 H & H caliber is a real finger buster.

L, I welded it to the main part of the lever at a location just far enough back to allow it to clear the trigger. Additional bending and shaping and filing had to be done before it was finished. So altered it is far less of a finger bruiser, believe me.

STOCKING

All of the FBW actions feature a throughbolt buttstock fastening and all have a flat-ended and hollow receiver at both ends. The hollow ends allow both the stock and forearm to be made with a tenon to fit into these hollows.

The stock bolt provided with these actions is a threaded rod with two nuts. The stock bolt is threaded into the receiver and one nut is used to lock it in place. The stock bolt can then be bent to accommodate the hole in the buttstock or to change

the drop of the comb line. Fitting a stock to these actions is not difficult. Both Fajen and Bishop make semi-finished stocks for the Models J and H and using these stocks is a great time and labor saver to the gun builder. I prefer the Fajen classic styled stock above all others.

Fitting the Fajen classic stock to the Model J or H action is a snap. After it is fitted to the action, and the buttplate and grip cap installed, the excess wood beyond the edges of the receiver, grip cap, and buttplate are planed, rasped, and sanded off just about as easily. The comb will be of ample height for scope use but a trifle too high and too thick for use with open sights.

The Fajen stock made for the Model J can also be used to stock the FBW Model K, but unless it is well trimmed all over it will be out of place on this small action. If you do want to use this stock for the Model K, I suggest using a small buttplate and smaller-than-average grip cap and reduce the stock accordingly, and this would include reducing the size and thickness of the cheekpiece.

I made the stocks and forearms for my FBW Model H, J, and K rifles from scratch. However, before I started building my rifle on the Model L Express I had obtained the Fajen Classic Model J stock and forearm. One thing I disliked about the Model L action was the width of the receiver and the large circumference of the rear, or grip end, of the receiver. An idea hit me on examining this big action—why not make it thinner at the grip end?

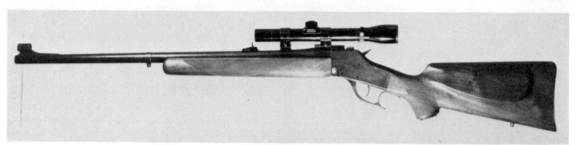

Fig. 4-28. My .375 H & H Magnum sporter is built on the FBW Model L Express action. A Federal 26" heavy sporter barrel was used for this rifle and the Bushnell 2.5× Banner scope mounted with Weaver top detachable mounts. Auxiliary open sights consist of a William's Open Guide rear sight and a gold bead front sight mounted on a William's sweat-on ramp base. The classic-styled stock is the one that Fajen makes for the FBW Model J and H actions, but by tapering the rear of the receiver down to a width of 1.275", it could be used on this larger action. See text for details. The forearm is attached to the barrel via an anchor block and 10×32 fillister head screw, with the block fastened to the barrel with two screws. In addition to the screw fastening, the anchor block was sweated in place with soft solder. The sling swivel band and the front sight ramp base were also sweated in place. Without scope this rifle weighs 8.5 pounds. This shows the rifle with the finger lever altered.

Thus I had a machine shop grind the rear third of the receiver to a taper on both sides, starting just to the rear of the breechblock mortise and tapering back to leave the grip edge of the receiver 1.275″ in width. Removing this metal in no way affects the strength of the action; it reduces the action weight a few ounces and a slimmer pistol grip is the result. Then to my surprise I found that the Fajen classic stock would fit the thinned action perfectly. I also found that the matching forearm that Fajen had sent with the stock fitted the heavy sporter barrel to a tee. The photos of my Model L Express show this stock and forearm in place. I can recommend this stock.

As for the installation of the forearms on my FBW rifles I employed the anchor block method as described in Chapter 12. It is a block fastened to the

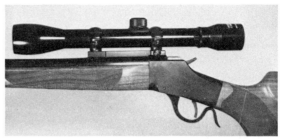

Fig. 4-30. Close-up of the FBW Model K rifle showing the Redfield Jr. scope mount. The base of this mount is one made for the Rem. M-760. The rear end of this base was machined flat to fit the receiver ring and the base attached to the barrel and receiver with three screws.

barrel with two screws, the forearm inletted over it and secured in place with the forearm screw threaded into the anchor block. I tenoned the forearms into the receiver and used glass bedding compound to bed the forearm over the block.

After testing each rifle for accuracy and point of impact change as described in Chapter 12, I either left the forearm in full contact with the barrel or floated it forward of the anchor block, whichever proved best.

MORE IDEAS

The makers of the FBW actions make six alternate finger levers: five styles for the Model S, two styles for the Model K, three styles for the Model J action (Fig. 4-29), and two for the Model L Express action. If you are interested in building a Schuetzen-styled target rifle on a modern single-shot action, then consider the FBW Model J or S actions and use one of the two Schuetzen-type finger levers that FBW can furnish. One of them is called the "Schuetzen" and the other the "International." Both are styled after the finger levers once popular in most Schuetzen-styled target rifles.

The third lever that FBW makes for the Model J action is a loop lever, not unlike one on a common lever-action repeating rifle. The loop is slightly curved for a semi-pistol grip stock. The alternate levers available for the Model L and K actions are straight or semi-pistol grip loop levers. If the loop parts of both of these levers are annealed, I am sure that they can be reshaped to fit any style of grip you might want.

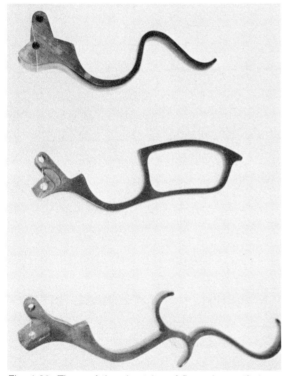

Fig. 4-29. Three of the six styles of finger levers that are available for some of the FBW actions. The three styles shown here are the International (bottom), S-shaped (top), and loop (center). The S-shaped lever is standard on the Models K, J, S, and L. A pistol grip loop lever is available for the Model K, a loop and two Schuetzen levers for the Model J, two styles of loop levers (straight and pistol grip) for the Model L-action, and all five are available for the Model S.

All five of the FBW actions have provisions to adjust the sear engagement to achieve a short trigger let-off. No other trigger adjustment is provided. However, with a minimum safe sear engagement and perhaps a bit of careful honing of the sear engagement surfaces, a trigger pull of around 2.5 pounds can be achieved and still leave the rifle safe to use. I have investigated the possibility of installing a set trigger mechanism in the FBW actions, but I see of no practical way that this can be done. If a fly were fitted in the safety notch of the hammer then it would be possible to fit a Canjar single set trigger mechanism to the trigger of any one of these actions. It would not be an easy job, but it can be done.

There you have it, all the ideas you will ever need when it comes your time to build a rifle on an FBW action. A lot more ideas are scattered throughout this book on attaching the forearm, selecting a scope mount (Fig. 4-30) or other sights, other finger lever designs, etc.

Chapter 5

Stocking the No. 1 Ruger Barreled Action

Most riflemen find the Ruger No. 1 single-shot rifle very appealing. It is made in several of the most popular calibers and in several classic styles, including a light, short-barreled sporter, a medium sporter, a medium-weight long-barreled sporter, a varmint rifle with a medium-weight barrel, and a big-bore, magnum-calibered classic. All are beautiful rifles, with excellent handling and shooting qualities. The Ruger No. 1 action is a very strong falling block with an internal swinging hammer, a sliding shotgun-type tang safety, and an adjustable trigger. Outwardly the action resembles the famous British Farquharson, perhaps the most admired falling block action ever made.

Compared to most commercial high-power bolt-action rifles, the Ruger No. 1 is comparatively high-priced. At least many shooters seem to think so. Single-shot rifle buffs know better and realize that there is a lot of value in the No. 1. However, for those who want a No. 1 for less and can do some stock work, barreled actions in the several styles are available.

Buying a barreled action and a low-cost semi-finished stock and forearm affords a considerable saving over the cost of a complete new rifle. If you are skilled at stockmaking and can make the stock and forearm from scratch, even greater savings are possible. But if you are like most amateur gunsmiths, you will prefer to get the semi-finished and inletted wood from a stock company and then do the final fitting and finishing yourself. This is the procedure I follow and describe here.

While the total cost of the Ruger single-shot may be substantially reduced by fitting your own wood, it is rather difficult to improve on the lines of the factory stock and forearm which are conventional and in keeping with the classic lines of the rifle.

I purchased the Ruger No. 1 Standard Model .22-250 barreled action with a 26″ barrel, which seems to be the most popular style (Fig. 5-1). The semi-finished and inletted stock and forearm were ordered from Reinhart Fajen Inc. Wood is available in various grades from plain to ultra fancy. I chose American walnut classic style in Fajen's extra-fancy grade and, as the photos show, it is considerably

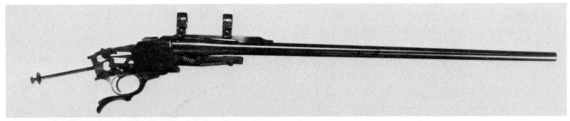

Fig. 5-1. The Ruger No. 1 Standard model barreled action.

fancier wood than normally found on the factory Ruger rifle. If you want wood comparable to that which Ruger uses, order Fajen's semi-fancy grade. In this grade the buttstock and forearm will cost about $43.00, and to this must be added the cost of the buttplate and pistol grip cap. I used the classic Niedner checkered steel plate and cap costing about $3.00 each, and if you intend to use this type of plate you can order the stock machined to accept it. The Niedner plate and cap, as well as other buttplates and caps, are available from Fajen and from Brownell's Inc., Montezuma, Iowa.

FITTING THE BUTTSTOCK

To fit and finish the stock and forearm to the barreled action, you will need a workbench with vise, pads of some sort for the vise jaws so the blued finish on the barrel won't be damaged when holding the barreled-action in the vise, a bottle of inletting black, sharp pocketknife, rubber-tipped hammer, several small carving chisels, 10″ round rasp, medium rough half-round rasp, fine half-round rasp, sanding block, screwdriver for the buttplate and forearm screws, and a long screwdriver for the stock bolt. A barrel inletting rasp of ⅝″ diameter may come in handy, but sandpaper wrapped over a dowel will also do. A hand-held grinder, such as a Dremel Tool, may also be useful (Fig. 5-2). You will also need several sheets of garnet or production paper in a variety of grits and a couple of pieces of 2″ × 2″ very thin steel or copper shim stock. And of course, you'll need some stock finish of your choice.

Before starting on the stock fitting, it is a good idea to protect the polished and blued metal of the barreled action as much as possible by putting masking tape on most of the assembly. Wipe the oil from the barrel and receiver and lay strips of the

tape on the sides and top of the receiver, finger lever and the front half of the barrel.

Start the stock fitting job by putting the barreled action in the padded vise, holding the assembly by the barrel. Remove the stock bolt and washer and test-fit the stock on the action. Don't force it on very hard as this may cause the wood to split or pieces to break off, but the chances are the stock can be slipped to within ½″ or so of its final position. With the stock partly in place, carefully note if there are any unduly tight places or if there is some extra wood on the two tenons at the front of the stock which must be removed.

Remove the stock and trim off any extra wood that you may have noted. Brush a thin coat of inletting black on the action where wood and metal will contact, and again slip the stock carefully in place and push it as far on the action as you can. If all goes well at this point, you might insert the stock bolt

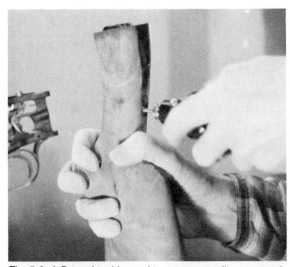

Fig. 5-2. A Dremel tool is used to remove small amounts of excess wood in some of the inletted areas.

and washer in the stock and using a long screwdriver, draw the stock close to its final position. The chances are that the fit is too tight for this, so remove the stock and scrape the insides of the inletting cuts with a knife blade. If the stock sticks, it may be removed by holding it in the padded vise and driving the rear of the receiver ring forward with a rubber- or plastic-faced hammer.

Also check the surface of the inletting where the tangs of the receiver join and into which the stock bolt threads to see that there are no high spots to keep the stock from being fully drawn against the receiver. When a very close and tight fit is obtained, remove the stock again, wipe off all the inletting black from the receiver, and carefully scrape away as much of the black from the wood as you can without removing any wood. Or use a piece of cloth with a little turpentine.

FITTING THE FOREARM

At this point I would suggest putting the buttstock away for a time and fit the forearm. I ordered the forearm for the standard rifle barrel and the inletting was almost 100% complete. You may find this to be the case with the one you get. Fit the escutcheon into its hole in the forearm. If it is a loose fit (as mine was), mix up a couple drops of epoxy, spread this in the hole, and then push the escutcheon all the way down, tapping it with a ¼" flat-end drift punch if necessary. Any ridges at the rear end of the forearm must be filed off, leaving the rear surface flat. It is a good idea to sand the sides of the forearm hanger inletting smooth, or at least take a fine rasp and cut down the high spots.

Next, wrap some sandpaper around a dowel and sand the barrel channel smooth, and test the forearm on the rifle. If the barrel channel inletting is too small, then it will have to be enlarged. On this forearm I believe this is best done with a dowel and sandpaper. The chances are that the channel inletting will be okay except for sanding it smooth.

Now test the forearm on the rifle, and you'll probably find that the forearm tip won't contact the barrel, which means that some wood will have to be removed from the bottom front end of the inletting for the forearm hanger. This wood can be removed

with a bent carving chisel or, if you are very careful, with the hand grinder. Now is the time to brush the inletting black on the metal parts which are to contact the wood, but mostly on the front of the receiver and the front part of the forearm hanger. Slip the forearm in place and use the forearm screw to draw the forearm in place. If the forearm tip is not drawn snug against the barrel, remove more wood from the hanger inletting area until it does. At the same time rasp and sand the rear of the forearm, both flat and concave surfaces, until the inletting black shows this end to be a close fit with the receiver. I removed enough wood from the hanger inletting so that after the forearm was screwed in place it took around eight pounds of pressure to force the forearm tip away from the barrel. More on this later. When a close fit is achieved, remove the forearm and clean away the inletting black.

BUTTPLATE, GRIP CAP, AND FOREARM TIP

The next job is to fit the buttplate, pistol grip cap, and a forearm tip if you want one. The plate and the cap can be fitted with the stock off or on the rifle. I prefer to do it with the stock off. If a Niedner plate is used and the stock butt semi-machined for it, the fitting is mostly that of getting the pointed tip at the top of the plate properly inletted. I like to use the sharp castrating blade of a stock knife to do this. Use the inletting black on the back of the plate and carefully press it in place. Rasp away the high spots until good contact is achieved. Use the rubber-tipped hammer to gently nudge the point in place slightly below the top surface of the stock.

The Niedner plate is quite thin, so don't force it. But when it starts to fall into place and a fairly even black is left on the butt, spot and drill the two screw holes and turn in the screws. Now remove the plate, sand away most of the black from the butt, put some new black on the plate and screw it on again. Gently tap around the plate with the rubber hammer and remove the plate once more and again sand down any high spots. Repeat until there are no gaps left between the plate and butt when the plate is screwed down.

The grip cap comes next. With the stock held in the vise, rasp the end of the pistol grip flat and square. Center the cap on it and spot the screw hole. Drill the hole and screw on the cap. If there are any gaps showing between the cap and the wood, remove the cap, put some inletting black around the edges, and carefully rasp or sand the high spots until there are no gaps left.

At this point reattach the stock to the rifle. Clean off the black from the buttplate, grip cap, and wood. Now wipe a very thin smear of silicon grease on the under surfaces of the plate and cap as well as on their screw threads, and then spread a good layer of white glue on the wood surfaces where the plate and cap fit. Try to keep the glue away from the screw holes and then screw the plate and cap on tightly. Now you are ready to rasp and sand excess wood from the buttstock.

SHAPING

The first step here is to remove the extra wood from the top and bottom of the grip—the wood that projects above the receiver metal. This extra wood should be cut off flush with the metal, but unless you want to repolish and reblue the metal afterwards, you will have to work very carefully to avoid scratching the blue while cutting this wood down. I do this best with sharp straight and bent shank carving chisels, gently cutting off the extra wood with the non-cutting part of the chisel blade riding on the receiver as a guide. The final cuts are within paper thickness of being flush. This last small amount is removed with the final sanding. Start with the straight chisel where the grip meets the top of the receiver and work back past the safety and to the end of the receiver grip frame (Fig. 5-3). Then turn the gun over and with a bent chisel repeat the process, starting at the end of the frame and working rearward.

For the final rasping and sanding, I hold the barrel of the rifle in a vise with the butt angled down and resting on the workbench. I then nail a piece of wood to the bench behind the butt to serve as a stop to keep it from moving while rasping. The surface of the cheekpiece will not have to be rasped down except perhaps with a fine rasp to remove machine marks. Sanding should not be done until the rest of the stock, except the grip panels, is rasped and sanded. The two side grip panels should be the very last surfaces to rasp and sand. Up to 1/16″ of wood must be removed from all the rest of the stock so that the surface is flush with the grip cap and buttplate.

I start with the stock held so the pistol grip cap

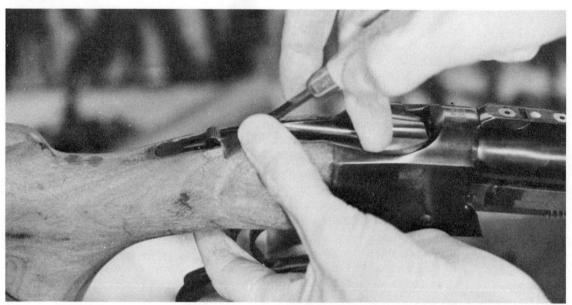

Fig. 5-3. A carving chisel is used to remove excess wood from the top and bottom of the grip areas.

92

is facing me. With a fine half-round rasp, I start removing wood first from one side of the grip, then turn the rifle over to do the other side of the grip. Next, I turn the rifle top side up and do the top and work down the sides, then with rifle bottom side up, rasp the inside curve of the grip and down the sides. Rasp carefully and leave enough wood to sand off to bring the surface flush with the cap. Enough wood should be removed so that no part of the grip is wider, or narrower, than the cap. The inside curve of the grip should be perfectly rounded. Work right up to the edges of the grip panels and, if one panel is longer than the other (as it was on my stock), shorten the longer panel. Use a small fine half-round rasp for this, preferably a well-used one that is a bit dull. Rasp around the edges of the panels very carefully to avoid taking out any wood below the level surface. The edges must be left sharp to give the panels that clean offset effect.

Now I place the rifle so that the side of the butt opposite the cheekpiece is up and begin rasping this surface down. If the grain in the wood is straight, perhaps a small block plane can be used. I first use a sharp medium-cut rasp to remove most of the surplus wood, then a fine rasp (Fig. 5-4). However it is done, the important point is that only enough wood is removed to leave the surface flat and level from the flush edge of the buttplate to the grip. The final smoothing is done with sandpaper under a sanding block. While working on this side, I also work partly over the top and bottom edges of the stock.

Now turn the stock over and remove the surplus wood from behind and below the cheekpiece. If you want to leave the profile edge around the cheekpiece, first sand the curved surface, being careful not to remove too much from the profile edge. After this is done, take a short piece broken from a 1″ wide mill file and file around the profile edge, thus keeping the corners clean, square and sharp, and the surface up to the edges flat. If you don't like this profile edge or find it hard to manage, merely remove it using medium coarse sandpaper over a dowel, as I did with my stock. Rasp over the rear of the stock down to within paper thickness of the buttplate. Use a round file to remove the surplus

Fig. 5-4. Wood rasps are used to trim off excess wood from the stock and forearm.

wood from the area behind the pistol grip.

Start sanding with a medium-coarse grit, using a sanding block, and sand until all the rasp marks have been removed, all other minor blemishes are gone, all surfaces are flat and level, straight lines straight, and the wood is flush with the buttplate and grip cap. I sand until the entire edges of the plate and cap have been brightened by the sandpaper in order to get a perfect match. Use a finer grit of paper to sand around the edges of the cheekpiece and grip panels and be careful to keep from rounding the edges that should stay sharp.

Keep on sanding with finer grits until the entire stock, except the grip panels, is level, very smooth, and free of previous sanding marks.

Now do the grip panels, which so far have not been touched except around the edges. Remove the buttplate, loosen the stock bolt several turns, and pull the stock back a fraction of an inch from the receiver. Take two pieces of .002″-.003″ steel or copper shim stock about 2″×2″ square, and insert one edge of each piece between the stock and receiver on each side of the rifle. Then draw the stock tight up against the receiver again with the stock bolt. Strip the masking tape from the receiver sides. Hold the shim stock forward against the receiver, and you can dress down the grip panels flat, level, and smooth to within the thickness of the shim stock of being flush with the receiver sides. If much wood has to be removed, first use the flat end of a fine half-round rasp, and then a wide mill file. Finally, with a piece of sandpaper under a block, sand right down to the shim stock (Fig. 5-5). Now you will have very distinctive panels that you can be proud of.

Fig. 5-5. To prevent scratching the blued finish of the receiver while sanding the grip panels, a piece of thin shim stock is placed between the stock and receiver.

If you want a forearm tip or schnable, or if you want the forearm shorter, I suggest this be done first. Then put the forearm on the rifle and note about how much can be removed from the bottom. If you want the forearm slimmer than it is as furnished by the stock company, now is the time to do it. Use a plane if the grain is straight; otherwise use a rasp and the sanding block. When you get it to the size you want, put it back on the rifle, insert the pieces of shim stock that you used before between the forearm and the receiver and dress down and sand the forearm side panels flush with the receiver. Then dress down the bottom line of the forearm.

FINISHING

After final sanding of the forearm, you are ready to apply the stock finish of your choice. I wanted to duplicate as close as possible the finish that Ruger uses on their factory stocks and achieved a very close match by using GB Lin-Speed oil. Remove the wood from the rifle, but leave the buttplate and grip cap on. After the stock is finished, remove the buttplate and cap and clean off any finish on them with paint remover. If you sand as I do, it

will be necessary to polish and reblue their edges. A cold blue can be used for a temporary job. When reinstalling the buttplate and cap after the stock is finished, tighten their screws so that all the slots are aligned. To achieve this you may have to switch screws.

The checkering should always be done after the stock is completely finished. I sent my stock and forearm to Ahlman's in Morristown, Minnesota for checkering.

In bedding the forearm as described earlier, I merely removed enough wood from the end of the forearm hanger channel so that when the forearm screw was tightened, the forearm tip put 8 to 10 pounds roughly measured) upward pressure against the barrel (Fig. 5-6).

With my pet .22-250 handload of 35 grains of IMR #4320 powder behind the Sierra 55-grain semi-pointed bullet, the first record five-shot group measured .850". I hardly expected this sort of accuracy with so little bedding effort. Until I can test the rifle (Fig. 5-7) more thoroughly, I plan to do no more to it. Your Ruger No. 1 rifle may be more critical than mine in respect to bedding and accuracy, but

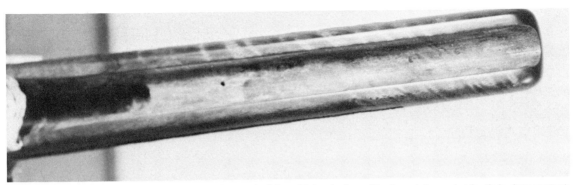

Fig. 5-6. The forearm was inletted the same as factory bedding with two inches of the barrel channel at the tip in close contact with the barrel, exerting some upward pressure against the barrel when the forearm screw is tightened.

Fig. 5-7. The Ruger No. 1 Standard model as I stocked it.

regardless of how you bed the forearm, the proof is in the shooting. If accuracy is within MOA, you have done well. If accuracy is worse than MOA, try bedding with more or less forearm pressure.

Ruger No. 3 barreled actions are also available, as are semi-finished and inletted stocks and forearms. The preceding instructions also apply to this model.

Chapter 6

Bedding the Ruger No. 1 Forearm

My son Mark, an experienced shooter and capable gunsmith, assisted in the experiments and tests described in this chapter.

The Ruger No. 1 falling block single shot rifle has a two-piece stock and forearm. The buttstock is securely attached to the action with a through-stock bolt, which is surely the very best method of attaching a buttstock to the receiver. With the wood well mortised and fitted to the receiver as is the case with the No. 1, and if the stock bolt is drawn up tight, the stock is about as secure as it can be made, and the accuracy and zero retention of the rifle are in no way affected because of the buttstock part of the two-piece design of this rifle.

The separate forearm, however, and the way it is attached and bedded on a single shot rifle can (and often does) affect both the accuracy and zero retention of the rifle. This is especially true in regard to the Ruger No. 1 forearm.

While most Ruger No. 1 shooters are interested in getting the best accuracy from their rifles, those shooters who use this rifle for varmint shooting are just as interested in having the rifle

stay in zero as in getting top accuracy. One is as important as the other to the varmint shooter and hunter. By manipulation of the forearm on the No. 1, it is often possible to get the finest accuracy that the barrel is capable of delivering, and have the rifle stay perfectly sighted-in over a long period of time as well. Obtaining and maintaining both with the factory-bedded forearm is often very difficult if not impossible.

FACTORY BEDDING

A great amount of time and effort was spent in designing the Ruger No. 1 rifle, with special emphasis on the forearm and its attachment and bedding. Due to the design of the action, some of its parts had to be mounted in front of the receiver below the barrel. Not wishing to attach any of these parts to the barrel, the designers chose to make a projecting arm forward of the receiver on which to mount these parts, making this arm a permanent part of the receiver. In so doing they made it long and heavy enough so that it could also double as a hanger for the forearm (Fig. 6-1).

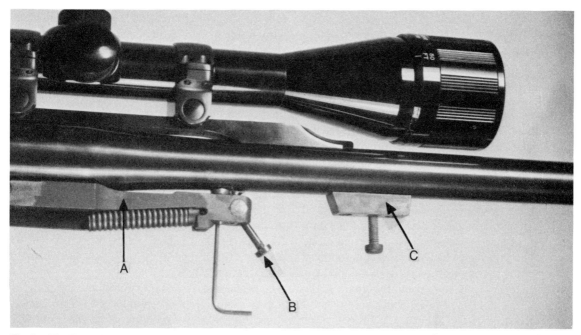

Fig. 6-1. The Ruger No. 1 action is made with an extension (A) foreward of the receiver which serves to house the extractor and mainsprings, and to serve as a hanger for the forearm. The forearm is secured to this hanger by an angle screw (B) which draws it against the receiver and hanger. One of the bedding methods described in this chapter uses a small setscrew threaded into the front of the hanger (its location shown here by the Allen wrench) to apply pressure against the barrel. Another forearm attachment we tested apart from the factory hanger method was an anchor block (C) with the forearm glass-bedded over it and secured with a forearm screw. The results of the various bedding tests are given in the tabulation.

A single screw was used to attach the forearm to the hanger, but instead of putting the screw at a 90-degree angle through the forearm and into the hanger, Ruger drilled the hole through the forearm and into the hanger at a rearward angle so that on tightening this screw the forearm would be drawn upward and backward—up against the hanger and back against the receiver. This fastening method positively prevents the forearm from moving forward due to the recoil of the rifle. On early No. 1 rifles the forearm screw was threaded directly into the hanger. Now the hanger is made deeper at its end, a hole drilled across it for a heavy pin, and this pin drilled and tapped for the forearm screw. This improved fastening arrangement allows torque-free tightening of the screw and some lateral movement so that the forearm tip automatically aligns itself with the barrel. By altering the bedding of the forearm against the hanger, the entire forearm could be made to be entirely free of the barrel,

contact the barrel its entire length, or have just the front part of the forearm contact the barrel at various amounts of pressure. Testing in the Ruger factory must have revealed that the best accuracy was usually obtained with the forearm so bedded that its tip contacted the barrel with considerable upward pressure, and this is the bedding method Ruger now employs on their No. 1 rifles.

Most Ruger No. 1 rifles are reasonably accurate with the forearm bedded in this manner. However, many owners of these rifles have found this not so. Or at least they think that in view of the relatively high cost of the No. 1, they should get better accuracy than their rifles are delivering. Many No. 1 owners have told us that they own lighter weight and much cheaper bolt action rifles in the same calibers as their No. 1s that are more accurate. This should not be so. Some of them have done some experimenting with the forearms on their No. 1s, and some of them have found that better accuracy is often possible with a bedding change. We have also heard from many shooters who are well satisfied with the accuracy they are getting from their No. 1s, but that their rifles do not maintain their zero. This is often an intolerable problem for the varmint hunter. Wood is a rather unstable material, and this being so, if the forearm is bedded so that its tip exerts pressure against the barrel, any slight change in the forearm such as warpage, shrinkage, or swelling is apt to have some affect on the barrel and consequently on the zero of the rifle. Further, in rest shooting, the zero and accuracy are affected if the rifle is not always fired with the forearm resting on a given spot. For example, a group fired with the forearm resting on its forward end may strike higher than a group fired with the rifle resting on the center of the forearm, and change again if rested on the rear of the forearm. The tension of the forearm screw, if not always the same, is also likely to affect the zero and accuracy.

IN SEARCH OF ACCURACY

The Ruger No. 1 rifle we used for our forearm bedding experiments was the Standard Model in .22-250 caliber with 26″ heavy sporter barrel. I stocked it with a Fajen semi-finished stock and forearm, making the forearm the same size and length as Ruger does on this model, and bedded it the same way with the forearm tip exerting upward to 12 pounds pressure against the barrel. All the test shooting was done from a benchrest using a handload of 41.0 grs. of #4831 powder behind the 53-gr. Sierra match bullet. Four to ten five-shot groups were fired for each test, sighting with a 10× scope, and all done under ideal weather conditions. Some tests were repeated several times, and in most instances 20 shots (four five-shot groups) comprised a test, starting with the barrel cold and the bore uncleaned since the previous firing, and ending with the barrel quite warm after firing at a rate of 60 to 90 seconds per shot.

I worked out and installed the different bedding methods, as well as working out the testing routine in order to get the best possible test data. Before any test firing was done the rifle was care-

fully sighted in to hit on a point of aim at 100 yards with the forearm as factory bedded and with the rifle resting on the front third of the forearm; no change was made in this sighted-in adjustment through all the subsequent test firing. The rifle was tested for any point of impact change with each bedding method over a period of several months. All of this was done over a period of nearly two years. After this groundwork of extended test firing was done, Mark took over the test shooting on his range, and in a planned routine order over a period of several successive fine weather shooting days, repeated all of the test firings, shooting with utmost care and precision. He did all the firing in ten-shot (two five-shot groups) relays, letting the rifle cool to about starting temperature, or up to one half hour or more, between relays.

In the test shooting to determine the point of impact change from different forearm resting positions (Fig. 6-2) he fired alternating shots on twin targets, alternating the forearm resting position with each shot. This resulted in the two groups being fired with an even upward temperature rise in the barrel, with one group being fired with the rifle resting on the front third of the forearm and the other group fired from the rear forearm position. In this way the point of impact change from one forearm rest position to another was instantly apparent and precisely recorded.

Afterward, we also tested the rifle by firing with it resting on the center third of the forearm, or more precisely a normal holding and resting position of about five inches long with the forearm screw as its center. In all cases of the four different bedding methods, the center rest position group sizes and point of impact change was midway between those fired from the front and rear rest positions of the same bedding method. This data is not included in the accompanying table except in the case of bedding method No. 3.

Following are the tests we conducted, with a description of the forearm bedding method employed in that test or tests.

Bedding Method No. 1: Factory bedding with forearm tip pressure against the barrel. Our best rifle was quite accurate bedded in this manner—

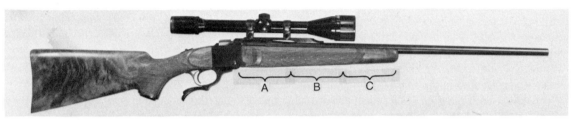

Fig. 6-2. In our forearm bedding experiment tests with the Standard Model Ruger No. 1 rifle, we found that the way the forearm was fitted and bedded to the rifle and what spot the forearm was rested on during firing greatly affected both the accuracy, point of aim, and zero retention. Three forearm rest positions were used; front end of forearm (A), rear of forearm (B) and center of the forearm (C). The test rifle always gave the best accuracy with the rifle resting on the rear end of the forearm. Sighted-in with the forearm rested on its forward end, the point of impact would drop if the rifle was then fired from the center position, and drop still more if fired from the rear position.

certainly accurate enough for varmint shooting. Without changing the load, sight setting, shooting position, or tension of the forearm screw, our test rifle retained its zero and accuracy during the first months of the test period.

After that the point of impact began to drop, enough so that after another three or four months the groups centered at least 1.5″ lower than at the beginning. Checking the forearm-to-barrel pressure at the tip, we noticed that the pressure had decreased so that now the forearm tip could be easily pulled away from the barrel. Apparently the forearm had warped or otherwise changed to cause the lessened tip pressure and the resulting lowering of the point of impact. With the lessening of the forearm tip pressure came a slight increase in the group size.

It was at this point that we made a demonstration as to the effect the forearm has on the point of impact and accuracy of the Ruger No. 1 rifle. By loosening the forearm and inserting a three-layer strip of target paper between the forearm tip and barrel and retightening the forearm screw, pressure between tip and barrel was restored to approximately what it had been in the beginning. Doing this, the rifle returned to its former zero and accuracy. Repeating the test with the strip removed and again with it in place, the same results occurred. A more dramatic demonstration of the effect the factory bedded forearm has on the rifle is to carefully test fire several groups with the rifle as factory bedded, and then follow it up after the rifle has cooled by firing the same number of groups with the barrel free-floating, which is easily done by

merely removing the forearm and firing the rifle with the tip of the forearm hanger resting on some support. With our standard rifle this change resulted in approximately three inches drop in the point of impact.

Another easily made test which may show similar results (but less dramatically) is to test fire several groups with the rifle resting on the tip of the forearm, then again with the rifle rested on the rear part of the forearm. In this test, the Ruger No. 1 Sporter model is likely to show a greater change in the point of impact, and perhaps in accuracy as well, than the heavier-barreled Standard model, and the still heavier-barreled Varmint model. In the case of our test rifle, with the forearm bedded with fairly light tip pressure against the barrel (estimated at about five to ten pounds), with the rifle resting on the rear third of the forearm, the point of impact would drop 1.3″ at 100 yards as compared to resting the rifle on the front third of the forearm. With the forearm bedded with fairly heavy tip pressure against the barrel (approximately 20 pounds), the point of impact at 100 yards was about 1.6″ lower with the rear forearm resting position as compared to the front forearm resting position. This last point of impact difference may seem insignificant at first glance, but to the varmint shooter it means that unless the rifle is rested on the same portion of the forearm as when it was sighted-in, he will miss most shots at small varmints at ranges of 150 yards or more.

In the above tests with our rifle, we discovered that the accuracy was also affected as to forearm resting position. Whether the forearm was bedded with light or heavy tip pressure against the barrel, the best accuracy was always obtained when the rifle was rested on the rear third of the forearm. It was most accurate with the heavy pressure bedding at the tip and rested in the rear position. The rear rest position with most of the forearm and barrel projecting beyond the benchrest pedestal made holding the rifle steady more difficult, but even so, this gave the best accuracy. At any rate, it was an easy overall demonstration that revealed how this rifle reacts to minor changes in the forearm.

Even though our Standard Model No. 1 Ruger rifle was quite accurate with the forearm bedded as the factory would have bedded it, we wanted to find out if there was not some other bedding method that could be applied to this rifle that perchance could make it a bit more accurate, but more importantly, find some way to eliminate the effect of the unstable wood forearm on the barrel and the resulting point of impact and accuracy changes.

Bedding Method No. 2: Hanger and forearm free of contact with the barrel (floating). Since the forearm hanger of the No. 1 Ruger is made free of the barrel, nothing had to be done with it in this bedding method and test. Two ways are open in test firing the rifle with this bedding method: with the forearm removed and resting the rifle on the tip of the forearm hanger, or with the forearm in place and either the channel sanded out or the forearm propped away from the hanger so that it is entirely free of the barrel while the rifle is resting on the forearm. We tried both methods, and with the forearm in place we chose to prop it away from the hanger rather than sand out the channel since we may have wanted to repeat some of the other bedding tests with an unaltered forearm.

To hold the forearm away from the barrel we merely placed enough folded cardboard between the forearm and the tip of the forearm hanger so that with the forearm screw tightened, the forearm tip was entirely free of the barrel with the rifle resting on the forearm.

While the forearm hanger of the No. 1 appears to be rigid, it is actually quite flexible. With the forearm removed it does not take too much finger strength to flex the end of the hanger several thousands of an inch, either by squeezing toward the barrel or pulling it away from the barrel. With the forearm attached to it and made free of the barrel, the effect on the hanger is about the same as doubling its length, thus making it even more flexible. To us, this condition was quite intolerable, because with the rifle not resting on the forearm, the gap between the forearm tip and barrel became considerable. At any rate, test firing our rifle bedded in this way, both with the forearm removed and with it in place, the rifle was fully as accurate as with any of the other bedding methods we tried. Quite to our surprise, however, there was a small but readily noticeable lowering in the point of impact from firing the rifle while resting it on the front of the forearm to that of resting it on the rear of the forearm. We cannot explain this, nor do we care to put forth a theory for the cause. In any event, had our rifle proved decidedly more accurate with this bedding method, we could not have tolerated the forearm gap necessary to achieve a free-floating barrel or the very limber forearm condition, and would have gladly chosen the second best bedding method instead. We would rightly suppose too that this condition would be a definite sales hinderance had the Ruger firm found the average No. 1 rifle most accurate so bedded and had chosen to make them this way.

Not expected, however, was that with this bedding method there was no change in the zero of the rifle over the entire period of our testing as we returned the rifle to this bedding at frequent intervals.

Bedding Method No. 3: The next bedding method we tried is one we call "forearm hanger pressure against barrel," a method which we found worked best on our Browning M-78 single shot rifle which also has a forearm hanger. This method is one in which a set screw is used near the front end of the hanger (Fig. 6-1) to contact the barrel, and in which the forearm is attached in the normal manner but altered or otherwise adjusted to be free of the barrel. In other words, instead of having the tip of the forearm applying a dampening effect pressure to the barrel, the forearm hanger is made to do this instead. And since the steel hanger is far more stable than wood, the pressure so applied will be more constant and perhaps there will be less point-of-aim and accuracy change than with any other type of forearm pressure.

To achieve this type of metal-to-metal bedding, we merely installed a set screw near the end of the hanger and adjusted it so that the hanger was pushed slightly away from the barrel. We used a ¼″ long 8×32 cupped-end set screw for this, drilling the hole for it approximately .650″ back from the end of the hanger, or just forward of the mainspring strut with the hammer in the fired position.

Then we made a thin V-block to fit loosely between the hanger and the barrel, positioning it over the set screw to serve as a pillar between the screw and barrel. A ⅜″ flat or round-ended set screw could be used, eliminating the need for the pillar block. After considerable experimenting and test shooting, we found that the best performance was obtained with the set screw tightened at least one full turn, which moves the tip of the hanger .031″ away from the barrel (with 32 thread set screw). We tested the rifle both with the forearm removed (resting it on the tip of the hanger on the benchrest stand) and with the forearm in place but with enough cardboard between the forearm and hanger tip so that with the forearm screwed tight, the entire forearm tip was free of the barrel even with the rifle resting on it. We found it much more convenient to fire the rifle with the forearm in place. Bedded this way there was no change in the zero of the rifle for a period of several months, and as long as the forearm does not touch the barrel when the rifle is fired, no zero change is expected over a much longer period. We found that our test rifle was much more accurate bedded in this manner than as factory-bedded, and just as accurate as the full-floated barrel (Method No. 2). In addition, we had a forearm sufficiently stiffened and rigid enough so that a wide gap was not needed to keep the forearm tip free of the barrel.

There still was the point of impact change from the front to the rear forearm resting position, which we could not explain and which bothered us a bit. However, when shooting the rifle in the normal forearm rest position (that is, resting the center of the forearm on the sandbag), the accuracy obtained delighted us. Further testing with the forearm resting just forward of the forearm screw and just to the rear of it, all within a five-inch length of the center section of the forearm, accuracy and point of impact remained stable. This was exactly what we were looking and hoping for—rigid forearm, top accuracy, no point of impact change, all with a normal center-of-the-forearm hold or rest. What pleased us even more was no change in the accuracy or point of impact from the first shot fired from a cold and uncleaned barrel to the last shot fired from the barrel heated up after firing a string of 20 shots in four five-shot groups.

Bedding Method No. 4: We also tried another forearm attachment and bedding method on our No. 1 test rifle. This method required that an anchor block be installed under the barrel, the forearm inletted over it and fastened to it with a separate forearm screw (Fig. 6-3) through the forearm and threaded into the block. The block was made from a piece of 5/16″ square rod about 1¼″ long and attached to the barrel with two 6×48 scope mounting screws. The side that contacted the barrel was grooved to fit the barrel closely and the ends angled off as shown in Fig. 6-1. It was attached about an inch forward of the hanger. Then a cavity somewhat larger than the block was chiseled into the forearm channel to allow the forearm to slip in place.

A 10×32 forearm screw was then installed, along with a brass escutcheon in the forearm for the screw head. The forearm was then glass-bedded over the block only, and both the factory and the new forearm screws used to hold the forearm in place while the bedding compound hardened. These screws were tightened so that the pressure between the forearm tip and barrel was approximately the same as the factory-bedded forearm. After the compound had hardened and the forearm removed, excess bedding compound in the forearm channel was sanded away, leaving the channel exactly as factory-made. Reinstalled and fastened only by the new forearm screw, the forearm tip still exerted considerable upward pressure against the barrel.

This was all done prior to the start of our experiments and all the prior testing was done with

Fig. 6-3. The forearm is shown here attached to the rifle barrel via a forearm screw threaded into the anchor block. Attached by this method and bedded so the forearm channel is free of the barrel, accuracy and zero retention was little different from that obtained by other bedding methods.

the block removed, which left the forearm as original except for the block cavity and forearm screw hole. Thus we could proceed with the bedding experiments without disturbing any other part of the rifle which might have affected the zero.

On testing the rifle with this forearm fastening and bedding method we found that the point of impact as compared to factory-bedded changed little. Also over a period of several months of changing weather conditions, the zero changed less from time to time than it did with the factory-bedded forearm under similar conditions. All of this is perhaps due to the fact that the point of attachment of the forearm with this bedding method is closer to the pressure bearing forearm area of the tip, which resulted in a more solid and stable pressure contact between forearm tip and barrel. With this forearm attachment method the forearm was held extremely rigidly in place, much more so than the factory attachment. Even if there was no accuracy improvement gained by the anchor block attachment method, this method would be the preferred one if the sling swivel is attached to the forearm and if the rifle is to be carried with a sling.

In regard to accuracy with the anchor block forearm attachment-bedding method, we did this in two stages: first with the forearm tip exerting pressure on the barrel, and then with the forearm fitted free of contact with the barrel. This last was done by merely placing a thick enough strip of cardboard between the bottom of the anchor block and forearm so that on tightening the forearm screw the forearm was just free of contact with the barrel—enough free space so that a strip of target paper could be slipped between forearm and barrel with the rifle resting on the forearm. Also noted was that the point of impact changed but little from the first shot with the barrel cold and uncleaned to the last shot with it warmed up—no more than that obtained with the rifle as factory bedded.

The anchor block forearm attachment method is a particular favorite of ours for use on full-sized single-shot rifles, and especially for hunting rifles chambered for a cartridge that produces considerable recoil. However, we have not found it a practical method to use on rifles having a forearm hanger such as with the Ruger No. 1 and Browning M-78 because we like to mount the block further back than could be done in this particular instance. We believe the anchor block fastening method would prove to be better than the method Ruger now uses on heavy caliber rifles if the unused hanger tip (about .750″) were cut off and the block mounted with two 8×40 screws .750″ forward of the hanger and with the bottom of the block made with a forward lip to serve as an additional recoil lug. In addition, we would recommend that the forearm channel from the receiver forward to one inch forward of the block, as well as the block, be glass-bedded in place, with the channel forward of that point made free of the barrel.

CONCLUSIONS

After all the tests with the different forearm bedding and attachment methods on our Ruger No. 1 test rifle had been made, we spread the many targets that we had fired on the floor and made our evaluation from them as to which was the best forearm attachment-bedding method to use for that rifle. We wanted the best accuracy that the rifle was capable of producing, but we were also just as much interested in zero retention so that the first shot

from it would strike very close to the last shot fired from it a week or a month or so before. The targets and the notes we made on them led us to the conclusion that with this particular rifle, best performance was obtained with the forearm hanger pressured against the barrel via the set screw and with the forearm completely free of contact with the barrel (Bedding Method #3).

Table 6-1 quite well sums up the results of our forearm bedding experiments with the Ruger No. 1 rifle. To be sure, we tested only one rifle, but the tests were extensive enough to lead us to believe that perhaps many other No. 1 rifles would react in a similar way.

Indeed, we are backed up on this statement by some No. 1 owners who have reported that their rifles as factory-bedded are difficult to keep zeroed

Table 6-1. Forearm Bedding Test Results.

Rifle: Ruger No. 1, Standard Model, Cal. .22-250
Range: 100 yards, 5-shot groups
Load: 41.0 grs. IMR-4831 with 53-grain Sierra HP Match bullet

		Tip Rest		Center Rest**		Rear Rest	
		average group size	point of impact	average group size	point of impact	average group size	point of impact
Bedding Method No. 1 (Factory bedding, forearm tip pressure against barrel)	Light pressure	1.115"	−1.4"			.750"	−2.7"
	*Medium pressure	1.275"	0*			.540"	− .9"
	Heavy pressure	1.420"	+1.0"			1.305"	− .6"
Bedding Method No. 2 (Barrel floated, forearm free of barrel)		.693"	−2.2"			.678"	−2.6"
Bedding Method No. 3 (Hanger pressure against barrel, forearm free of barrel)		.929"	+2.1"	.925"	+2.2"	.673"	+2.4"
Bedding Method No. 4 (Forearm attached to barrel with anchor block & screw)	No pressure	1.265"	−4.6"			1.150"	−5.2"
	Light pressure			1.070"	+ .2"		
	Heavy pressure	1.025"	+ .9"			.630"	+ .4"

* All point-of-impact figures are based on the rifle sighted-in to strike on point of aim and the forearm as factory bedded with medium tip pressure against the barrel.

**Center rest figures not given can be calculated as being the average between the tip and rear rest position data.

in, that the accuracy is seldom up to their expectations, and that the accuracy is better with the rifle resting on the rear of the forearm.

To sum up our findings with one rifle we found that the factory-bedded forearm is a problem maker in that the slightest change in the forearm wood for any reason whatsoever, or a variation in the location or position the forearm is held or rested during firing can, and usually does, cause a change in the point of impact, and unless the forearm is rested on nearly the same position during a string of shots, the accuracy will suffer.

The full-floated barrel (Bedding Method No. 3) eliminates the effect that the pressure bedded forearm can (and does) have on the barrel, does away with frequent point of impact change due to the forearm, and accuracy is substantially improved. However, so much gap is required to keep the barrel free of the forearm, and the forearm left so flexible, that most No. 1 owners probably would find this condition intolerable.

Bedding Method No. 3 seems to be the best answer to the forearm problem in that the forearm being free of the barrel cannot affect it in any way. Accuracy is as good as with any of the other bedding methods tried, it eliminates point of impact change due to the forearm, and the forearm is held quite rigidly so that only a minimum gap between forearm and barrel is needed and yet this holds the forearm free of the barrel. For best results, however, the shooter should always hold the forearm (or rest it) on one location or position only and the middle third of the forearm, or its normal checkered area, would be most convenient. We certainly suggest to No. 1 rifle shooters who are experiencing accuracy and point of impact change problems that they try this bedding method and test it against other methods.

We feel that Bedding Method No. 4 would have some merit on a No. 1 hunting rifle chambered for a heavy recoiling cartridge, and especially so if the sling swivel is mounted on the forearm or if the rifle is stocked with a full-length forearm.

Chapter 7

Remodeling the Ruger No. 3

The Ruger No. 3 carbine is a single-shot rifle based on a strong falling block action and is available in .22 Hornet, .223 Remington, .375 Winchester, and .45-70 calibers (Fig. 7-1). Its style is reminiscent of the military single-shot carbines that were popular before the turn of the century. But by present standards, or at least our own, the rifle did not quite have the lines and feel we wanted. Since the Ruger No. 3 is relatively inexpensive and does not have the premium finish of the Ruger No. 1, it is an ideal choice for the amateur gunsmith who wants to do some remodeling.

The No. 3 carbine has a 22″ round tapered barrel of moderate weight. On the barrel are open hunting sights: a bead front sight mounted on a typical band, and a folding leaf rear sight fitted in a dovetail slot cut into the barrel. The barrel is also drilled and tapped for several popular scope mounts. The buttstock and forearm are made of walnut. The buttstock has a straight grip and is fitted with a traditional carbine-styled curved buttplate made of black nylon or a similar plastic material. The forearm is full and there is a black

nylon split band fitted on the tip, with a screw to hold the band ends together and to hold it in place. The band is a decoration only, as the forearm itself is held securely to the rifle by a single screw through it and threaded into the forearm hanger.

ACCURACY TESTING

The No. 3 we chose for our remodeling project was chambered for the .22 Hornet cartridge, and we chose this caliber because it offered more rechambering possibilities than did the other calibers this carbine is chambered for. But before doing anything towards the remodeling or rechambering, we tested our factory-issued carbine for accuracy and made some forearm bedding changes that proved beneficial to accuracy and zero retention. For these tests, which were fired from a bench rest using various handloads, we mounted a 6× scope using Weaver top detachable mounts.

After a series of experiments, we determined that our No. 3 Hornet gave the best accuracy and held its zero best with the forearm band removed, the forearm made entirely free of contact with the

Fig. 7-1. The Ruger No. 3 Carbine.

barrel, and with the end of the forearm hanger bearing against the barrel with some tension so that it is pushed away from the barrel about 1/16" or so.

We accomplished this by drilling and tapping an 8×32 hole near the end of the hanger (Fig. 7-2) and fitting it with a socket-head set screw. (Wedging a narrow strip of hardwood or metal between the hanger tip and barrel will have the same effect as the set screw.) The hole was drilled just to the rear of the hole for the forearm screw cross nut and just forward of the end of the mainspring strut when the hammer is cocked.

From the factory-bedded gun we seldom obtain less than 3" five-shot 100-yard groups, but with our revisions the groups shrank by 50% or more with vertical dispersion all but eliminated.

We also obtained the best accuracy with the Hornet handloaded with 50, 53 and 55 grain bullets. We were puzzled about this at first but later on found that the barrel was rifled with a 1-in-14 twist. Normally, most barrels intended for the Hornet cartridge are bored with a 1-in-16 twist, a rate best suited for bullets lighter than 50 grains. Even with the lighter bullets we got the best results with .224" diameter bullets, which was also the groove diameter of the bore of our rifle.

RESTYLING THE STOCK

What we disliked most about our No. 3 Ruger

was the wavy surface of the machine-finished wood, the bulkiness of the forearm, and surplus wood on the butt. Simply resanding the wood with the sandpaper held under a sanding block to make the surface level would improve the looks of the wood but do little else. Planing the buttstock down first to make the wood flush with the buttplate and then sanding would be better; if this is done in conjunction with making the wood flush with the receiver, it would immensely improve the looks and feel of the gun. However, we decided to go all the way with the wood remodeling and refinish and thus completely changed the appearance and feel of this gun. We not only made the gun lighter in weight by a few ounces, but reduced the size of the gripping area as we considered both gripping areas too large.

For our carbine we decided on a schnable-tipped forearm patterned somewhat after the short and well-tapered forearm on the long-popular Model 99 Savage rifle. Because the No. 3 barrel is considerably heavier than the M-99 Savage barrel, we had to make the schnable larger than Savage does. To duplicate our forearm, saw the smaller tip off the No. 3 forearm and then plane the forearm down to a straight taper to the approximate size of the flare that the finished schnable will be.

Figure 7-3 gives the rough dimensions of the schnable on our forearm. After most of the surplus is removed, attach the forearm to the gun; holding

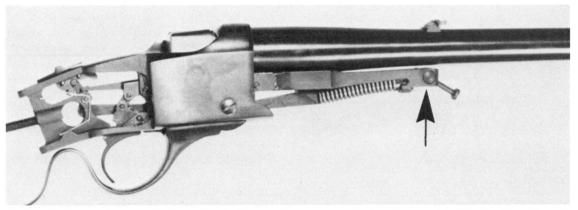

Fig. 7-2. The forearm hanger of the Ruger No. 3 with angled forearm screw in place. Arrow points to the location of the set screw which we installed to provide metal-to-metal pressure contact between hanger and barrel. This assures a stable bedding for the forearm, especially if the forearm channel is made free of contact with the barrel. The accuracy and point of impact variance was greatly improved on my rifle when bedded in this way. (See additional details in Chapter 6.)

the barrel in a padded vise, rasp the wood to near its final size, leaving the schnable. The bottom and side lines of the forearm should be straight, running from the receiver level to the small of the schnable. To obtain sufficient bottom line taper, plane and rasp the wood down to very near the level of the edge of the forearm screw head.

Schnables always look best if there is a short, pointed ridge running back an inch or more from its bottom tip, and if the edge of the rest of the schnable is also sharp. Keeping this line and edge well-defined requires careful rasping and sanding.

We also wanted to pattern the buttstock on the Savage M-99 carbine style, and we found that there was ample wood to do this. The factory No. 3 stock has a fairly large diameter wrist and its underside is

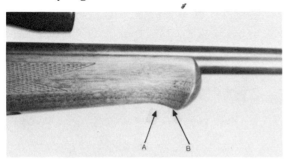

Fig. 7-3. This schnable is styled after the classic forearm tips long found on certain Savage rifles. At its thinnest point (A) it is 1.35″; at its deepest (B) it measures 1.5″ and its width at the tip is 1.35″.

nearly flat with squarish corners. It does not make for comfort or good trigger control. The widest part of the grip area on our stock was 1.60″ at a point where the panels would end, and the narrowest spot at a point about 3″ back was only 1.50″. By leaving a panel on either side and thinning the remaining portion of the grip to match the narrowest point, and by rounding up this entire area as a grip should be made, a far more comfortable grip can be achieved as well as a far better-looking one.

We used a rasp to work wood from the grip. The rasping was all done with the stock attached to the receiver and the barrel held in a vise. However, to work around the panels we removed most of the action parts including the safety, trigger, and finger lever and thus allowed better rasping access at the top and bottom of the grip and panel areas (Fig. 7-4).

We made the panels about 1.7″ long. When finished, the grip on our stock was approximately 1.3″ thick and 4.75″ in circumference. Most of the wood removed was from the area just behind the panels, and from the lower part of the grip just behind and below the panels.

Before rasping the grip to its final size, we tackled the major butt portion. A small block plane was used to remove most of the surplus wood, and we considered all wood as surplus that lay above a line from the smallest part of the grip to the entire edge of the buttplate. This meant that on our stock

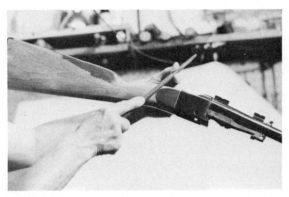

Fig. 7-4. A small round file is used to form the grip panels on the stock. Care must be used in doing this, as well as in the sanding, to keep the panel edges clean and sharp.

we had to remove as much as ⅛" of wood at spots. The important thing to remember here is to make the stock surface level. After the planing and some fine rasping, we used sandpaper held on a block to achieve the final flat and level surface that we wanted. When finished, the wood surface from the buttplate to the grip just behind the panels was straight, as checked by a straightedge.

The panels look best with clean, sharp edges, and to keep them sharp requires careful sanding (Fig. 7-5). The same caution applies where wood joins the receiver. There will be a few places where the wood is higher than the receiver and this should be made level, or nearly so. We found it best to sand this wood down, but doing it with the stock removed from the receiver. However, if you plan on rebluing the barrel and receiver, then merely sand the wood down level with the metal. In any case, sand right down to the level of the buttplate; if the sandpaper removes some bluing from the upper buttplate screw, merely repolish it and cold-blue it.

The wood on our No. 3 was very porous, so after the final sanding with fine sandpaper, we used a wood filler on it. We then followed up with GB Linspeed which gave us the finish we wanted.

Incidently, the buttstock of the No. 1 Ruger will fit perfectly on the No. 3. Thus, if you want a pistol grip stock on the No. 3, you can order one from the factory or commercial stock manufacturer. The forearm of the No. 1 Sporter or Standard model will also fit the No. 3, although it will be necessary to do some work in the barrel channel of the sporter forearm to make it fit. Procedures and instructions for fitting such a semi-finished stock and forearm on

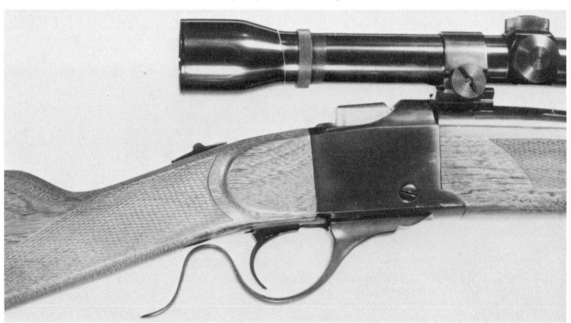

Fig. 7-5. Close-up of the finished grip panels. This remodeled grip greatly enhances the looks and the feel of the rifle.

Fig. 7-6. Ruger No. 3 barreled action.

a No. 1 Ruger are outlined in Chapter 5, and these instructions apply as well to the No. 3. Ruger No. 3 barreled actions (Fig. 7-6) are also available.

Was all this remodeling work on the No. 3 Hornet worthwhile? Yes, we feel that it definitely was. To us the remodeled rifle looks better and handles better (Fig. 7-7).

RECHAMBERING

We were not entirely satisfied with the results obtained with our No. 3 Hornet so we investigated the possibilities of rechambering it to another cartridge. The bore proved to be correct (.224″ groove diameter and 1-in-14 rifling twist) for any of the more powerful .22 centerfire cartridges such as the .22, .223, and .22-250. The extractor as made for the Hornet is also correct for the .222 head-sized case, and with only a very slight alteration to the extractor hook (shortening it), it is also suitable for the .22-250. Except for cutting in the larger chamber, nothing else has to be done for the No. 3 carbine to safely handle any of the common .22 centerfire cartridges.

Two problems must be overcome before the rechambering can be properly done—removing the barrel from the receiver in order to chamber it and replacing it again, and, in the case of rechambering

to a larger cartridge than any of the .222 family (such as the .22-250), boring out a short section of the Hornet chamber so that the reamer will start on center. At first we thought that the Hornet barrel could be rechambered to the .222 head-sized case without first removing the barrel from the receiver, but none of the reamers we owned would clear the loading groove in the receiver. There would be an exception here if the reamer had a small diameter shank so that it could be centered with the bore without touching the receiver, and, in addition, if the reamer were made to accept a threaded male extension, then it might be possible to do the rechambering without removing the barrel and doing the rechambering by hand. Even so, we would advise against any rechambering unless the barrel is removed.

Removing and replacing the No. 3 barrel is no chore provided the proper equipment and tools are used. A barrel vise and a suitable action wrench are almost essential to do this job.

The No. 3 barrel is set up very tightly into the receiver and considerable force is needed to unseat it. To securely anchor the barrel in our barrel vise, we used Brownell's Acraglas on the barrel to cement it in the wood vise block. Once the barrel was removed from the action, the cemented-on blocks

Fig. 7-7. My remodeled Ruger Carbine. Some will say that it is a better-looking gun than the factory version, but all who have handled it testify that it certainly is a better-handling gun.

were left in place during the rechambering and other work so that recementing them would not have to be done again. In order to remove the No. 3 barrel entirely from the receiver it is necessary to remove the rear sight, as well as any scope mount bases if they have been attached. And don't forget to remove the extractor before attempting the barrel removal.

Before removing the barrel it is necessary to measure the gap between the breech end of the barrel and the face of the breech, as this measurement is used in obtaining the correct headspace when chambering the barrel outside of the gun. Use thickness feeler gauges to make this measurement and do it with the action closed and cocked and then inserting the gauges from the top. The gap in our No. 3 was .015″. Whatever the gap measurement is in your rifle, to get the correct headspace when rechambering, the chamber must be cut only deep enough so that a *go* headspace gauge or a new empty cartridge case projects to within .002″ of that amount when either is chambered. After the chambering reamer is run into the chamber nearly the required depth, clean the chamber thoroughly, insert the headspace gauge or case into the chamber, and then check the amount the head protrudes from the breech face of the barrel and continue the chambering until the correct protrusion, the amount of the gap, is obtained.

Rechambering can be done with a tap wrench and the barrel held in a vise. However, it is more properly done in a metal lathe with the muzzle of the barrel held in the chuck and a center-rest to hold and center the breech end. Let the center-rest ride the barrel threads. Start the chambering by holding the reamer in a tailstock chuck until the shoulder on the reamer has cut past the extractor cut, and then finish the chamber with the reamer centered over the tailstock center and the reamer held from turning by a wrench. If rechambering to a cartridge larger than one of the .222 family, the old chamber must be bored out to about .20″ depth and to the diameter of the reamer shoulder in order to get the reamer started right. Always use plenty of cutting oil and clean the chips out frequently. The final headspacing can best be done with the barrel in a

vise and turning the reamer by hand.

When the correct headspace measurement is obtained, smooth up the new chamber edge with fine emery cloth, clean the chamber and threads, and then reinstall the barrel in the action. If you have done the job right the action should close easily with the *go* gauge or new cartridge case in the chamber, but not close on a *no-go* gauge or with a .003″ thick feeler gauge held between the new case head and the face of the breechblock.

On reinstalling the barrel and setting it up tight, the original position of the barrel can be determined by attaching a scope base to the barrel and checking its squareness to the side of the receiver with a machinist's square.

We have always preferred to have our falling block rifles "tight" or "close" breeched—that is, with the minimum possible space between the barrel breech and breechblock. In the Ruger No. 3, as well as in the No. 1, we prefer no gap at all, or at the most a .0005″ to .001″ gap or just enough so that the breechblock does not stick when the action is closed. The .015″ gap that was in our No. 3 carbine does not mean or in any other way indicate that it had excessive headspace, for in fact the headspace was perfectly normal. We just insist on a very close fit to eliminate the gap, to prevent the breechblock from rattling, and so that the correct headspace is achieved when the chamber is deep enough so that the head of the *go* headspace gauge or new cartridge case is flush with the breech end of the barrel. Therefore, as long as we had to remove the barrel for rechambering, we decided to set the barrel back one turn and eliminate the gap.

Fitting the barrel of the No. 3 Ruger and getting the zero breeching is not too difficult. A metal-turning lathe setup is required. This barrel has 16 threads per inch, and this means that exactly 1/16th inch (.0625″) must be turned off from the face of the barrel shoulder to allow the barrel to be turned in one turn farther. Since our barrel had a .015″ space from the breechblock, only .0475″ had to be removed from its face. This also meant that the extractor cut in the barrel breech needed to be made deeper by that much, which was quite easily done with a file. The barrel was then rechambered and headspaced with a new cartridge case, with a straightedge being used to determine when the head of the case was flush with the breech face.

We got a too-close fit between barrel and breechblock on our first attempt and had to remove the barrel once more and polish the barrel breech down another .002" and deepen the chamber that much. Finished, a .001" feeler gauge will now be jammed before the breechblock can be fully closed on it. *That's* the kind of breeching and headspace we like on falling block rifles.

Our rifle was definitely much more accurate after the rechambering to the .223 cartridge. Using our favorite handload of 21.5 grains of IMR #4198 powder and the Sierra 50 grain Blitz bullet, consistant MOA accuracy was achieved. We feel that a similar improvement in accuracy would have re-sulted had we rechambered our rifle to .222, .222 Magnum, .225, .220 Swift, .22-250 or .224 Weatherby Magnum.

A Ruger No. 3 in .223 caliber can be safely rechambered to any of the larger .22 center-fire cartridges such as the .22-250 and .220 Swift. I do not believe it advisable or practical to rechamber any of the other calibers of this carbine to larger cartridges although some of these rechamberings can safely be done. For example, the No. 3 in .30-40 can be rechambered to either the .30-06 or to the .300 Winchester Magnum or .300 H & H Magnum. The .45-70 No. 3 could be rechambered for the .45 RCBS Basic but who would want to fire it with a full load in that caliber? Always, after rechambering any rifle, obliterate the original caliber markings and stamp on the new caliber designation.

Chapter 8

Refining the Browning M-78

John Moses Browning designed and built his first successful rifle in 1878. It was a high-walled single-shot of the falling block type and was operated by an under finger lever. He patented it in 1879. Winchester bought the manufacturing rights for it in 1884 and reintroduced this Browning rifle in 1885 as the Model 85 Winchester. It became a very popular and successful rifle. It is regarded by many shooters as the best single-shot rifle ever made in the United States.

In 1973 the Browning Arms Company introduced a single-shot rifle which has many features and characteristics of the original Browning rifle. It's probably more aptly described as a modernized version of that rifle or of the Winchester Model 85 high-wall. Browning designated it as the M-78 in honor of John M. Browning, the founder of the Browning Company (Fig. 8-1).

Those familiar with the original Browning single-shot rifle can find few of J.M.B.'s holdovers in the new Browning M-78 action. Even so, J.M.B.'s touch for simplicity is not there. But more apparent to those who know the Model 85 Winches-

ter rifle as it was made can find no touch of Winchester in it, and especially not in its exterior finish. Every M-85 Winchester was superbly finished to the last detail. Not so are the M-78 Brownings that I have examined. In my opinion they are poorly finished, and this is the reason why I have retouched the M-78 I own. I think I would have J.M.B.'s and the Winchester craftsmen of the M-85 period's stamp of approval of what I did.

STOCK REFINISHING

What I disliked most on the M-78 is the poor finishing of the stock and forearm. It seems that no attempt was made to sand the surface of the wood level. Too much wood was left on the grip where it joined the receiver and unevenly at that. The pistol grip cap (Fig. 8-2) appears to have been attached after the stock was finished and its edges are not even with the wood. Ditto for the rubber buttplate. The checkered areas were wavy, with over-runs and many unpointed diamonds. The high gloss sprayed-on finish was not evenly applied; it could be creased with a thumbnail, and a lot of it extended

Fig. 8-1. The Browning M-78 single-shot rifle as it came from the factory (except for scope).

into the checkering. All of these things displeased me.

I started the retouching work on the buttstock. First I replaced the whiteline pad with a Pachmayr presentation pad which had no whiteline and dressed it down to wood level with a sanding disc. With several layers of masking tape protecting the receiver, I used rasps and sandpaper to dress down the pistol grip, making it level with the receiver and pistol grip cap. In doing this almost all traces of the original checkering was removed. Care was used in working around the grip cap; in one place, in order to level up the joint between cap and wood, some of the edge of the cap had to be removed. I then removed a similar amount from the rest of the cap to even things up.

After the work on the pistol grip was done, a pocketknife was used to scrape the soft factory finish from the rest of the stock. Before work started on the wood, the sling swivel bases were removed—easily turned out with a large screwdriver. To transform the wavy stock surface (Fig. 8-3) to a level one I sanded the stock with the sandpaper held under a sanding block. Sanding was continued until the lowest spot was made level with

Fig. 8-2. Close-up view of the M-78 Browning action and pistol grip as issued.

the rest of the surface. Final finishing was done with 400 and 600 grit papers. None of the basic contours of the stock were changed. The most noticeable change—and it was a needed and pleasant one—was that the grip circumference was made smaller.

The forearm was given a similar retouching. With it attached to the rifle and with tape on the receiver, the projecting wood around the receiver joint was made level with the receiver metal. Then the forearm was removed and with sandpaper under a sanding block it was sanded down.

I did consider doing a major retouch job on the poorly-shaped factory schnable and trying to re-shape it into a M-85 Winchester schnable, even to including inletting in a wedge of ebony, but decided against this at the last minute. Instead, I sanded the factory schnable off while sanding the rest of the forearm to a straight taper and a round contour following the original lines. The forearm was so wavy, especially in the checkered area, that by the time the surface was sanded level, almost all traces of the checkering was gone. Care was taken not to sand any more than necessary over the swivel base hole. At any rate, to level up the bottom line it was sanded down so that the forearm screw escutcheons were made level with the wood. Lastly, the tip was rounded up. The few remaining evidences of the original checkering would be obliterated on re-checkering.

After finishing the wood with G-B Linspeed oil, the grip areas were recheckered 22 lines to the inch.

DETAILING

I could have quit the retouching at this point but there were still three sore points that I wanted

Fig. 8-3. Browning M-78 stocks are not sanded level as this photo shows. A surface not perfectly level will show uneven light reflections.

to change. Two of these were minor sore spots but easily changed, and neither had any place on this fine rifle. The first one was the very unorthodox center-bored crown on the muzzle; for improved looks, as well as to get rid of the very sharp edges, I recrowned the muzzle with a conventional rounded crown.

Next, I not only did not want a cheap-looking chrome finish on the trigger, I also did not like the tight curve it had. To correct this, the trigger was removed, heated to red hot, and the fingerpiece straightened to a considerable degree. On so doing, the chrome finish came off. After a bit of steel brushing and polishing, a cold blue was used to blue it. A commercial replacement trigger (Fig. 8-4) with a full range or adjustments is available for this rifle.

The third point was the finger lever. I had nothing against the S-shaped lever; on a straight-gripped stock it is ideal, but on a pistol grip stock I find it less than perfect. I also disliked so much gap between the lever and the grip. Altering the finger lever as I wanted it was not too difficult. With the base of the lever held in an aluminum-padded vise, the rest of the lever was heated to red hot and straightened out. After this initial heating and straightening it could then be filed and bent cold. As

shown in Fig. 8-5 the end of the straightened lever was cut off and welded back on in a different location to form the behind-the-trigger part of the guard bow. After some more bending, filing, and polishing, the lever was blued and reinstalled. The altered finger lever allowed the trigger hand to be positioned to get full use of the pistol grip and made for better trigger control and gun handling (Fig. 8-6). For rifles in calibers which produce more recoil than the 6MM cartridge, the bent end of the rear part of the bow should be longer than I made it so that the middle finger will hold the finger lever closed during firing.

Except perhaps for the finger lever alteration, my retouched M-78 Browning is much more of a finished rifle than Browning makes it (Fig. 8-7). I feel it is much more like John Browning would have insisted on its being finished were he still alive to demand it. I think I have given this M-78 his touch.

GLASS-BEDDING

Bolt action rifles have been bedded and rebedded to such an extent that bedding techniques in these guns have been pretty well refined, whether

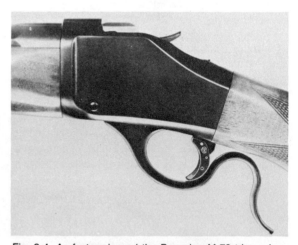

Fig. 8-4. As factory issued the Browning M-78 trigger has considerable slack or takeup and overtravel and there are no adjustments provided to eliminate this excess trigger movement. The weight of pull adjustment is also very limited. The best way to improve this trigger is to replace it with the Canjar single-set trigger mechanism as shown here. With this trigger mechanism you have the choice of either an adjustable single stage trigger or a single-set trigger that is adjustable to a pull of only a few ounces. (Courtesy Canjar.)

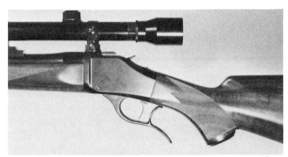

Fig. 8-5. The retouched M-78 Browning finger lever and pistol grip.

Fig. 8-6. The retouching not only improved the appearance of the Browning M-78, but the gripping and triggering of the rifle as well.

for a bench gun or a sporting rifle to be carried into the woods. Single-shot rifles require entirely different bedding systems, and like bolt action rifles, different models may require slight variations in bedding for the best accuracy.

The Browning 78 is no exception. Although the conventional two-piece stock has the fairly standard through-stock bolt in the buttstock, the M-78 forearm has an important role in regard to the accuracy of the rifle. Depending on how the foreend is inletted and bedded, it can affect the accuracy, point of impact, and day-to-day zero of the rifle.

The M-78 Browning forearm is long and slim. It is attached to the rifle with two small screws which affix it to a forearm hanger (Fig. 8-8). This hanger is an integral part of the receiver, projecting forward about six inches. The hanger, which is also the mounting for the automatic ejector system, tapers from rear to front and does not contact the barrel at any point. It takes up considerable space, especially the first four inches ahead of the receiver, and a lot of wood must be removed from the inside of the forearm for clearance. The hanger is steel, and despite its generous size, is not as rigid or as stiff as one might suppose. An adult with average strength in his fingers can easily move the end of the hanger a fraction of an inch either away from or towards the barrel.

The forearm of the M-78 is factory inletted and bedded so that when it is tightened in place by the two forearm screws, the front few inches of the forearm exerts considerable pressure against the barrel. The amount of pressure may vary from rifle to rifle, but on each of my two M-78s I estimated this pressure at around 15 pounds. The M-78 barrel, whether round or octagon, is of the heavy sporter weight—ideal for a combination varmint/sporter rifle, which the M-78 is.

At the midway forearm pressure contact point with the barrel (at the front sling swivel base location), the round barrel is .915" in diameter. Even though the barrel from the breech to this point is heavy and stiff, the forearm tip exerts enough pressure against the barrel to affect it. This may be for the good as Browning intended it to be, and it is generally conductive to the best accuracy. However, the reverse could be true in individual M-78s.

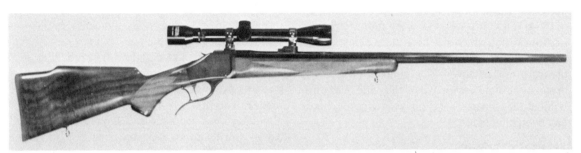

Fig. 8-7. My finished Browning M-78. Note the absence of the white line in the butt pad, chrome plating on the trigger, and schnable on the forearm. Also note the altered finger lever and the slimmed forearm and pistol grip.

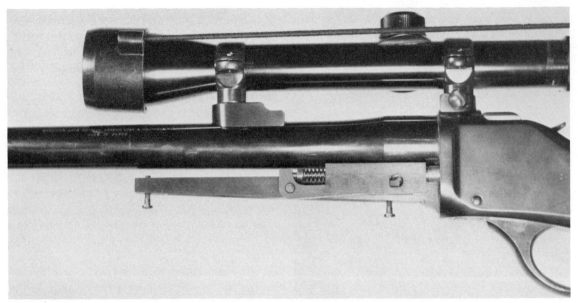

Fig. 8-8. The Browning M-78 forearm is attached to the forearm hanger by two small screws shown here. The forearm is so bedded that when it is attached to the rifle, the tip end exerts some upward pressure to the barrel. Although the forearm hanger appears to be rigid, it is in fact quite flexible at its end and it can be flexed several thousands of an inch toward or away from the barrel by finger pressure.

Another effect of this pressure is in the point of impact, which can vary with the pressure on the barrel. This effect is easily demonstrated by a simple shooting test. For example, with my round-barreled M-78 in 6MM, the 100-yard impact point drops from three to four inches with the same load when fired with the forearm removed or completely floating, compared to the factory-bedded forearm with pressure against the barrel.

On two M-78s that I experimented with, forearm pressure also produced a point of impact change to the side. This sideways change seemed to indicate that the forearm tip was exerting some side pressure. This later proved to be the case with both of these rifles. After checking the forearm channel inletting to find which side bore the heaviest against the barrel, I sanded it down until the uneven side pressure was removed. The point of impact then dropped straight down when the rifle was fired without the forearm—the sideways impact change had been eliminated.

ACCURACY TESTING

Browning evidently found that the M-78 is generally most accurate with forearm tip pressure against the barrel. But wood is not always stable over a period of months, weeks or even days; the forearm of a M-78 can be affected by a change in temperature or humidity. Any slight change in the tip pressure due to slight warping, swelling, or shrinkage of the wood can (and usually does) affect the zero of the rifle.

Not only does bedding affect accuracy, but with the pressure-against-barrel type of bedding in the forearm, changes in the way the rifle is held can also produce point of impact changes. For example, if the rifle resting on the forearm just to the rear of the sling swivel base, and afterward is fired with the forearm held or resting on a spot much farther to the rear, chances are that the point of impact will shift. If a sling is used to steady the rifle while shooting, sling tension on the forearm will also affect the forearm pressure and consequently the point of impact. The pressure-bedded factory forearm can also affect the accuracy and impact point as the barrel warms from repeated firing. The target shooter and the varmint hunter will want his M-78 to be as accurate as possible. The varmint hunter also wants his M-78 to stay zeroed from shot to shot and from month to month. The pressure-bedded forearm will probably give the best accuracy in most M-78s, but as mentioned, this method of bedding has its drawbacks. The thing to do, therefore, is to test your M-78 to find just how accurate it is with the factory pressure bedding and then follow up with one or more alternate forearm bedding methods to determine which one results in the best accuracy.

In these experiments, the accuracy testing should be done from a benchrest at a range of approximately 100 yards or more. All the testing should be done with the same ammunition, preferably a handload that has proven accurate in that particular rifle.

A minimum of at least four five-shot groups should be fired with the rifle in each of the three bedding stages described below. The change from the factory bedding to the two alternate methods is simple and this allows all the firing to be done in one session at the range.

To prepare for this, take along a screwdriver that fits the forearm screws. A small washer about .075" thick is also needed to serve as a spacer between forearm and forearm hanger in one of the tests. This washer must be small enough (or its sides filed straight) that it will fit into the forearm hanger inletting groove. For the round barreled M-78 take along a 6-inch piece of ¾" dowel and a piece of medium grit sandpaper to fit over it. If the rifle has an octagon barrel, get yourself a piece of wood about six inches long and either ⅜" square or ⅜" thick and glue a couple of ⅜" wide strips of sandpaper to it. These sanding sticks are for smoothing and widening the forearm channel.

Lastly, to carry out test No. 3, drill and tap the forearm hanger to accept a socket-head setscrew (Fig. 8-9) and make a small pillow block to fit between this screw and the barrel. I used an 8×32 setscrew for this, drilling the hole for it about ⅜" to the rear of the front forearm screw hole. The support block is a .20" piece of ⅜" aluminum rod countersunk on one end for the end of the setscrew. If

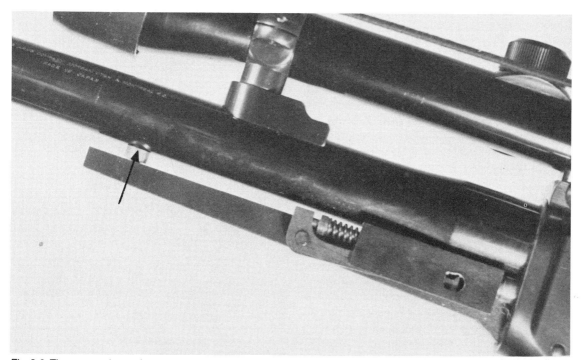

Fig. 8-9. The arrow points to the set screw and spacer block I added to shore up the forearm hanger. Its use, as explained in the text, along with sanding out the forearm channel so it is free of the barrel, resulted in better accuracy and zero retention.

you don't mind having a small hole in the forearm of your rifle, drill a hole through it to align with the setscrew and in this way the screw can be turned, and barrel tension adjusted, without removing the forearm.

Bedding test No. 1 is with forearm-against-barrel pressure, as factory issued. This should be the first test, but it should follow preliminary testing to find an accurate load for the rifle. The rifle should also be properly sighted in to strike on point of aim. The test targets will then show the accuracy of the factory bedded rifle and the targets serve as reference index for the following tests.

Bedding test No. 2 is with the barrel floating or free of forearm pressure. This test can be done in two ways—with the forearm completely removed and the rifle fired by resting it on the forearm hanger, or the forearm rigged so that it is free of the barrel. This test is best done with the forearm removed. However, if firing the rifle this way poses a problem for you, the same results can be obtained by placing a small washer about .075″ thick over the front forearm screw between the forearm and the forearm hanger. With both forearm screws tightened, the washer will separate the forearm tip from the barrel and the rifle can then be fired in the normal way. However, before firing, and with the rifle resting on the forearm, make a test by attempting to slide a strip of thin target paper between the forearm and barrel (Fig. 8-10). If this cannot be done then it will be necessary to sand the forearm channel smooth or a bit wider, or use a thicker washer, so that the forearm is completely free of the barrel. Fired either with forearm removed or propped away from the barrel, the groups will reveal whether the rifle being tested is more accurate, less accurate, or equally accurate with the barrel free-floated or with forearm pressure against the barrel as factory issued.

This test will also reveal the point of impact change that will occur when forearm pressure is removed. The vertical change need be of no concern, but if there is a horizontal change, it most likely indicates that the forearm tip is exerting some side pressure on the barrel as well as upward pressure. In this case, check to determine which

side of the channel is bearing more heavily against the barrel and sand it down. This done, it is a good idea to repeat test No. 1 as this uneven side pressure might have affected the accuracy. At any rate, the forearm pressure bedding will likely produce better accuracy than the floated barrel and in this case an even all-around forearm pressure is less apt to disturb horizontal point of impact later. The forearm channel inletting is not very smooth, and in addition it is liberally and unevenly coated with stock finish. Just sanding the channel to smooth out the humps and ridges may be all that is needed to

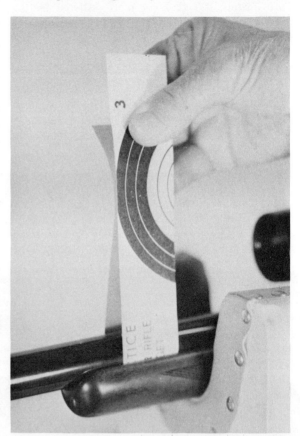

Fig. 8-10. The correct way to test for a free-floated barrel is by resting the rifle on its forearm, then with a strip of paper check the space between the barrel and forearm. If the strip of paper can be easily passed between barrel and forearm, this indicates a floating barrel. If not, the barrel is not free of the wood and thus not floated. A forearm that is free of the barrel cannot affect the barrel in any way and the rifle will retain its zero better. A free-floated barrel may result in better accuracy for the rifle, but this can only be determined by tests.

obtain even contact and pressure with the barrel.

Bedding test No. 3 consists of forearm hanger-against-barrel pressure. This is a bedding method which transfers barrel pressure duty from the forearm to the forearm hanger. The point of pressure contact is moved back several inches from the tip of the rather unstable forearm to the end of the much more stable forearm hanger.

As described previously, the pressure is produced by the setscrew installed in the forearm hanger, with a pillar or support block fitted loosely between the hanger and the barrel over the setscrew; the screw can be adjusted to apply almost any amount of pressure to the barrel. Unlike the pressure supplied by the factory-fitted forearm, this hanger pressure method is stable, even, and constant. Moreover, it's readily adjustable. In addition, it makes the forearm hanger as rigid as the barrel, which in turn provides a rigid mounting for the forearm either in contact with or entirely free of the barrel. With my round-barreled M-78, after firing test No. 2 (in which I had to smooth out the forearm channel to widen it a bit) I removed the spacer washer from between the forearm and the hanger, then inserted the pillar block and tightened the setscrew enough so that with the forearm installed it would have just enough clearance to slip a strip of paper freely between barrel and forearm. In a subsequent test I found no advantage whatsoever in having the forearm tip contacting the barrel.

In my forearm bedding experiments with two Browning M-78s, I fired 60 shots in each test with each rifle, and then repeated tests No. 2 and No. 3 to further verify the results with one of the rifles. This was a lot of shooting, but actually I had the accuracy evidence after firing four five-shot groups for each test. You can fire more groups if you want, but if you have good ammunition, are firing in good weather from a solid bench, and go about the testing properly, four carefully fired groups for each bedding test is all the information needed.

At home, with the targets marked and using a micrometer caliper, measure each group and figure the average for the groups in each test. If there is not much difference in the accuracy with the different bedding methods, you may want to do the tests again, perhaps with a different load. Or you may find at the time you are firing the rifle that accuracy is noticeably better with one of the methods, and of course that's the bedding method that should be used for that particular rifle.

If there is no significant difference in the accuracy with the three different bedding methods (as was the case with my round barreled M-78 in 6MM), then you have the choice of the three. You might prefer to retain the factory bedding, in which case just remove the pillar from under the hanger and attach the forearm again. However, you are still left with the rather unstable forearm bearing against the barrel and the likelihood of the zero changing with the first big change in the weather. To eliminate this possibility, choose one of the other methods.

In choosing between the completely floated barrel method and the forearm hanger-against-barrel pressure method, I would recommend the latter. The reason for this is that using the washer to keep the forearm away from the barrel is not a very good idea for a permanent arrangement, and to free-float the barrel with the forearm attached in the normal manner, the barrel channel in the forearm has to be deepened and widened considerably, leaving a fairly big gap. Remember that a barrel is not free-floated unless it remains free of the forearm no matter how the rifle is held or rested.

In my 6MM M-78, I chose to use the forearm hanger-against-barrel bedding method. As described before, the setscrew and pillar are used to supply upward pressure against the barrel which may help dampen barrel vibrations. This arrangement serves more or less as a prop between the hanger and barrel, and actually pushes the front end of the hanger away from the barrel and holds it there rigidly. With the forearm attached in the normal manner and with the setscrew adjusted so the front of the forearm is free of the barrel, the original forearm channel does not have to be deepened to any extent and neither the forearm nor the hanger can give, no matter how the rifle is held when fired. A possible side advantage of this bedding method is that at any time the pillar block can be removed and the forearm reinstalled, leaving the rifle bedded just as it originally was. Besides all this, the main advantage of this bedding method is that warpage or shrinkage of the forearm cannot affect or cause a change in the zero or point of impact of the rifle. There was no change in zero of this 6MM during a seven-month period, checking it on the range at least once a week. Also, this rifle showed no loss in accuracy as the barrel warmed from firing a long string of shots.

By the simple bedding tests and modifications described you may be able to significantly improve the accuracy potential and stability of your M-78 Browning, resulting in a much better "one-shot" hunting rifle.

Chapter 9

A Custom .45-70 Rolling Block

Late in 1972 I decided that I should have a .45-70 rifle for shooting during the centennial year of that cartridge. I have owned a number of rifles in this caliber in the past but all were rather ordinary, and I never shot any of them very much. Most of them were single-shots, but none was of exactly the style that suited me.

I've always wanted a really fine rifle for this cartridge—a Winchester high-wall, for example, or better still, a Remington or Whitney rolling block of the Creedmoor style. I considered remodeling my Model 1873 trap-door Springfield into a fine sporter like that done by the late Alvin Linden and described in the July, 1936, issue of *The American Rifleman*, but I'm at an age now where I respect old single-shot rifles in their original condition and decided not to rework this particular specimen.

Anyway, newly manufactured rolling block actions became available that year, and I decided to have my cal. .45-70 centennial rifle on this action. My rifle turned out and shoots so well that I'd like to describe it in detail and tell what was needed to make it and how it was made.

The action was ordered from its importer, Navy Arms Co., of Ridgefield, N.J. Although rather expensive compared to the surplus rolling block actions available in the 1950s, the action is well-made and finished and appears to be every bit as strong as the best of the original Remingtons. It is made in Italy, and is so marked on the front of the receiver. It is a close copy of the original Remington No. 1 rolling block action although none of the parts are exactly alike or interchangeable.

This action (Fig. 9-1) is large, being about 1.410″ thick, 7.87″ long, and weighs about 3 pounds. The sidewalls are .330″ thick. The cast steel receiver is very nicely finished and color case-hardened. The trigger guard with integral lower tang is brass, as is the plate which holds the breechblock and hammer pins in place. These two pins, which are as important to the strength and proper functioning of this action as are the thick sidewalls, are .470″ in diameter, and are ground precisely to fit snugly into the equally precisely reamed holes in the receiver walls and in the hammer and breechblock which they support. This pre-

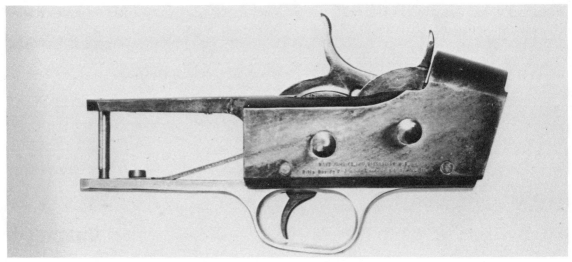

Fig. 9-1. The Navy Arms large rolling block action has a color case-hardened finish on the receiver and a polished brass trigger guard-lower tang. It is a well-made Italian import.

cise fitting eliminates most of the excess play and "give" so common with rolling block actions in which the breechblock is locked closed by the hammer. With the tight breeching of the Navy Arms action, the handloader won't have any problem with most rimmed cartridges.

BARRELING

The action also has a mechanically-retracted .076″ diameter firing pin. The size and close fit of the pin makes the action safe enough for most rimmed cartridges that do not develop over 40,000 c.u.p. This would include cartridges like the .219 Zipper, .25-35, .30-30, .32-40, .38-55, .44 Magnum, and .45-70.

I would not advise using this action for any commercial or wildcat cartridges like the .225 Winchester, .219 Wasp, Improved Zipper, .22/.30-30, .25 Krag, etc. The extractor design makes this action unsuitable for any rimless cartridges or belted head cartridges. I had a fine Buhmiller .45 caliber chrome-moly blank on hand and decided to use it for this rifle. The barrel has 12 narrow lands with a 1-in-16 twist. A rifling twist of 1-in-22 is standard for the .45-70 cartridge, but the faster 1-in-16 twist is satisfactory, especially with the heavier bullets.

The blank was turned to make a 1.20″ diameter cylindrical portion 1.75″ long forward of the receiver. A short radius reduced the diameter to .935″, and from there the barrel was turned on a straight taper to .775″ diameter at the muzzle. Finish turned and cut to an overall length of 25.5″, it weighed 3.5 pounds.

The barrel shank and thread specifications are shown in Fig. 9-2. When turning and threading the shank (which is done after the barrel is turned down) I always leave the shank a bit longer than required so that some metal must be shaved off to achieve close breeching when the barrel is turned tightly into the action. By "close" breeching, I mean that the action can be closed and the hammer fully and easily lowered on the breechblock, but it will not accept a .003″ feeler gauge between breechblock and barrel face.

After this fit was obtained, I set the barrel up tight in the action. While holding the extractor in place against the barrel face and receiver wall. I used a scribe to mark the extractor hook position and width on the barrel face. I then removed the barrel from the action and, using a milling attachment on my small lathe and a ⅛″ end mill in the lathe chuck, milled the necessary extractor hook recess cut. The recess was made the full depth of the extractor hook, and almost as wide (within a few thousandths), so that the final fitting could be done with files.

This milling, while not difficult, took considerable time in order to get everything properly lined up, and then several passes had to be made to get the correct width and depth. The extractor on this action is of the rotary type and the action design is such that the barrel must furnish the left-side support to the hook. This support is best obtained by making the extractor cut with a mill setup. However, if a mill setup is not available, the extractor cut can be filled in. This file cut setup is shown in Fig. 9-2. In order to leave a support wall, first make the horizontal cut.

After the horizontal file cut is made, make the vertical cut. In filling in the extractor hook recess, the necessity of making the horizontal cut does cut away some of the support wall that otherwise would be there if the recess is milled in, but enough wall is left below the horizontal cut to give adequate side support to the extractor hook. With a milled-in recess, the top left corner of the extractor hook should be filed round to match the recess, but when the recess is filed, leave the extractor hook square and flat on top.

After the extractor hook recess is made and the extractor hook is fitted into it outside of the action, screw the barrel back into the action tightly.

Then fit the extractor hook into its recess, and, if necessary, dress the hook down with files and emery paper until a good fit is obtained. It must be fitted so that the hook does not interfere with the full closure of the breechblock.

CHAMBERING

The chambering comes next. All that is needed for this is a finish chambering reamer. If the barrel is a rather soft one and an extension is used on the reamer, it may be possible to do the chambering by hand with a large tap wrench on the extension. This method requires that the breechblock be removed from the action. If the chambering is done this way, I would suggest doing it with the receiver completely stripped. It helps if you can find an assistant to hold the extractor in place for you while you do the chambering. Use plenty of cutting oil on the reamer, clean out the chips often, use steady pressure to push the reamer in, and use an even motion to turn the reamer. If you feel that the chambering reamer is not cutting smoothly, or if you feel any sort of chatter, stop reaming, clean the chamber and carefully inspect it. If you notice any ridges or other unevenness you will have to discontinue the hand reaming and do the chambering with the barrel in a lathe. The barrel I used was a hard one, and I quickly found that to prevent reamer chatter, I had to feed the chambering reamer into the barrel slowly under

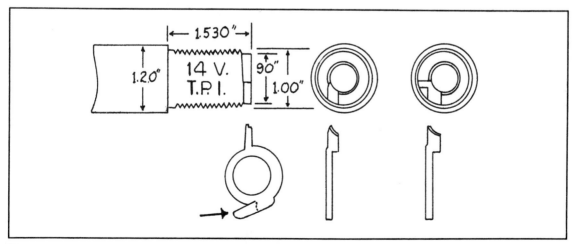

Fig. 9-2. Breech end of barrel cut for extractor by milling or filing. Horizontal file cut is shown at right. Stop (arrow) was added to prevent cartridges from chambering ahead of extractor.

the power of the tailstock feed screw.

The problem then arose of how to finish the extractor hook to match the chamber as the chamber was being cut. I solved this by removing the barrel from the lathe at about every half-inch of deepening the chamber. I could then place the barrel in a padded vise, and while holding the extractor hook in its recess in the barrel, with the other hand slowly turn the chambering reamer until the extractor hook was cut level with the chamber. This switching from the lathe to the vise was continued until the chamber was within a few thousands of an inch of being deep enough, and the final deepening and extractor cutting were done in the vise. I stopped the reaming at the point when a new .45-70 case chambered flush with the breech face. I then polished the chamber and rim recess edges with fine emery paper, finishing with #500 grit. When this was done, I screwed the barrel back into the receiver, assembled the action, and then tested the chamber and extractor by trying a case in it.

Everything worked, but like many Navy Arms rifles on the same action, the extractor tipped so far back that a cartridge can be chambered ahead of the extractor hook. This annoyance was corrected by silver-soldering a small projection on the lower part of the extractor so that it would contact the underside of the hump on the trigger guard when the extractor hook was tipped back about ¼″. I spotted the location where this projection should be by removing the trigger guard assembly from the receiver, opening the action, and with a finger holding the tipped-back extractor forward, scribe-marked the spot on the circle part of the extractor where the projection would touch the trigger guard.

I then cut a small dovetail in the extractor at this spot, made a projection to fit, and silver-soldered it in place. I then dressed down the oversized projection to stop the extractor at a point just a trifle past the maximum point where the breechblock would tip it back on the action being opened (Fig. 9-3). Figure 9-2 shows the extractor, approximate location and finished size of the stop, and its dovetail (plus silver-solder) attachment to the extractor.

STOCKING

My son did the stock work. A piece of good American walnut, large enough that the forearm could be cut from the same blank, resulted in a perfect match. The buttstock was made along the lines of an original Remington No. 1 rolling block sporting rifle stock, but heavier. The buttplate used was a steel one of the pre-'64 Model 70 Winchester type. Any other buttplate or pad can be used, but it should be about 5″ long and 1.6″ wide. I decided against bending the lower tang to form a pistol grip, which simplified the stock making. The lower line of the stock was made straight with the lower tang. The M70 buttplate was fitted to give a down pitch of 1″ and 14″ length of pull (I am 6′ 4″ tall). From the top line of the receiver, the stock has a 2.75″ drop at the heel and 2.12″ at the comb.

The forearm was made somewhat longer and heavier than the original Remington sporting forearm. It is 11″ long, has a slight schnable tip, and is 1½″ wide at its widest point. It is held in place by a single screw threaded into a studded barrel band, with the band locked on the barrel by the two socket head screws in the stud.

Inletting the forearm snugly over the band's stud prevents the forearm from moving forward when the rifle is fired. He made very neat half-rounded panels on the buttstock and forearm where the wood butts against the receiver and this produces a pleasing design and adds much to the final appearance of the finished gun.

While the wood was being finished, I polished the barrel by hand with emery paper, starting with #200 grit and finishing up with #500. This produced a fine level finish which, when blued later on, added much to the custom touch.

SIGHTS

I decided to use the Navy Arms tang sight (Fig. 9-4) and a globe front sight of some kind, preferably a windgauge sight as used on many old Creedmoor target rifles. The tang of the rifle was already drilled and tapped for the tang sight so it was easy to install with the screws furnished. The front sight was something else. Since windgauge sights are not

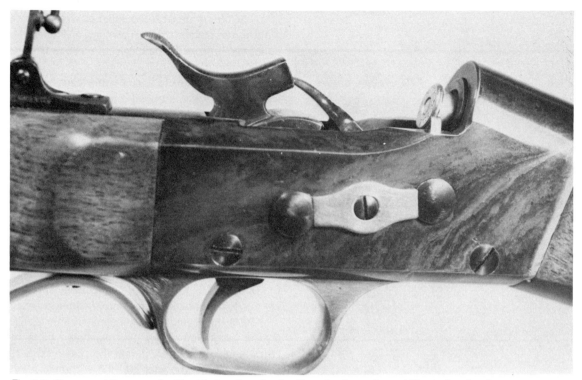

Fig. 9-3. Close-up of the opened rolling block action showing the extractor and a cartridge in the chamber.

generally available, I made my own. I found that was not as difficult as it first seemed. A Lyman No. 66A receiver sight was modified and combined with a band and the Lyman No. 17 AHB front globe sight. The result was a very satisfactory recreation of the old-time windgauge sight (Figs. 9-5, 9-6).

I filed the No. 66A sight base (where it normally contacted the receiver) flat. A band to fit the muzzle was then turned from a piece of steel tubing, the underside of the sight base was grooved slightly to fit the band, and the two were silver-soldered together. A hole drilled and tapped through the base and the band for a small socket head screw held the sight on the barrel.

Next, the windage arm of the sight slide was sawed off and discarded. The remainder of the slide was disassembled and the No. 17 AHB globe sight was silver-soldered to the slide. To achieve the lowest sight possible, I filed the dovetail base off the globe sight before attaching it to the slide. The

little graduated scale from the slide was attached to the front of the base, and an index line was filed on the bottom of the globe.

When I blued the barrel I also included the front sight, buttplate, and the four exposed action screws.

This particular Navy Arms rolling block action had a very good trigger pull as received—about three pounds, short, and free of creep.

The last thing I added to the rifle was the Numrich brass grip piece which they make for their under-hammer muzzle-loading rifle. This was attached with two 8×40 screws, and to me at least looks and feels like it ought to be there.

The rifle proved very accurate from the beginning, and I have had a lot of fun shooting it. I believe that this rolling block action is entirely strong and safe enough to handle the heavier handloads usually recommended for use only in strong rifles such as the Model 1886 Winchester.

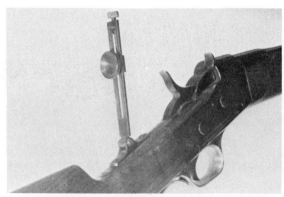

Fig. 9-4. This long-range tang aperture sight obtained from Navy Arms is a replica of a sight used long ago on target rifles such as the one described here.

Fig. 9-5. I designed and built this windgauge front target sight. See text for details.

The 300-grain jacketed bullet proved accurate with various charges of 3031 powder, and this is the bullet and powder I would use if I were to use the rifle for hunting.

Just for the fun of it I tried some lead round ball loads. A .456″-diameter ball can just be pushed into the necks of sized cases. I tried a load of 10 grains of Unique powder topped with cornmeal to fill the case. The ball is pushed flush with the case and a bit of lithium automotive grease spread on top. Accuracy at 50 years was fair. Last, I tried some .45 Minie bullets cast in a Lee mold. These bullets measured .445″ in diameter and weighed 290 grains. I loaded these into sized cases using a strip of bond typewriter paper 1″ × 1¾″ as a patch around the bullet. The paper was moistened and wrapped, or rolled tightly around the bullet in such a manner that about 5/16″ was left below the base. This was twisted to a point and pushed into the hollow base.

After the paper dried I put some lithium grease on the paper and seated and patched bullets by twirling and pushing them into the cases. With 10 grains of Unique powder and the cornmeal filler, accuracy at 50 yards is good, the bullets cutting clean holes in the paper targets. No leading occurs with the round ball or paper patched Minie ball loads.

This rifle, fitted with different sights, would make a suitable big game hunting rifle (Fig. 9-7). A

Fig. 9-6. Plan drawing of my windgauge front sight.

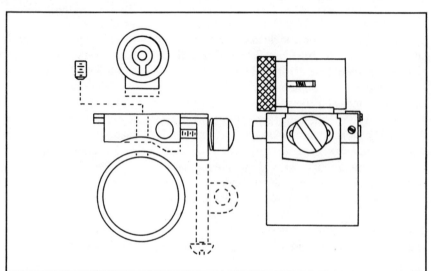

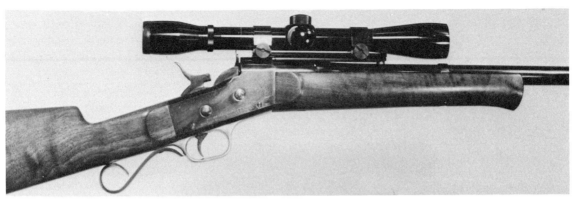

Fig. 9-7. The long barreled .45-70 target rifle proved to be very accurate and I have used it for testing various handloads with jacketed and cast bullets. For this shooting a scope was fitted using Weaver top detachable rings on a No. 70 one-piece base.

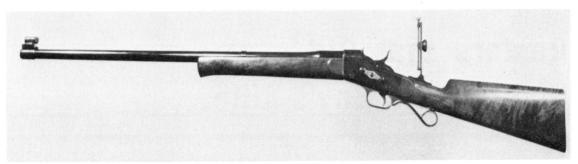

Fig. 9-8. My .45-70 target rifle built on the Navy Arms rolling block action.

scope can be mounted using a No. 70 Weaver base. For close-in work, the Williams Guide open sight would be ideal.

Sighted as shown, with tang and wind gauge front sights (Fig. 9-8) it is best suited for serious competitive target shooting from benchrest or off-hand. Readers interested in this sort of sport with single shot rifles should contact the American Single-Shot Rifle Association. This organization sponsors various shoulder-to-shoulder and postal matches throughout the year wherein only single-shot rifles (other than bolt actions) with lead bulleted loads can be used. For information write to American Single-Shot Rifle Association, L.B. Thompson, Sec./Treas., 987 Jefferson Ave., Salem, Ohio 44460.

Chapter 10

Restore that Old Single-Shot Boy's Rifle

That old well-used and perhaps little-cared-for single-shot rifle you had when a boy—or the one your father or grandfather owned—can again become a useful arm although it may not have been fired for years. Restoring one of these old rifles (Fig. 10-1) need not be difficult and can be a lot of fun. Restoration will increase its sentimental value and perhaps even its dollar value.

RESTORE OR REMODEL?

The old-time single-shot boy's rifles discussed in this chapter have two-piece stocks and actions other than bolt-action type. Many rifles are becoming collector items; all predate 1945, with some dating back as far as the 1880s. While most have collector interest, they are not necessarily more valuable as collector items than as shooters. Some were mass-produced over a long period of time and consequently are still fairly common today.

The most valuable of these rifles are the rarer models and better-known makes (such as Stevens, Remington, and Winchester) that are original and in

very good or better condition. To retain their value as collector arms, such rifles should not be touched. Neither should any other boy's single-shot rifle that is completely original, has 50% or more of its original finish (Fig. 10-2) and has a perfect or near perfect bore. The countless boy's rifles falling short of this condition are prime candidates for restoration.

The maker's name and model number are usually found on the barrel or action. Books can tell you exactly what it is, when it was made, what its original finish was, what it might be worth, etc. *Boy's Single-Shot Rifles* by James Grant is probably the most complete work on the subject. My book, *Single-Shot Rifles And Actions*, contains sectional-view drawings and photos of the rifles discussed here, and may be very helpful if your rifle lacks parts (Fig. 10-3). Other publications including reprints of old arms catalogs may show and describe your rifle and often have parts lists. Learning everything you can about the rifle may be half the fun of the project.

At the same time, study the rifle itself. Clean it

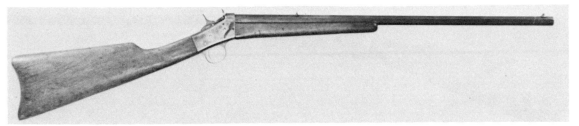

Fig. 10-1. The sentimental value of this Remington No. 4 low-cost boy's rifle can be greatly increased by restoration.

up and decide what restoration it needs. If the action does not function correctly or is overly loose, take it apart and check for missing, damaged, worn or broken parts.

If parts are missing, identify them by checking drawings, photos, and parts lists of the action. If the part is a major one, such as a breechblock, it may be too difficult or expensive to make. In this case, your best bet is to contact firms who deal in used gun parts. A listing of these firms can be found in the trade directory in the *Gun Digest*.

Damaged, worn, and broken parts which cannot be replaced can often be repaired. A common problem with many old single-shot boy's rifles is that the sear and safety notches on the hammer are worn off or broken. This part can be repaired by cutting out a section where the notches were, silver-soldering in a piece of tool steel, and filing new notches. Bent, worn, broken, and missing pins are best replaced with new pins made from drill rod. Replacement firing pins are available today for many old single-shot rifles, but most firing pins are quite readily made from drill rod. The firing pin hole in the breechblock is all the pattern you need to fashion a new one. Screws can often be made from other gun screws. It is best to get the action in good

tight working order before you begin the rest of the restoration.

If cleaning shows the chamber and bore to be in excellent condition, it is probably best to leave the rifle in its original caliber. If the bore is good but the chamber is not (you can best determine this by firing a test round in it; if the case splits, bulges badly or can't be extracted, then the chamber is bad), it is often possible to bore out the ruined chamber and put in a sleeve and then chamber this sleeve. Otherwise, the entire barrel can be relined. If the bore is dark, pitted, or if the rifling lands are badly worn, only relining or reboring will restore the barrel.

Most .22 rimfire boy's rifles with ruined bores are best relined to the original caliber—in fact that is about the only thing that can be done safely. If the rifle is a .25 or .32 rimfire (.25 and .32 rimfire ammunition is expensive and hard to find) and you want to make the rifle shootable, it may be best to reline the barrel with a .22 rimfire liner and chamber it for the .22 long rifle cartridge. This will also require that the extractor hook be lengthened. If originally a .32, the old firing pin hole must be filled, a new hole made, and a new firing pin made and fitted.

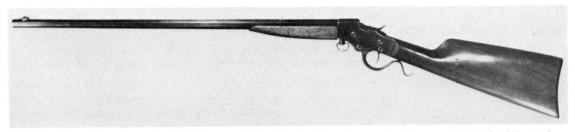

Fig. 10-2. This Stevens Favorite boy's rifle has over 50% original finish and an excellent bore; no attempt should be made to restore it.

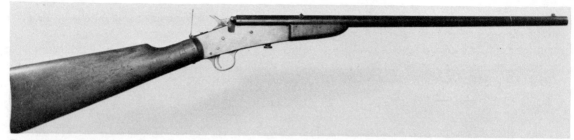

Fig. 10-3. There are two versions of this Remington No. 6; the parts of both are illustrated in the book *Single-Shot Rifles And Actions*.

None of the "small" boy's rifles in .22, .25, and .32 rimfire chambering are generally suitable for reboring or relining for centerfire cartridges. The larger rifles such as the Winchester low-wall and Stevens No. 44 originally chambered for low-pressure centerfire cartridges may be relined or rebored for centerfire cartridges not exceeding the size and pressure of those originally used with the action. It is often possible to change from rimfire to centerfire, or vice-versa, although this requires additional work to change the extractor and firing pin. Except for .22 rimfire, relining and reboring are jobs for a professional gunsmith who can usually advise you as to cartridge choice. Charges for relining or reboring usually run from $30 to $50 depending on caliber, barrel length, and who does the work. Rimfire reline jobs are often less.

Installing a .22 rimfire liner is not too difficult as epoxy cement can be used to secure it in the barrel. Low-cost liners 27″ long are available from Numrich Arms Corp., West Hurley, N.Y. A drill for drilling out the barrel is also available from them. Besides the drill and an extension for it, the only other special tool needed is a .22 rimfire chambering reamer (also available from Numrich). Several gunsmiths offering reboring and relining services are listed in *Gun Digest's* trade directory. Gunsmiths offering relining services for larger calibers seldom sell these liners separately. Properly done, relining or reboring is a a very satisfactory way to restore an old worn-out barrel to shooting condition.

COLOR CASE-HARDENING

Most of the older boy's single-shot rifles hav-

ing exposed receivers or frames were made with color case-hardened frames. If good mottled case hardening colors remain on the receiver of your rifle, and the receiver is not rusted, pitted or damaged, you are lucky. In such cases you can brighten up the old case-hardened finish by rubbing it with fine, lightly-oiled steel wool. But if the receiver has no color left, or is otherwise in need of refinishing, this is your next job. The receiver must be sent to a firm specializing in color case-hardening to have this work done; it can't be done at home. To save yourself time and money and to assure that the polishing will be done right, do all preparatory work yourself. This means putting a high polish on all parts that are to be case-hardened and shoring up the receiver.

The best way to achieve highly polished flat receiver sides is to prepare up to eight polishing boards, using 12″×12″ fiberboard ceiling tiles having smooth and level faces. With rubber cement, fasten to each tile a sheet of wet-or-dry auto body finishing emery paper, in 220, 240, 280, 320, 360, 400, 500 and 600 grits. With the receiver grasped firmly, and with one flat side against the paper, rub it back and forth over the paper, starting with the 220 and finishing with the 600 grit.

With the boards bracketed or nailed down, and the pressure of both hands applied to the receiver, flat polishing is quick and thorough. When the sides are done, take strips or pieces of the same paper, held under a dull file or flat paint stirring stick, and polish the top and bottom of the receiver. Hand polishing gives a much better finish than that produced by a power-driven wheel.

Certain receivers will have to be shored inside

to avoid warping and caving of the receiver walls during the quenching part of the case-hardening process. Small, one-piece receivers do not have to be shored, but longer receivers with flat, thin sides, such as the Remington No. 2 (Fig. 10-4) and Winchester low-wall, must be shored or they are likely to warp inward.

For shorings I use sections of an old .22 rifle barrel with the ends turned flat and cut to a length that gives a tight push-fit between the receiver walls.

With the Remington No. 2, I insert the polished trigger guard/tang into place in the receiver and put two loops of stovepipe wire through the guard screw holes, and then wedge a shoring between the walls at about the center of the receiver between the holes for the breechblock and hammer pins. With a low-wall Winchester, I use three shores: one near the top and one near the bottom of breechblock mortise and one at the point of the tang screws.

The finger levers of most single-shot actions which had color case-hardened receivers were also case-hardened and should be polished and sent along with the action. Some also have a case-hardened buttplate. The parts you send should be polished and wired together. Don't send parts that do not have to be hardened. The usual charge for color case-hardening if you do the preparatory work

is from $10 to $15, depending on size of receiver and number of other parts to be treated.

Some single-shot boy's rifles had nickel-plated frames (Fig. 10-5). If much of the plating has peeled off, have a commercial plating firm strip off the remaining nickel. Then polish the frame as outlined before, and have the plating firm put on a new nickel plate. Whether the receiver (frame) is to be color case-hardened, plated, or blued, the higher the parts are polished, the better the final finish will be.

REFINISHING

The final steps in restoring the rifle are polishing and bluing the remaining metal parts and refinishing the stock and forearm. I sand the stock and forearm before any of the metal parts are polished. (More about this later.) First, check the stock and forearm carefully for cracks, splits, nicks, dents and missing slivers. If the wood retains any original finish, remove it with varnish remover or scrape it off with a knife or piece of broken glass. Dents can usually be raised by placing a wet Band-Aid (Fig. 10-6) on the spot overnight and/or steamed out with a hot clothes iron. Nicks and other holes can usually be filled and concealed by using shellac sticks (Fig. 10-7) which are available in different colors. Minor splits can be ignored, although in some cases the split can be spread apart and some glue run into it and the split bound until

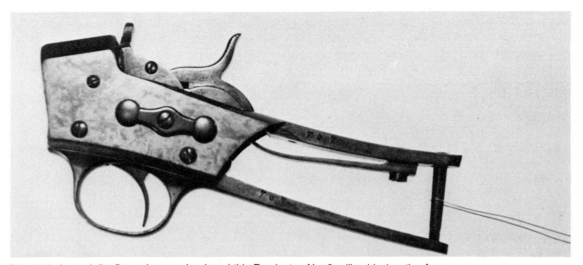

Fig. 10-4. A speciality firm color case-hardened this Remington No. 2 rolling block action for me.

Fig. 10-5. This long-obsolete Quackenbush boy's .22 rimfire rifle is worthy of a complete restoration—rebluing the barrel, renickeling the frame, color case-hardening the breechblock, and refinishing the stock.

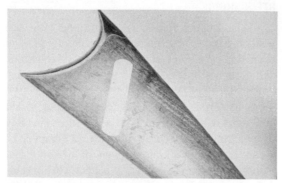

Fig. 10-6. An overnight bandaging of a dent with a wet Band-Aid will level most dents.

the glue has set. If small pieces of wood are missing it is usually possible to patch in another piece of similar wood from another old stock. If the stock is unrepairable, there is a good chance that Reinhart Fajen Inc. can furnish a new replacement for it.

Next, put the stock in place on the unpolished action and install the buttplate. Now is the time to sand the stock, working right down to the buttplate, receiver and other surfaces where the wood is supposed to be flush with the metal (Fig. 10-8). There is usually extra wood all over the stock and sanding down right to the metal will probably remove all evidence of prior use. Treat the forearm similarly,

Fig. 10-7. Small cracks, holes and damaged spots in the stock wood can be hidden by filling with sealing wax stock filler stick. Glass-bedding compound dyed to match the wood can also be used.

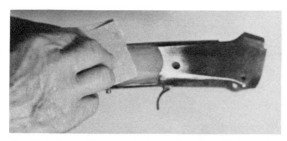

Fig. 10-8. To avoid rounded edges where wood joins metal, the sanding of a stock should be done attached to the gun. This is always best done before the metal parts are polished.

doing most of the sanding with it in place on the rifle. If the forearm has a black tip insert and this tip is loose, pry it out and reglue it in place. If the black insert is missing, make and fit another from a piece of ebony. After sanding, remove wood parts and finish them while the action and barrel are being readied.

Most boy's single-shot rifles had varnished wood. The wood on some of the cheaper Stevens boy's rifles was light-colored and stained to look like walnut. If your rifle has this sort of stock, treat it with walnut stain and then varnish it. If the wood is walnut and has sapwood in it, also treat it with walnut stain. If the wood shows much open grain it is a good idea to use a filler such as Birchwood-Casey Filler-Stain first. Then varnish the wood with common clear floor varnish. Alternatively, you can duplicate the original finish very closely by using a spray-on clear lacquer which is much easier to use than varnish. With either, you have to apply more than one coat and do some fine sanding between coats to achieve a smooth and level finish.

The final restoration step is the finishing of the remaining metal parts. If the receiver was originally blued, polish it as outlined for receivers to be color case-hardened. Resist the temptation to use polishing or buffing wheels. If you must use a polishing wheel, stay away from barrel and receiver markings, and edges and holes. The closest approximation of the original finish will result from doing all metal polishing by hand using emery cloth first and then the wet-or-dry paper. Finish with 600 grit paper and you will have a polished surface close to that of the original factory polish.

Take special care with octagonal barrels and the octagonal part of half-octagon barrels in order to keep the flats flat and the edges sharp. This is best done with emery paper backed by a file or other piece of flat metal. Polish in lengthwise strokes, starting with 220 grit and finishing with 600 grit papers. Also polish in lengthwise strokes on the final stages of polishing round barrels or the round part of half-octagon barrels. The polish obtained with buffing wheels will be a dead giveaway that the metal was refinished. It is necessary to keep the markings clean and sharp, which is impossible if you polish over them with a buffing wheel. Polish all screwheads and ends, as well as all pin ends by holding them in a drill press or electric hand drill chuck. With the drill rotating at medium to average speed, and using a fine-toothed flat file, remove any burrs and round up the ends. After this, polish the ends by pressing a piece of folded emery paper against them (Fig. 10-9).

The metal parts of most of the old single-shot boy's rifles were not blued by the modern hot-dip salts bluing method. However, this produces a durable blue-black finish which is desirable if the rifle

Fig. 10-9. Polishing screwheads is best done with emery paper and the screw held in a revolving chuck of a drill.

Fig. 10-10. Having inherited his grandfather's Stevens Favorite .22 rifle, the owner had it engraved with hunting scenes before giving the rifle to his son. The engraving was done by Neil Hartliep, Fairmont, Minnesota.

is to be used. If the rifle is intended to become an heirloom and will not be used much, Birchwood-Casey Perma-Blue or Brownell's Dicropan cold blues are satisfactory. Both are quite easy to use and will produce a blue finish similar in appearance to that of the slow rust process originally used on most of these old rifles.

If the restoration job is done with forethought and care, you will be proud to pass the result on to your son or heir (Fig. 10-10).

Chapter 11

Gunsmithing Ideas
for Two Break-Opens

The Savage Model 219 break-open single-shot rifle was introduced in 1938 and discontinued in 1966 and in that time a lot of them were made and sold. There were four variations: the Model 219, 219B, 219C and 219L (Fig. 11-1). All were based on a hammerless, break-open action and all were made with a fairly heavy 26″ round tapered barrel. The models 219, 219B and 219C had actions operated by a top-snap while the 219L featured a side lever. At one time or another they were made in calibers .22 Hornet, .25-20, .32-20 and .30-30, with the .22 Hornet and the .30-30 being the most popular.

The Model 219 (Fig. 11-2) was always a low-cost rifle among the centerfires—a plain-folks rifle, a rifle to keep in the outbuildings or in the back of the pickup. It was the poor man's .30-30 or a youngster's first varmint rifle. It was often the very first rifle to be remodeled or practiced on by many an amateur gunsmith. Even today I can't suggest a more suitable rifle for the beginning gun tinkerer to work on, unless it might be the H & R Topper. You may ask, "Where can I get a Model 219?" Try dealers who handle used guns, attend gun shows, dealers who handle used guns, attend gun shows,

and start reading *The Shotgun News*. And if you have not heard of *The Shotgun News*, send two bucks to *The Shotgun News*, Hastings, Nebraska, and get a sample copy.

The following gunsmithing information applies to all four models.

As produced by the factory the Model 219 Savage single-shot rifle is mechanically sound and reliable, and for the average shooter this rifle was made without frills, and evidently little handwork or hand-fitting went into it. However, the more critical and fussy shooter, on firing the Model 219 rifle for the first time, will find that the action is difficult to open and close, and that the trigger pull is far from ideal. Also the Model 219 is not finished as well as it could be. There are also some rechambering possibilities with these rifles. Carefully planned and executed gunsmithing can correct the mechanical deficiencies and turn the Model 219 into a classy sporter.

Lapping and/or polishing some of the action parts can relieve much of the opening and closing stiffness. The principal cause of the stiffness is in

Fig. 11-1. Model 219L Savage, so designated because it was operated by a side lever, was the last of the several variations of the M-219 that Savage made. A Model 219 in any variation chambered for the .22 Hornet cartridge, scoped and properly sighted in, makes a good short range varmint rifle.

the hinge joint where the forearm metal contacts the frame. Polishing the curved end of the frame and the inside curved surface of the fore-end iron will do away with the grating of these surfaces. I have found that it is best to lap these two parts first with coarse valve grinding compound and then polish them very smooth. The hinge pin and the groove in the barrel lug which contacts the hinge pin usually are quite smooth and should not be polished. The sides of the barrel lug can be polished, although this may not make the action work smoother. The face of the standing breech against which the extractor slides when action is closed can and should be polished smooth, as well as the face of the extractor and breech end of the barrel.

If desired, some of the action parts can be polished or lapped to make the action function more smoothly. Contacting surfaces of the top snap and locking bolt assembly can be lapped or polished to make the unlocking motion smoother and lighter. The front of the locking bolt and the bottom front corner of the barrel lug can be polished smooth, so that on closing the action, the locking bolt is depressed smoothly. The locking surfaces on the locking bolt and barrel lug should not be polished except as explained later on. Parts of the action which cock the hammer or striker can also be

polished. After polishing or lapping, all the parts should be thoroughly washed and lightly lubricated before reassembling. A high-grade paste lubricant should be used on the hinge joint parts.

SAVAGE M-219 TRIGGER WORK

When new, most of the various models of the 219 Savage rifles have a very heavy trigger pull, usually in excess of five or six pounds. In all cases, such a heavy trigger pull can be reduced to a safe three or four pound letoff, but doing this requires skill and know-how. In some cases there is a lot of roughness and creep in the trigger pull and this can be removed, and in so doing the trigger pull is usually made lighter at the same time. In some cases the trigger pull may be overly long, and this too can often be corrected very easily. All of this work can usually be done by just honing the sear surfaces on the trigger, sear, hammer, or striker, depending on the variation of the 219 action. Except for the tools needed to remove and replace the action parts to be worked on, the only tool needed for the honing is a small medium-hard triangle Arkansas stone.

On the Model 219 with the sear and striker (Fig. 11-3), and using a very small diamond-shaped hone, the sear surfaces (end of the sear and notch in

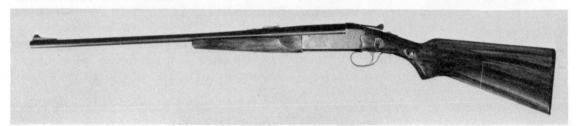

Fig. 11-2. This abused but mechanically sound Model 219 Savage rifle is a prime candidate for restocking and remodeling.

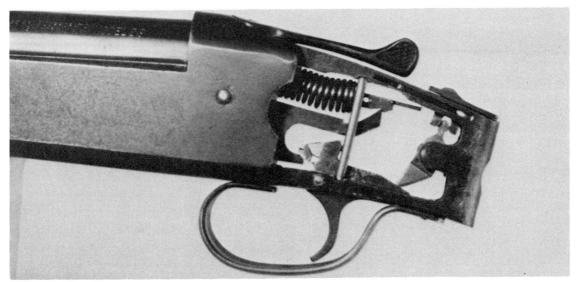

Fig. 11-3. The original Model 219 Savage action with stock removed showing the striker, mainspring, and trigger mechanism.

the striker) can usually be honed without taking these parts from the action. Also hone to leave the surface flat with sharp edges, and except when the trigger pull is extremely heavy, never change the angles of the sears. If a slight angle change is indicated, then work most carefully and slowly, and test the trigger often. A shorter letoff can be had by reducing the depth of the sear notch in the striker by honing down the peak of the notch.

On the actions with the swinging hammer (Fig. 11-4) it will be necessary to remove the hammer and trigger in order to hone them, but otherwise the same instructions apply. This is not a job which can be done in a hurry, and this is the reason why professional gunsmiths do not want to take on these jobs.

OFF-CENTER IGNITION

With several of the Model 219 Savage rifles I have owned and used, the firing pin would strike below center on the primer, often striking the near bottom edge. In all cases this was due to the fit of the breech end of the barrel in the receiver—being fitted so the breech did not close as far as it could have been made to close. On one particular Model 219 Savage rifle in .22 Hornet which gave poor accuracy when new—and in which the firing pin

struck the bottom of the primer—I thought perhaps that the poor accuracy was due to poor ignition on this account. I therefore experimented with this rifle and corrected this condition by filing the breech face of the barrel down until the firing pin struck in the center of the primer. This necessitated building up the locking surface of the barrel lug so the locking bolt would hold the action closed. This was done by adding steel to this area with electric welding and dressing it down as needed. After this the chamber was deepened to compensate for metal removed from the barrel breech. A desirable side effect in lowering the breech was that the stock drop was decreased, making the rifle better for scope use.

However, in subsequent thorough testing there seemed to be no improvement in the accuracy after the rifle was modified. Based on this experiment, it would seem that the Model 219 rifle will perform as well when the firing pin strikes the edge of the primer as when it strikes the center.

M-219 RECHAMBERING

The Model 219 Savage rifles offer several rechambering possibilities. The 219 also happens to be one of the easiest rifles to rechamber due to the break-open design. However, just because this rifle

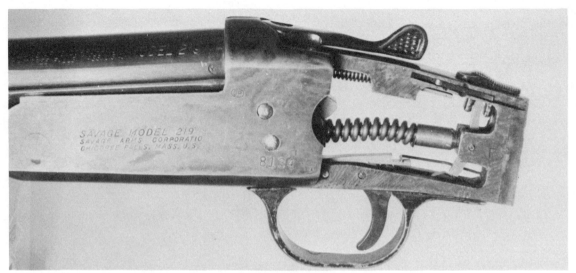

Fig. 11-4. The Model 219B Savage action with stock removed. The Models B, C, and L M-219 actions had inside swinging hammers rather than a striker as in the original Model 219.

can be rechambered to some other cartridges, or because the rechambering can sometimes so easily be done, is no reason to rechamber one of these rifles without a good practical reason to do so.

An entire book can be written on the rechambering of rifles, but I will limit my discussion here to the four calibers in which the Model 219 was made, and to only the cartridges these are suitable to be rechambered for. It must be remembered that rechambering one of these rifles to another cartridge is not likely to make the rifle more accurate, and that most of the rechamberings are only practical if you are a reloader. In most cases the rechambering will increase the sure *killing* range of the rifle, but seldom if ever increases the sure *hitting* range.

The Model 219 Savage rifle in the .25-20 caliber can be rechambered for the .255 Dean, .256 Magnum, or .25-35. The .255 Dean is a wildcat cartridge, or a so-called improved version of the regular .25-20 cartridge. This cartridge must be handloaded, but regular .25-20 cartridges can be fired in the Dean chamber. Rechambering to the .256 Magnum cartridge would be more practical, and it is perhaps the best cartridge for which this rifle is suited. The .256 Magnum cartridge may become obsolete in a few years, but the cases can be made from .357 Magnum brass.

The Savage 219 barrel in the .25-20 caliber has a .257″ groove diameter and a rifling twist of 1-in-14. This is correct for all .25 caliber (.257″ diameter) bullets up to 87 grains in weight, but best suited to the 60 and 75 grain bullets. This rifle is suitable to be rechambered for the .25-35 cartridge, but only if handloaded with suitable lightweight bullets. It would be very unwise to rechamber this rifle to any larger .25 caliber cartridge than this.

The Model 219 Savage in the .32-20 caliber, which by the way, is quite scarce, offers no practical rechambering possibilities.

The Savage Model 219 in the .30-30 caliber could be rechambered, although I would see little point in doing this. Perhaps the best rechambering would be to the .30-30 Improved cartridge—provided you are a handloader. With this rechambering, regular factory .30-30 ammunition can be used. I have heard of others rechambering to the .30-40 Krag cartridge, and even though the Model 219 action would likely be more than ample in strength for this cartridge, the recoil would be severe in this lightweight rifle.

This rifle in the .22 Hornet caliber offers the best rechambering possibilities. The bore of this rifle usually has a .223″ to .224″ groove diameter, and is made with a rifling twist of 1-in-16. This rifling twist is best suited to bullets of 45 grains or less in weight. My own tests have shown that this barrel will not give good accuracy with the pointed 50 grain bullets, or with any bullet heavier than 50 grains. Therefore, rechambering should only be considered if you are a handloader.

The most common rechambering of the Model 219 Savage in the .22 Hornet caliber is to the .22 K-Hornet caliber. For readers who are unfamiliar with the K-Hornet, I will describe this cartridge briefly and list its advantages and disadvantages. The "K" in K-Hornet stands for Lysle D. Kilbourn who is credited with originating this and other similar cartridges. The K-Hornet cartridge is merely a regular Hornet cartridge with a sharper shoulder angle. This comes about by simply reaming out the regular Hornet chamber so the shoulder area is nearly as large in diameter as the base. The K-Hornet case is then "formed" by merely firing a regular .22 Hornet cartridge in this enlarged chamber, expanding the case walls to fill the new chamber. If you are a handloader the advantage of the K-Hornet is that its case will hold more powder and thus it is possible to handload it to achieve from 100 to 300 fps more bullet velocity than is possible with the regular Hornet.

If you are not a handloader then there is no advantage to having a Hornet rifle rechambered to the K-Hornet. In fact it is a disadvantage because in firing regular Hornet ammunition in the K-Hornet chambered rifle, some of the velocity is lost.

Some gunsmiths have rechambered the Model 219 in .22 Hornet caliber to the .218 Bee, or .218 Improved Bee, but since the .218 Bee case is quite a bit shorter than the Hornet chamber, the bullets will not be throated properly and accuracy will be affected. A much better cartridge choice is the .22 Super Jet, which is a wildcat based on the blown-out .22 Jet case. Properly handloaded with 40 or 45-grain bullets the Super Jet cartridge is a formidable varmint cartridge equaling the .222 Remington.

If handloaded with 40 or 45-grain bullets, rechambering this rifle to the .219 Zipper cartridge might also be practical. I have seen some of these rifles which had been rechambered for the .219 Wasp and Improved Zipper cartridges, but the usual load recommendations for these cartridges are far too hot for this action. Likewise, I consider the .225 Winchester cartridge as being *far* too hot for this rifle.

The Model 219 Hornet rifle is also suited for rechambering to the rimless .221 and .222 Remington cartridges. Rechambered for the .221 FireBall cartridge, and used with factory loads, I would estimate the muzzle velocity would be in the 2950 to 3000 fps range, with accuracy fully equal to the rifle in its original Hornet caliber.

Chambered for the .222 Remington, and used with the factory 50-grain bulleted loads, the Model 219 may perform quite well. In this rifle, however, the .222 will perform best when handloaded with lighter bullets. The .222 Magnum and the .223 Remington cartridges are loaded to higher pressures than the .222, and I would advise against rechambering this rifle to them.

The mechanics of rechambering the Model 219 Savage rifle vary as to the size of the cartridge it is to be rechambered for. Rechambering to any of the "improved" cartridges is a simple job, requiring only a finish chambering reamer, cutting oil, and a suitable tap wrench. Remove the ejector spring from behind the extractor, and with extractor in place, merely cut the chamber until the rim recess of the reamer just touches the rim recess in the old chamber.

In rechambering to a larger cartridge it is usually necessary to do this in a lathe setup. This is because the reamer probably will not have a pilot long enough to reach in the bore at the start of the chambering, and without this guide it is about impossible to start the chamber correctly by hand. With a large lathe, the breech end of the barrel can be chucked and centered in a four-jaw chuck and the reamer held and fed in with the tailstock. With a small lathe, about the only way the barrel can be held for chambering is with a milling vise attachment on the carriage to hold the barrel, and with the reamer held in the headstock chuck.

In this setup, the barrel can be aligned by placing it between lathe centers, then adjusting the carriage and milling vise to hold the breech end of the barrel in this alignment, then replacing the headstock center with the reamer. The chambering, (or at least the chamber started in this manner) is then done by slowly feeding the barrel into the revolving reamer with the tailstock. This is done with the extractor in place (with ejector spring removed) so that the reamer will cut evenly. As soon as the shoulder of the reamer has cut past the extractor cut and the pilot entered about ¼″ into the bore, then the remainder of the chambering can be finished by hand.

Modifying the Model 219 Savage extractor to extract rimless cartridges is not too difficult. Figure 11-5 clearly shows the system I used on my own rifle which was chambered for the .222 Remington. In cutting the .222 chamber, the extractor is left in place so that on finishing the chamber the end of the extractor hook is level with the chamber. Metal is

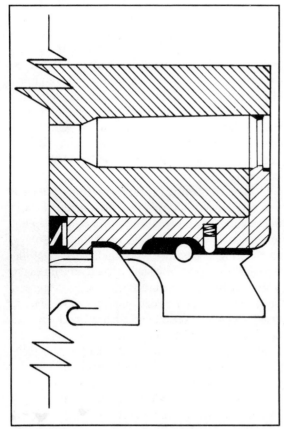

Fig. 11-5. Rimless cartridge extractor alteration for the Model 219 Savage rifle. See text for details.

then filed away from the top of the extractor stem to allow the hook to rise about .020″ into the chamber. The end of the hook is then recessed across its top front face for the cartridge rim (this can be done with a file) and the top inside edge beveled off to match the angle of the extractor groove in the cartridge. Finally, a small spring and plunger must be installed in the extractor stem as shown, this is to provide upward tension to the extractor so the hook will engage the groove in the cartridge.

A 1/16″ hole is drilled in the stem about 5/16″ back from the extractor face, and a small round ended plunger fitted. I used a small spring from a tumbler from a Yale lock under the plunger. I found it necessary to shorten the extractor travel to keep the plunger within the extractor hole, and this was done by shortening the extractor stop pin groove by filling in with steel weld. Unlike the original extractor, which on opening the action after firing a cartridge would eject the empty case several yards, this rimless extractor would extract the empty .222 case only about halfway out of the chamber, whereupon it can be grasped and drawn out with the fingers. This makes it most convenient for the reloader as the empty cases are not ejected clear of the rifle.

M-219 RESTYLING

The low cost Model 219 Savage rifle is quite ideal as a gunsmithing "practice" gun for the amateur gunsmith. If you are a beginning amateur gunsmith you may not want to undertake all of the action and chambering work already described, but rather want to try to doll up its outside appearance. There is plenty of room to take up where the Savage people left off in refinishing these rifles to your heart's desire. This is especially desirable on the later Models B and L.

You can start by just refinishing the buttstock and forearm. In doing this there is usually ample wood in both the stock and forearm for some slight reshaping.

For one thing, just making the surfaces level—planing down the hills—will do much to improve the looks. Contouring the rear end of the forearm to be flush with the fore-end iron also im-

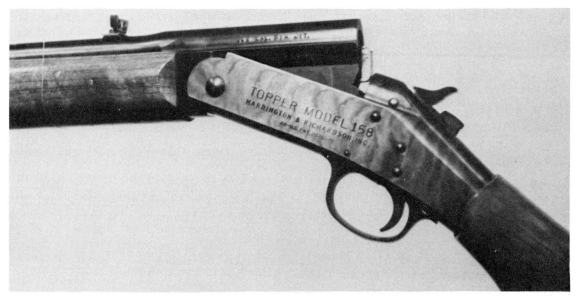

Fig. 11-6. Close-up of the H & R Topper rifle action.

proves the looks. Considerable wood can be trimmed from the B and L models to make the forearms more graceful. The comb of the stock can be undercut and the end of the pistol grip can be "set out" to improve its appearance. A horn pistol grip cap can be added, as well as a horn buttplate. Finally, with a new finish applied to the wood and the grip and forearm decorated with a neat checkering pattern, the Model 219 becomes more than just a "shooting" rifle.

If you want to replace the wood then you can purchase custom semi-finished stocks and forearms for these rifles from Reinhart Fajen Inc.

THE H & R TOPPER

The H & R Topper rifle, like the Savage Model 219, is nothing more than a rifle barrel fitted to a single-barrel shotgun frame. In fact, the Topper has long been made as a "combination" rifle/shotgun, a frame and stock and interchangeable rifle and shotgun barrels. At the same time it was and is still being sold as a rifle with only the rifle barrel. The Topper action (Fig. 11-6) is a manually cocked hammer type with a pushbutton-operation locking lug. It is fitted with a round tapered sporting weight barrel on which is mounted open sights. The stock

and forearm are made of some hardwood other than walnut but stained to look like walnut.

The 1980 listing of Topper rifles are as follows: Model 158 (Fig. 11-7) in .22 Hornet and .30-30, 22" barrel; Model 155 in .45-70 (24" or 28" barrel) and .44 Magnum (24" barrel); and Model 157 in .22 WMR, .22 Hornet, and .30-30 (22" barrel). The Model 155 was once chambered for the .444 Marlin.

The Topper single-shot rifle was first offered chambered for the .22 Jet cartridge. From the start this cartridge was branded an oddball, and this proved to be right. For one thing it was loaded with a non-standard diameter bullet for a .22 centerfire, a .222" bullet for a groove diameter bore of that size as compared to the long standard .224" bullet and groove diameter bore for most other .22 centerfires. However, it did not take long before the .22 Jet caliber was dropped and replaced with the .22 Hornet. The Topper rifle is a sturdy one and the three in .22 Hornet caliber that I had a chance to range test for accuracy were all quite accurate—good enough if scope-sighted to keep most shots within an inch and a half circle at 100 yards.

The H & R Topper rifle is a good rifle for the beginning gunsmith to start with. It can be remodeled and dressed up in a number of ways and there is

Fig. 11-7. The Model 158 Harrington & Richardson Topper rifle. This rifle in .22 Hornet caliber is a good choice for the beginning centerfire shooter, reloader, and gunsmith.

a good chance that its accuracy can be improved upon by some change in the forearm bedding. Here are some ideas:

Replace the blade front sight with a bead sight. Remove the factory sights and ramp and replace them with a Williams Guide rear sight and a bead front on a Williams ramp base. Shorten the barrel and crown the muzzle. Polish the internal moving parts to smooth up the operation of the action, including the sides of the barrel lug. Polish and reblue the barrel. Replace the plastic trigger guard with a steel one (you will have to make it). Straighten the fingerpiece of the trigger and round up its front surface. Carefully hone the sear surfaces on the hammer and trigger to achieve a smoother and lighter trigger pull.

Here are some stock remodeling ideas:

Remodel the buttstock and forearm similar to that on a Ruger No. 3 as described in Chapter 7. There is ample wood in the grip area of the buttstock to leave neat half-circle panels. In the process of thinning the grip, you should thin the entire stock. The comb can be fluted. There is also enough forearm width to leave panels on it where it abuts the frame. Put a schnable on it, or an ebony wood tip. Then sand the wood to a level and very smooth surface, stain it and then put the finish of your choice on it. After that, checker the grip areas, or try your hand at carving these areas with a simple leaf pattern.

If you do not like the very plain factory wood or if you have botched up the stock remodeling job, then get a semi-finished, shaped and inletted stock and forearm of good American walnut from Fajen. They make a dandy for this rifle, with a full pistol

grip, high comb, and cheekpiece perfect for use with a scope on the gun.

If you restock the Toppers in the .30-30, .44 Magnum, .444, or .45-70 caliber I would urge that a recoil pad be installed on the buttstock, and my preference would be the Pachmyer solid, no white-line pad.

If your Topper rifle is in .30-30, .44 Magnum, .444, or .45-70 caliber then you probably will not be interested in a high degree of accuracy from it. I feel confident that this rifle in any of these calibers right out of the box and using factory ammunition has deer hunting accuracy. However, if the Topper you have is a caliber .22 WMR or .22 Hornet (in which case you may want to use it for hunting small game and varmints), you will certainly want to get top accuracy from it. In this case the very first thing you have to do is mount a good scope on the rifle and with a box or two of ammunition and some targets, do some serious shooting with it—benchrest shooting if possible.

Find out first how the factory-issued rifle will do accuracy-wise. During this testing it might be a good idea to take along a cleaning rod with bronze brush and some powder solvent, cleaning patches, and a jar of J-B bore paste. After every ten shots or so brush the bore with solvent as well as giving the bore a real good J-B treatment. I would suggest a J-B treatment after every 25 shots until you have fired one hundred shots. After that it probably will not do much good. Anyway, the scrubbing and the J-B polishing will take some of the roughness from the new bore.

Following the initial accuracy testing with the rifle as issued, I would suggest you do a bit of experimenting with the forearm. One test could be firing three or four five-shot 100 yard groups with the forearm removed and resting the barrel on a sandbag at the point of the forearm stud. If you find a noticeable change in accuracy (*either* better or worse), then you know that the forearm has something to do with it. Another test is to place a half-inch square of folded target paper or plastic between the forearm and the barrel at a point just forward of the forearm stud. The piece should be thick enough that the forearm channel ahead of that point is free of the barrel. If the accuracy shows an improvement with the forearm bedded this way, then you can leave the piece of paper or plastic in place or you can remove it and sand out the forearm channel from that point forward until the wood is entirely free of the barrel. The way to check this is to rest the rifle on the forearm as if you were firing the rifle, and in this position there must be enough space between the forearm and barrel to pass a strip of target paper.

You should also fire a few groups with the rifle resting at different places on the forearm. For example, fire two five-shot groups with the sandbag at the front end of the forearm, then another two groups with the sandbag in the middle, and another two groups with the sandbag at the very rear of the forearm and partly under the frame. This test will show you if the point of impact changes with respect to the forearm rest position. If the accuracy is not affected but the point of impact *is*, then this tells you that you should always hold and rest the forearm at one position when firing it. You can learn more about this forearm bedding business in Chapter 6.

Chapter 12

Miscellaneous Ideas and Techniques

No matter what single-shot rifle you want to put a scope on, there is a mount available to do the job. You might not be able to find the mount listed in any of the manufacturers' catalogs, and you may have to improvise a little, but there *is* a mount that will do the job. It won't be practical to mount an over-the-bore target scope on the H & R replica Trapdoor rifle, but mounting a long eye relief handgun scope on it may be practical, and there are several mounts made to do the job. Nowadays, with so many scope mount manufacturers in business, you can even be quite selective in your choice of mount.

SCOPE MOUNTS FOR SINGLE-SHOTS

Let's begin with some of the commercial single-shot rifle models.

The Ruger No. 1 in its several styles is a very popular rifle, and Ruger furnishes bases and mount rings with the standard barrel weight styles and target/varmint scope bases with the heavy barrel model. The Ruger ring mounts are very good, but there are shooters who prefer other mounts instead. Many Ruger No. 1 shooters find that with the

Ruger rings they cannot get the eye relief they want; the usual complaint is that the scope is too far forward. The solution for that problem (other than shortening the buttstock) is to have the rear scope ring mounted on the receiver ring instead of forward of it.

One solution for this problem is to discard the Ruger mount and use instead two-piece blank mount bases of another make and fit them to the barrel and receiver to obtain proper eye relief. Blanks, unmachined at the bottom, are available from Buehler and Redfield. Installing them will require machining or hand-filing the bases to fit and drilling and tapping some holes. I have used these blank bases on several of my single-shots, and I recommend them highly. Their use is not only the answer to the Ruger eye relief problem but also the answer to scoping many other single-shot rifles. Incidentally, in selecting a scope for use on the No. 1 with Ruger mounts—if you are below average in stature or otherwise expect an eye relief problem, it might be a good idea to select either a Weaver or Bushnell scope since these two makes have their reticle cells placed well forward on the scope tube, allowing positioning the scopes well to the rear.

Buehler, Redfield, Weaver and Cone-trol make mounts for the Ruger No. 3 carbine.

The idea here is that any one of these mounts can be readily adapted to other single-shot rifles having a barrel with a similar shoulder contour. You should keep this in mind, and it would not be a bad idea to keep one or two of these mounts on hand for mounting a scope on that FBW or other single-shot action that you may be using. Also remember that Weaver, as well as some other mount makers, make extension rings and the use of these can solve some of the eye relief problems you may encounter.

Having just mentioned the Weaver mounts (and I am referring to the top detachable mounts), I have to say that they are a boon to the single-shot gunsmith. This mount system is sturdy, reliable, and low in cost. Besides the bases made for the Ruger No. 3 being adaptable to some other single-shot rifles, so is the No. 60 one-piece base (Fig. 12-1) suitable for more rifles than the H & R Topper. In fact, this particular base is ideal for the small Martini rifles including the Martini Cadet and the Ithaca Saddle Gun (last made by Savage-Stevens). I have used other Weaver one-piece bases on various single-shots, such as the No. 70 base mounted so

that it overhangs the reciver. All gunsmiths should have the complete assortment of Weaver bases, both the one and two-piece designs, and with them almost every scope mounting job can be accommodated. There is one Weaver base that I have not yet used on a single-shot, but that I expect to, and that base is the No. TO-9 as made for the Ruger Model 10/22. It will accommodate either the regular detachable rings or the tip-off mounts.

Speaking of tip-off mounts, this system seems to be here to stay. It certainly is a good system for .22 rimfire rifles. The Redfield tip-off base for the Marlin Model 39A rifle is one that I have used often on .22 single-shot rifles and I have used it on some rifles in calibers up to .25-20. I have also used the Redfield tip-off base made for the Browning .22 Automatic rifle on some single-shots. Another tip-off base that every single-shot gunsmith should have in stock is Brownell's (Fig. 12-2). Get the blank base in both radiuses; you will find uses for it. On most .22 rifles two 6×48 or 8×40 screws are adequate to secure this base to a rifle. Counterbores for Weaver-type screws of these sizes are available from Brownell's.

I have a special liking for all-steel mounts and especially for the Redfield type with a one-piece base. Mounts of this type that I have found very

Fig. 12-1. The Weaver No. 60 base for use with the Weaver top detachable mount rings is adaptable for use on a number of single-shot rifles such as on most Martini actioned rifles. Here it is used on an Ithaca .22 Model 49.

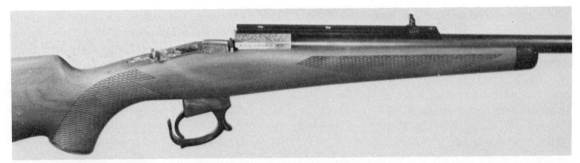

Fig. 12-2. On this F.D.H. Chicopee .22 single-shot rifle I used the Brownell tip-off blank base to mount a scope and the rear sight. It is not too unlike a half-rib, common on some foreign-made single-shot rifles. It is attached with three 6×48 screws; one at each end and one in the center. The rear sight is dovetailed into the front of the base, a very neat arrangement for a .22 rimfire rifle.

suitable for single-shot rifles are the ones made for certain non-bolt action rifles which have rather short bases with the bridge being centered in the base (Fig. 12-3). The ones that I have used are those which Redfield makes for the Marlin Model 336, Remington Models 740, 742, and 760, and for similar rifles. In most instances these bases need some altering—the underside machined or filed to fit the barrel and receiver it is to be mounted on, an original mounting hole or two in the base filled by welding, a section of the bridge cut out and the base welded back together again to shorten it, and perhaps a new hole or two drilled and counterbored into it. I often install these bases with the rear end

of the base extending over the receiver ring (Fig. 12-4), but with all of the mounting screws through the bridge and threaded into the barrel. In this style mount I prefer the Redfield (Fig. 12-5) over the Buehler because Redfield offers a greater range of ring heights.

Some single-shot shooters prefer target or target/varmint-type scopes which have the external adjustment rear mount. Target-type scope mounting blocks are required to mount these scopes and in most instances the same blocks that are standard on the Model 52 Winchester target rifle will be correct on a heavy-barreled single-shot. As furnished by the Unertl firm, the bases are A and

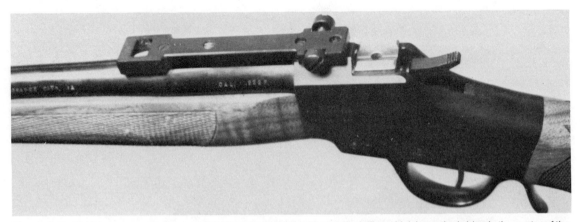

Fig. 12-3. Redfield Jr. scope mount bases made for a number of non-bolt action rifles which have the bridge in the center of the mount such as this one are adaptable for use on many single-shot rifles. The Redfield Jr. bases of this type include those made for the Remington Models 121, 241, 81, 141, 740, 742 and 760; Winchester Models 63, 61, 88, and 100; Marlin Models 39, 39A, 336, and others. On the FBW Model K actioned rifle shown here I used a base made for the Remington Model 760 and the only alteration it required was to machine or file the rear end of it flat underneath to fit the flat-topped receiver.

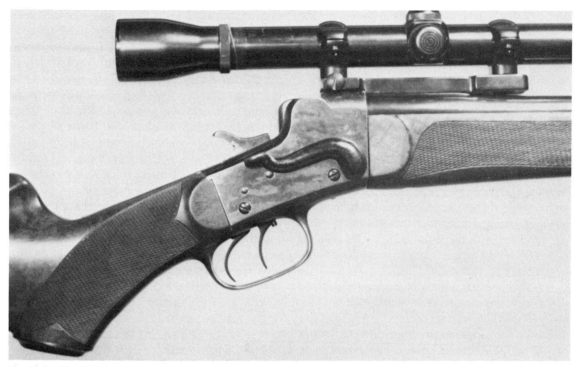

Fig. 12-4. A Redfield Jr. scope mount base made for the Remington Model 742 rifle was altered underneath to fit the barrel and receiver ring of this custom Remington-Hepburn varmint rifle. Three 6×48 screws threaded into the barrel adequately hold the mount in place.

B. However, it may happen that on certain rifles a different base or bases may be required. It may prove convenient to have a small assortment of target blocks on hand. You should also have the chart (Unertl will send it out on request) which shows actual-size side and end view drawings of all the different blocks they can furnish. Height and screw hole spacings are also shown as well as other important information. I prefer the long or two-position front blocks over the short ones—blocks SS, MM, and BB.

Altering the underside of scope mount bases is not always easily done. The job can be done most precisely with a milling machine, if you have the

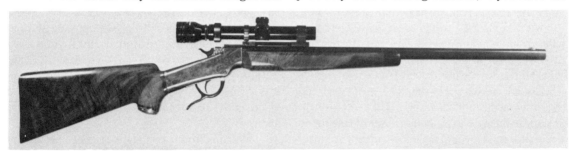

Fig. 12-5. My custom Marlin Ballard .22 LR small game rifle; the 2.5—5× Tasco scope is mounted with a Redfield Jr. mount having a flat bottomed base to fit an octagonal barrel. A Redfield Jr. base made for the Remington Model 760 rifle could have been used, with or without flattening the bottom of the base. The base could also have been mounted part on the receiver top and part on the barrel and this might have been necessary had a different scope been used—a hunting scope with an enlarged objective end, for example.

proper mill cutters. The one-piece bases are the most difficult to work either by machine or by hand. The job is sometimes made much easier by first altering the bridge, removing metal from its bottom and sides to leave it much thinner, and this makes it easier to file, grind, or mill the ends to fit the rifle. A drill press can be used to grind the underside of two-piece bases. This works best with an Atlas crossfeed table mounted on the drill press table and a drill press vise mounted on the crossfeed table. Use arbor-mounted grinding wheels dressed down to about the radius you want; with the drill press belted to its highest speed, very slowly feed the block against the stone which you continually move up and down with the drill press as the grinding proceeds. The hardened target scope blocks are best altered by this method also.

A drill press is a must in any gunshop, and if you do any amount of scope mounting that requires holes to be drilled and tapped then I strongly advise you to obtain a scope mounting jig. Mine is a Forster and during the years that I have used it I have never drilled a misaligned hole with it. I recommend it highly. It will accommodate almost any firearm and not only for drilling and tapping scope mounting holes but for front sight ramps, open rear sights which screw on, ribs, and forearm anchor blocks.

OPEN SIGHTS

I cannot offer you much help in obtaining original open sights for old single-shot rifles. What I am offering here are a few suggestions as to open sights that are available and that are suitable for the single-shot rifles that you have remodeled or built.

At first glance it would seem that the simplest solution for installing open sights on a rifle barrel is to select a set of the common dovetail sights, cut dovetail slots in the barrel, and drive them in place. This is not necessarily true. The problem is not obtaining these sights (Marbles still makes a good variety of them), the problem is that of cutting the dovetail slots. Dovetail sight slot cutters are available from Brownell's, and if you have a milling machine to use this cutter in then the job is not too difficult. The job is also not too difficult to do with a milling attachment on an eight-inch or larger lathe,

or even with a drill press that has an Atlas crossfeed table attached to its table. The sight slot cutter is easily broken if the milling setup is not a solid one. Anyway, before attempting to cut dovetail slots in the finished barrel I would urge you to make a few practice slots in a piece of discarded barrel to familiarize yourself with the operation. Then, when you are ready to cut the slots in the barrel, just make sure everything is right—the cutter is at the correct depth, the barrel is held solidly, level, and square. Just keep in mind that it is nearly impossible to correct a botched-up slot-cutting job.

If you are handy with a file and have an eye to keep the filing level and square, a sight slot is not too difficult to cut with a doctored-up three-cornered file. Every gunsmith needs one of these files. It's just a slim tapered saw file from which you have ground the teeth off of one of the flats. Grind it to a flat and level surface. To make a dovetail slot, first cut out as much of the metal as you can with a hacksaw, making four or five closely spaced cuts, and then finish it with the two-cutting-sided three-cornered file. Even if you make the dovetails with the dovetail cutter mill in a milling machine you will want the file to make the final fit for the sight that has to go into it.

I dislike putting slots in a barrel because they are so permanent. Instead, I much prefer open sights with bases that attach to the barrel by screws. In particular, I am referring to the Williams Guide open blade sight and the Williams front sight ramp bases. The Guide rear sight certainly is a marvel of design. It is very light in weight, small in size, and adjustable for both windage and elevation. Replacement sight leaves of various heights and different notch styles are available for it. This sight is attached with two 6×48 screws spaced the same as the screw holes in front target scope blocks, and it is a good idea to keep this in mind in choosing the place on the barrel to install it. I recommend this sight.

Williams front ramp sight bases come in several styles and in different heights. They are extremely well-made and finished and look good on most any sporter-sized rifle barrel. There is the regular long base which is recommended for use on high-powered rifles. It is available with or without a hood. The screw-on style is drilled and counter-bored for two 6×48 screws (which are furnished); attached with these screws the ramp is solidly mounted and removable. The other style is the sweat-on ramp furnished with one screw located under the dovetail slot. It is no trick to sweat this ramp in place and so attached it is not likely to be knocked off.

Then there is the Williams Shorty ramp (Fig. 12-6) which I especially like when I want open sights on a short-barreled rifle or one in .22 rimfire. It is attached with one 6×48 screw under the sight slot—a strong enough attachment if the rifle is not knocked around, but easily sweated on besides.

All of the Williams ramps are slotted to accept the standard dovetailed front sights as made by Marbles and Lyman. Since both the ramps and sights came in various heights, you can come up with a combination that will be correct for your particular requirements. The slots in the ramps are usually a bit undersized. Before a sight can be started into it you may need to use that special two-sided/three-cornered file in it.

The Williams Guide rear sight (Fig. 12-7) is also made to fit a barrel or receiver that is grooved for tip-off scope mounts. Incidently, the sight slot cutter is also a perfect tool for cutting the tip-off grooves into a barrel or receiver, an operation that is easier to do than cutting a sight slot dovetail.

In planning an open sight setup on a rifle it is important to consider the positioning of the rear sight so that it will not interfere with a scope should you want to mount one on it. Anyway, plan ahead for this. If you do not want to remove the rear sight when the scope is in place, then position the rear sight accordingly. If the use of the Williams Guide presents a problem in this setup, you might consider using a Lyman folding leaf sight mounted on a dovetail base. With the sight folded down most scopes will clear it if mounted over it. Of the scope mounts now made I consider the Weaver top detachable mounts best suited for most single-shot rifles on which open sights are also mounted if you wish to make use of them on occasion. These mounts allow the scope to be quickly removed and replaced with the scope bases low enough for sighting over and still have the scope mounted relatively low.

SILVER-SOLDERING

The gunsmith who plans to remodel and rebuild old single-shot rifles sure ought to be skilled in silver-soldering techniques and have materials and a heat source with which to do silver-soldering, sometimes referred to as silver-brazing. Learning the technique is easy; a few dollars will buy the materials needed, and an acetylene torch outfit will be sufficient to handle most silver-soldering jobs. If you have an oxygen-acetylene welding outfit, so much the better.

The materials needed for most silver-soldering jobs are a roll of free-flowing silver-solder in wire form, a jar of paste silver solder, and a jar of silver-solder flux. Silver-solder is also available in thin ribbon form and for certain jobs this is sometimes preferred over other forms. All are available from Brownell's Inc., and a roll of silver-solder wire will last you for years if you are not wasteful. You will need a few holding tools such as a parallel clamp

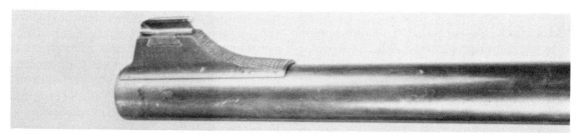

Fig. 12-6. The Williams Shorty front sight ramp makes an ideal base for front sight mounting on a small-caliber single-shot rifle. The single screw mounting is generally adequate if the rifle is used and handled in the normal manner. However, if the rifle is to be knocked about, the ramp can be sweated in place with soft solder or even silver-soldered in place.

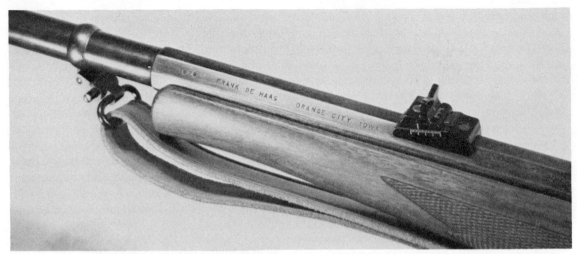

Fig. 12-7. This is the Williams Guide open sight, a fully adjustable sight that is hard to beat. On a single-shot rifle used for hunting, I recommend a shorter-than-normal forearm with the front sling swivel mounted to the barrel ahead of the forearm tip as shown here. I prefer using the Jaeger-type quick detachable swivel and here its stud is attached to a thin band sweated to the barrel.

or two, C-clamps, and visegrip pliers. A pair of the adjustable arm visegrips that Brownell sells will solve many of the holding jobs. I hold fully half of my silver-soldering jobs with pieces of clothes hanger wire.

A perfect silver-soldering job depends not so much on the actual brazing of the parts together as on the work needed prior to it because before you can succeed you have to prepare the parts for silver-soldering, and most important of all, hold the parts together during the heating and soldering step. It is generally only if you have performed the first two steps that you can succeed with the last.

I will describe a typical silver-soldering repair job and show you what I mean. Let's take a repair job on the extractor of a Remington No. 4 rifle. This is a half-moon extractor, and its rim recess is badly eroded and battered; you have relined the barrel and before chambering the barrel the extractor has to be rebuilt to match the new chamber. Here is how I do it:

I begin by filing a square or round notch in the extractor hook to remove the entire original cartridge rim recess and the eroded metal surrounding it, finishing up the file work as smooth and level as possible. After that I file the front, rear, and top surface of the notched extractor hook to remove

burrs and leave the surfaces bright. Next, I take a piece of mild steel slightly thicker than the extractor hook and file or machine it to fit closely into the filed square notch. If I decided on a round notch, I turn a piece of rod to match the notch and use a slice off its end for the new insert and silver-solder in that entire slice. If the notch is square-cornered I not only make the insert thicker, but ⅛″ or so higher so that there is metal to file off the top after it is soldered in place. Whether made square or round, I strive for a close fit without gaps so that when finished only a very faint silvered line will show.

Getting a close fit is the first part of any silver-soldering job, and the next part is holding the parts together. With this particular job I use a six or eight-inch piece of spring clothes hanger wire to do the job, clamping one end of this wire together with the base of the extractor between the vise jaws and with the extractor in the horizontal position. I then bend the piece of wire into a loop so that its free end contacts the bottom of the notch in the extractor. Now I take the insert and slip it into the notch and place the end of the holding wire on it to hold it in place. If necessary I readjust the holding wire so that it presses in a straight line against the insert, remembering that the end of this wire will get red hot in the silver-soldering process.

When I am sure that the parts are being held together correctly, I remove the insert and spread a thin layer of flux on the edges where it will contact the extractor and then reinsert it as before. Now I cut off three very small pieces of wire silver-solder and carefully place the pieces along the edge or seam where the two pieces will join. Now everything is ready for the torch, which I direct on the parts from below. I watch the pieces of silver-solder as the extractor and insert heat up and begin to turn red and as soon as the silver-solder melts and disappears in the joint, I remove the flame and the silver-soldering is done. When cooled, the extractor is then ready to be dressed down and fitted.

In the silver-soldering process it is important to have the parts that are to be joined filed clean, closely fitted together, and held together sufficiently for the remainder of the operation. Remember that only a minimum of flux need be used, and a minimum of silver-solder. From long experience I have found that placing small pieces of the silver-solder along the joint is a much surer route to a successful silver-solder job than touching the end of a length of silver-solder wire to the joint after the parts are heated. The main problem with the latter method is that you might move the part being soldered and you use much more silver-solder than needed. If the part is moved the result may be that you will have to do the entire job over again and in this case it means just that—you have to start again from the beginning.

It is just about impossible to repair a botched-up silver-soldering job, and your only recourse is to heat the parts until the parts separate and begin anew. Using more silver-solder than needed is not only wasteful but it is also difficult to remove, as it is not nearly as easily filed away as steel is.

With many jobs I employ gravity to hold parts together—for example, if the parts can be held vertically in the vise with the part to be silvered on above the other part. For this I place a box or tin can approximately the same height as the parts about ten to twelve inches away from the vice holding the part and lay a mill file with its broad end on the support and its pointed handle end on the parts to be

soldered. Sometimes I can make the parts to be joined fit together in such a way that they are held together of their own accord and then the soldering can be done without a holding wire, weight, or clamp. When a clamp or clamps have to be used, just make sure that they do not interfere with getting the parts heated up quickly for a good fitting job.

Some silver-soldering jobs require more ingenuity in holding the parts together than a holding wire, weight, or clamps. On these jobs I often use pins or screws, sometimes hidden and sometimes not. Sometimes a hole can be drilled in some place in the two parts to be joined and a pin used very effectively to hold the parts in position and together during the soldering. If the pin is fluxed and if you can get solder to it, the solder will flow throughout the joint.

Sometimes when I have two fairly large pieces to silver together, to assure myself of getting solder throughout the entire joint, I drill a small shallow hole or two near the center of the joint and place small pieces of solder in these holes.

From the time I did my first silver-soldering job many years ago to the one I did yesterday, I have found that this process is an indispensable one for me when repairing and rebuilding single-shot rifles. It can't be beaten for extractor alterations and repair, but I also use it to install tool steel sear tips on triggers, sear notch and safety notch inserts on hammers, installing replacement firing pin tips, bushing in breechblocks, new heads on screws, etc., etc., etc.

STEEL WELDING TIPS

Most amateur gunsmiths do not own steel welding equipment—that is, an oxygen-acetylene torch or an electric welding unit. Either unit will be very useful in the remodeling, restoration, or rebuilding single-shot rifles. If you decide to purchase an electric arc welder, do not make the common mistake of getting a "cheapie." Spend a hundred or two more and get a good one. Next, if you buy either the torch or electric welder, or both, learn how to use them. Almost every community offers adult education courses sometime or another each year in welding and you should not pass up these chances, even only if for refresher courses. It is too bad that courses in silver-soldering are not offered.

Anyway, welding on a gun part (such as in the alteration of a finger lever) requires a high level of skill if you want the welded area to finish up undetectable. You will know what I mean not only on your first welding job but on your tenth or twentieth as well, unless you know and practice every trick and skill of the trade.

I am not a welder, but take my welding jobs to the best welder in town. This short piece is written for you who have to do the same. The problem is that few skilled welders will want your work unless you bring it in all prepared for the welding operation, and you had better be prepared to pay the welder a good price.

The method then is to prepare the parts you want welded so that the welder can do the welding with no fuss or bother. That means, for example, if you want two parts of a finger lever welded together that you should have the parts so jigged up and arranged so the welder has ample access to the area to be welded. In other words, it is up to you to figure out how to hold the parts and make the holding fixture beforehand so all the welder has to do is weld.

I go about it in this way: Using the finger lever example again, if I want a spur welded on it, I prepare the two parts to be joined so there is ample room for the welder to lay in a bead on all sides, and then rig up a holding fixture to hold the parts exactly where I want them. Sometimes I use a small clamp-on bench vise to hold the parts, often with another clamp or two attached to the vise in some way to hold the parts in line. Sometimes I use a board with nails and screws and clamps to hold the parts to be welded, sometimes only good enough for a temporary holding job or just enough for the welder to "tack" the parts together. These holding fixtures of mine are usually Rube Goldberg contraptions—sometimes it's a whole armful holding two or three small parts together for welding. My welder looks at it, smiles, and lays a tack or bead; I loosen a vise or clamp, remove the tacked part from the contraption, and then let him have a free hand to finish the welding. I have told him beforehand what amount of metal I want at the joint and he lays on more than enough to cover it. Then I pay him, clear out with my junk, and do the dressing down and the finishing up of the welded areas myself. The gunsmith doing a bolt altering job on a turnbolt rifle can purchase a bolt handle welding jig but the single-shot rifle gunsmith has to contrive and make the jigs himself.

FOREARMS AND FOREARM ATTACHMENT

In my gun cabinet I regularly have up to 20 single-shot rifles of the two-piece stock design and on no two are the forearms alike. There is not a forearm style or shape that I haven't tried at one time or another. I have tried full-length Mannlicher style forearms, stubby ones, fat ones, skinny ones and everything in between. There were extreme beavertail forearms and forearms with built-in palm rests and other target and so-called varmint-style forearms of all shapes and sizes. And I have made sporting-styled forearms galore, all sorts of them, with all sorts of tip styles. Further, I've attached forearms in every way imaginable—with screws, bands, crosspins or wedges, with anchor blocks and hangers, tightly bedded with and without some type of bedding material, and free-floated others. As forearms go—and ways to fasten them on—I like to think I've tried them all.

As you may expect, there are forearm styles that I dislike—for example, the large and bulky ones that were once in style on varmint rifles in the 1920s and '30s. The tastes of single-shot rifle fans differ, but I dare say that if you are a young shooter and your liking is for a large forearm on a varmint rifle (or any other style single-shot rifle) that within the next ten years your taste will change to a shorter and thinner forearm. If that proves true, then all you need to do is to shave those large forearms down and I will wager that you will then say, "Why didn't I make it this size to begin with?" I do not like toothpick forearms either, and I no longer like to attach any forearm with a screw threaded into the barrel. Since tastes do differ, the best I can do is to offer some suggestions about single-shot forearms.

In making a forearm, proportion it to the rifle it is to be put on. It seldom need be longer than half the length of the distance between the trigger and the muzzle.

An exception here is for a target rifle, and in this case a target forearm need not be an inch longer than the forward most position of the sling swivel. Proportion the size of the forearm to the size of the barrel too; if the barrel is a slim one, make the forearm on the slim side. If you want sling swivels on a hunting rifle, consider making the forearm an inch or two shorter and then mounting the front swivel or swivel stud on the barrel ahead of the forearm tip. This is especially recommended if the rifle is of a large caliber. Remember this: the shorter and slimmer the forearm, the less likely it will be to warp and the less it will affect the accuracy or the zero of the rifle. Putting a large and long target style forearm on a slim-barreled sporting rifle won't make that rifle more accurate nor will it allow you to shoot it with more accuracy; it may result in just the opposite affect. Good examples of well-proportioned forearms are those on the Ruger No. 1 rifles. The forearm on the Browning is also well-proportioned but they are not as well finished as the Rugers.

As for forearm fastening methods and the bedding for them, I will only describe those which have proved the best and most practical for me. On sporting single-shot rifles in all calibers I prefer the single anchor block method (Fig. 12-8) in which a block of around 5/16″ square and 1.5″ long is attached to the underside of the barrel, with two screws about midway the forearm length, the forearm carefully inletted or glass-bedded over it and with a single screw threaded into it to hold the forearm in place.

If carefully inletted over this block, the forearm cannot move and will stay put even on a rifle of heavy recoil. I generally favor glassing the forearm over it. I sometimes like to bed the entire forearm channel in glass but most often prefer to first bed the channel with wood-to-metal contact and only the block bedded in glass. Then I'll test the rifle for accuracy and for any point of aim changes due to resting the rifle on the forearm at different places.

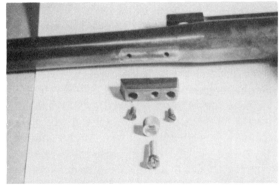

Fig. 12-8. The anchor-block forearm fastening method is one that I favor. It consists of a 5/16″ square block about 1¼″ long, with one side concaved to fit the barrel and attached to the barrel with two scope mounting screws. The forearm is inletted over the block and fastened in place with an escutcheoned fillister head screw. The ends of the block should be angled toward the bottom, especially so the rear end, to facilitate the removal and replacement of the forearm. This is most important if the forearm is glass bedded over the block, and this is recommended. The block is best positioned an inch or so rearward of the center of the forearm. A 8×32 size screw is adequate for light small caliber rifles, but for heavy recoiling rifles, or if the forearm is longer than 12 inches, a 10×32 screw is recommended. On heavy recoiling rifles, the anchor block should be sweated in place with soft solder in addition to the two screws.

At the same time I make a free-floated forearm test by simply inserting some paper shims between the block and the forearm. If accuracy is best this way, I sand the forearm channel out until wood no longer contacts the barrel. If the forearm is not too long or heavy and if the barrel is of standard sporter weight or heavier, it most often does not make much difference how the forearm is or is not bedded.

A second fastening and bedding method that I like real well is a forearm free of contact with the barrel and mounted on a single long block with two screws, which is in turn fastened to the breech end of the barrel with two 8×40 screws. This method is not ideal for rifles developing much recoil unless some sort of additional recoil block is in turn attached to the anchor block. I also prefer this method on rifles with actions that have no provision for a forearm tenon to fit into the receiver. On hunting rifles I use a ½″ square aluminum block about five to six inches long and fasten it to the cylindrical breech end of the barrel with two screws, spacing them as far apart as the length of the cylindrical section allows. Then I always install an 8×32 setscrew in its forward end. (I will explain its possible use later.) Then I inlet the forearm over the block and use two 8×32 or 10×32 screws with escutcheons to hold the forearm on, spacing the screws three to four inches apart. At the start I usually inlet the forearm to contact the barrel and do the initial accuracy testing bedded that way. After testing the rifle that way, I place shims or washers between the forearm and block to free the forearm of the barrel. The last test I make is with the setscrew turned to bear with about two or three turns of tension against the barrel. The testing will usually reveal that the best and most consistant accuracy will be achieved with the forearm free of contact with the barrel and with the setscrew bearing against the barrel. At least, that has been my experience. The use of the setscrew not only serves as a possible accuracy improvement gimmick but I have found that when it is used, the point of impact is not affected no matter at what place the forearm is held or rested on when the rifle is fired. Also, the setscrew under tension allows you to make and hold the free-floating gap between forearm and barrel to a minimum.

The above forearm fastening and bedding method can also be used on a target rifle. In this case I would suggest using a ½" square steel bar about eight inches long and attaching it to the barrel breech with three 8×40 screws spaced two inches apart and filing metal away from this bar ahead of the screws so that the forward half of the bar is free of the barrel. Put a setscrew in the front end as you may want to use it. Attach the forearm to the bar with two or three 10×32 screws.

The last method of attaching a forearm that I will briefly describe here is not adaptable to all rifles, but when it can be used it is the only really good method I know by which the forearm is fastened to the receiver rather than to the barrel. This method is a throughbolt hanger—in other words, the forearm is attached to the receiver just like a throughbolt buttstock is attached to the receiver (Fig. 12-9). It is adaptable only to rifles with a large flat frontal receiver area to which a rod can be secured. My F.D.H. System action is ideal for this

method. It is the only positive way I know of to entirely free-float a barrel in a forearm.

Briefly, the so-called hanger is a rod silver-brazed to a plate which is in turn attached to the front of the receiver with four screws. A smaller rod is threaded to the larger hanger rod and with it the forearm is drawn against the receiver. The function of the rod with plate affixed to it and the throughbolt (Fig. 12-9) is to draw the forearm tight against the receiver, and that, more than the rigidity of the rod, is what secures and holds the forearm in position and rigid.

GLASS-BEDDING

Most amateur gunsmiths, as well as many professionals, are familiar with glass-bedding compounds. This material is used most often in bedding a bolt action into a one-piece stock. For this purpose it is quite ideal, especially for the beginning stockmaker. This fiberglass bedding compound is a useful product, and its range of usefulness extends beyond bedding a bolt action rifle. I will now show you how this material can be used in connection with single-shot rifle gunsmithing.

Perhaps the most popular brand of glass-bedding compound is Acraglas as sold by Brownell's. It is the brand I have used a lot and it is the brand I am discussing in the following paragraphs. It is furnished in a kit form—enough for several jobs, complete with resin, hardener, dye, release agent, mixing cups, and instruction booklet. You can mix up only as much as you need and store the remainder in the freezing compartment of a refrigerator; it will keep for many months.

There are three basic steps or operations in all glass-bedding jobs. Step one is the preparation for the application of the mixed compound, the second is the mixing of the compound, and the last is the separation of the parts and the final clean-up work. Read the instructions first.

I prefer to do any glass-bedding after the metal parts have been polished and before they are blued.

Always remember that hardened fiberglass material is unyielding and in order for you to remove a forearm from a barrel after glass-bedding

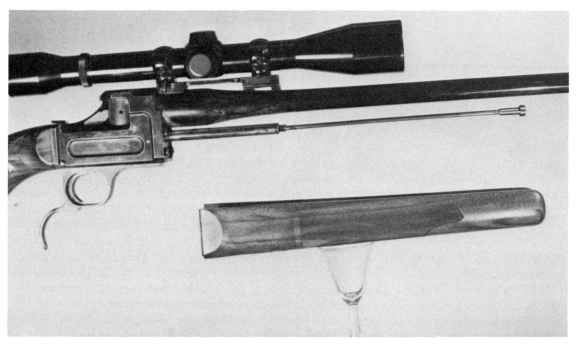

Fig. 12-9. Forearm removed from a rifle that is rigged up for a throughbolt forearm fastening method. The base of this fastening is attached to the receiver with four screws and the thin large-headed drawbolt threaded into it as it would if the forearm were in place. The base with its heavy rod does little to secure and support the forearm in the free-floating position; rather, the rigidity needed for this is obtained by perfect glass-bedded inletting of the forearm against the front of the receiver and a tight drawbolt to hold it there.

without the possibility of damaging it, you must prepare for this in advance. Use Magic tape to cover open seams and holes where you do not want the compound to get into. Then brush on a generous coating of release agent. Screws that will come into contact with the bedding compound must be coated with silicone paste. In the example glass-bedding job discussed here, that of a forearm, cover the forearm screw hole in the anchor block with a layer or two of tape so that no compound can get into it. Later, when the glassed forearm is put into place, the forearm screw will perforate the tape as it is screwed in.

The other part of the preparation job is to prepare the wood to accept the compound. In the areas where you want the compound there must be some room for it. If the inletting is sloppy, then there is already enough room and nothing more need be done. However, if the inletting is a close metal-to-wood contact then the wood where you

want the bedding compound must be relieved so that after the compound is spread in that area and the wood fastened to the gun, a thin layer must remain to harden. It is always a good idea to provide extra purchase areas for the compound in close inletted areas and this is best done by making some V grooves near the edges of the inletting with a V chisel.

Clear your workbench and on it arrange the parts of the gun that you are working on so you won't have to fumble around finding things after you have the compound mixed and ready to go.

The main use for glass-bedding compound on a single-shot rifle is on the forearm. There is nothing wrong with glass-bedding the entire forearm channel in glass, although you should always strive to do the inletting accurately enough so that this will be unnecessary. However, one of the good features about glass-bedding is that no matter how poorly you have inletted a forearm to the barrel and re-

155

Fig. 12-10. The escutcheoned head of the drawbolt in the top of the forearm that is attached to the receiver via the throughbolt method.

ceiver, a perfect bedding job will result with the bedding compound.

A favorite forearm attaching method of mine is with an anchor block as described elsewhere in this book. When I use this method, especially if it is on a varmint or big game rifle, I glass-bed the forearm over the block. This absolutely assures that the forearm is securely positioned so that it cannot slide forward or twist. If at the same time the forearm is tenoned into the front of the receiver, I also prefer to glass that area as well. In this case I glass the entire area from just forward of the anchor block to the tenon in glass, including that part of the forearm channel. Then I finish up by sanding out the forearm channel in front of the anchor block so that it is entirely free of the barrel. The effect is a halfway free-floated barrel.

When attaching a forearm to a rifle by the drawbolt method, in which case you will want the forearm to be fully free-floated, by all means glass-bed the rear of the forearm against the receiver to ensure the fullest amount of contact in this area, and to ensure a permanent contact.

Fitting a buttstock to many single-shot actions is usually a complicated gunsmithing task. Even skilled and experienced stockmakers do not relish tackling a stock job on tanged rifles such as the Winchester M-85, Stevens No. 44½ and the Farquharson. On such rifles the amateur stocker certainly can benefit by the use of a bedding compound—that is, if it is used judiciously. I also rec-

ommend its use on buttstocks of heavy-recoiling rifles.

Always do the inletting to the best of your ability; do it as if you are not intending to use any glass-bedding, for in this way little of the compound will show when the stock is finished and on the rifle. Then, if the inletting is not perfect and the stock does not fit tightly when fastened in place, use the glass-bedding to snug it up—for example, glassing in the upper tang, where the front of the stock abuts the receiver, and the rear of the lower tang. Then prepare these inletted cuts to receive the bedding compound by using a V or small U carving chisel and undercutting the edges of the tang inletting cuts and cutting a fairly deep groove on both sides of the front end of the stock. Remove all parts that are attached to the tangs or provide a tape covering for them, brush on the release agent, and you are ready to mix and apply the compound.

Glass-bedding compound is also an excellent material for certain repair jobs on stocks of old single-shot rifles. I is especially good for tightening up buttstocks that have become loose. On tanged actions follow the same procedure as outlined in the preceding paragraph. However, if the wood is somewhat oil-soaked, a radical undercutting job is required, perhaps even drilling some holes into which the compound can get a purchase. Just use your ingenuity. If a forearm on a Winchester M-85 has become loose, just remove some of the old wood from the area around the forearm screw stud and glass it in.

Glass-bedding compound, suitably dyed to match the wood, is also an excellent filler material for checks and knot holes in stock wood. Try it the next time you run into an open place in a stock when shaping it.

Now come the final operations in a glass-bedding job. Your workbench is cleared, you have the metal parts of the gun well taped and coated with the release agent, and it is within easy reach, the wood is properly prepared to receive the compound, and you have the forearm screws coated, a screwdriver handy, and you have the compound mixed.

Pick up the forearm and with a popsicle stick

spread the compound in the area where you want it. Now pick up the gun, put the forearm carefully in place, insert the forearm screw, and turn it home. If necessary, use a rubber mallet and tape the forearm in place, especially rearwards. Use a cloth, paper towel, or a thin piece of wood to wipe away the surplus compound that has been squeezed out. Save a little gob of the compound on a piece of paper so that you can check it from time to time as it hardens.

I do not like to wait several hours for the hardening process so I hasten it. In the winter I do this by using a couple of heat lamps to warm up the glassed area of the gun or place the gun in front of a heat register or above a stove. In the summer I place the gun in the warm sunshine. At first, before the compound begins to set, I hold the gun this way and that and turn it over now and then so that the compound stays put and doesn't run out. This takes fifteen minutes or so. After that I lay the gun down and then every fifteen minutes or so check the test gob of compound. Just as soon as it has hardened enough so that it takes some force to indent it with my thumbnail, I set about to unscrew the forearm screw and loosen the forearm from the barrel and receiver. At this stage in the hardening process the compound is still a bit elastic and breaks away from the metal quite readily if the metal has been properly coated with the release agent.

As soon as I detect that the forearm has loosened, I tighten the forearm screw again and leave the gun alone for another hour or so. After that, or when the compound has fully hardened, I remove the forearm entirely. Even if it has been previously loosened it may require considerable rapping with a rubber mallet before the forearm comes off. Anyway, at this point I usually try to remove any surplus compound from the wood and metal, replace the forearm again and then let the gun stand for a day so the glass-bedding compound can cure.

ESCUTCHEONS

If you do not already know what an *escutcheon* is, you will find out if you do any work at all on a single-shot rifle. The escutcheon is the little metal ring or cup in the bottom of the forearm that sur-

rounds the forearm screw. It is usually made of yellow brass and its purpose is to provide a solid foundation for the head of the forearm screw and to protect the wood around the forearm screw hole. It looks good, too. You will need one or two of these little cups almost every time you stock a single-shot rifle and since you cannot buy them, you will have to make them. This is not hard to do.

When building a single-shot rifle, my preference for attaching the forearm is to use either the number 8 or 10 size fillister or socket head screws. With these screws I prefer the escutcheon to be ⅜″ in diameter. I prefer to make my escutcheons from yellow brass if I have it, but I like red brass just about as well. Otherwise I use aluminum; a piece of an old ⅜″ aluminum shotgun cleaning rod is a suggestion for a source of that material.

Making a couple of escutcheons is not too much of a task with a metal-turning lathe, although it does take time. The procedure is as follows: Chuck the rod in the lathe chuck, face it off, drill the hole for the forearm screw body, bore out the recess for the screwhead, and cut it off.

If you want to serrate the outside surface similar to factory-made escutcheons—and I recommend that this be done—you can do this before doing anything else by using one roller of a knurling tool, rolling on a neat spiral serration.

I prefer to make my escutcheons a bit faster than one at a time. To do this I made a simple drill/counterbore from drill rod for each of the forearm screw sizes and head styles I use. Figure 12-11 shows the details and the dimensions for the common 8×32 slotted fillister head machine screw. After it is turned, filed, and sharpened, I harden and draw it.

Using such a drill/counterbore, I follow this procedure in making escutcheons: Chuck the ⅜″ brass or aluminum rod in the lathe, leaving enough rod exposed for three escutcheons; serrate the exposed section. With the drill/counterbore in a tailstock chuck, drill and counterbore the end to a depth slightly deeper than needed for the screwhead and then with a cutoff tool, cut the escutcheon off. Repeat the counterboring and cutting off on the remainder of the exposed rod. The last operation is

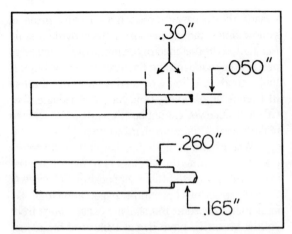

Fig. 12-11. Simple counterbores such as this one are easy to make and serve many useful purposes for the single-shot gunsmith. The dimensions of this one is for counterboring escutcheons for 8×32 fillister-head screws.

to chuck each escutcheon in the lathe to face off its bottom and to put a slight bevel on the outside edge so that it can be pressed into its hole in the forearm.

Installing an escutcheon in a forearm and getting everything right is not the easy job you might at first think. Let's suppose you are stocking a two-piece stocked single-shot rifle and have the forearm about ready to fasten to the barrel or an anchor block.

The forearm is still unshaped. You are faced with the task of installing the escutcheon, drilling the hole for the forearm screw in both the wood and metal, tapping the hole in the metal, making the hole for the escutcheon and getting it centered and to the correct depth—all separate operations but not necessarily in the order given, but operations that must be done right. Anyway, what you want to finish up with is a forearm snugly held against the barrel and receiver and with the head of the forearm screw and escutcheon in the centerline of it and flush with the bottom of the finished forearm. Before you drill a hole, I would suggest you stop and do some thinking about the best way to proceed.

This is the procedure that works best for me: After the barrel is fitted, drill and tap the rifle for scope mounts, doing this with the Forster jig and making sure the mounting holes are squarely on top. Using the jig again, drill the holes for the

forearm anchor block. Inlet the forearm over the barrel and against the receiver. Remove excess wood from the bottom of the forearm. Attach the anchor block and inlet the forearm over it. Remove the forearm and fasten the barreled action via the scope mount in the drill press vise.

Center the anchor block under the drill chuck and bolt the vise on the drill press table. Replace the forearm on the upturned barrel and hold it in place with a clamp. Using a short-length drill the size of the body of the forearm screw, drill through the forearm and drill-point depth into the anchor block.

Replace the drill with a 5/16″ end mill and use it to bore the forearm screw hole larger to the approximate depth needed for the escutcheon. Replace the small end mill with one of ⅜″ diameter and enlarge the hole to the depth needed. Remove the forearm and with a drill of correct size to tap the threads for the forearm screw, drill the hole in the anchor block. Replace the drill with the correct tap and, turning the drill press chuck by hand, start the tap several threads into the hole. Remove the barreled action from the drill press vise. Mark the front end of the anchor block and the barrel with a prickpunch so that it can be returned to the same position again, remove the block, and finish drilling the hole way through. Replace the block on the barrel, put the forearm in place, and while holding it securely against the barrel and receiver, tap the hole in the block as far as possible through the forearm screw hole.

Remove the forearm and the anchor block and complete the tapping entirely through the block. Remove burrs from the block and reattach it to the barrel. Use the drill press with a flat-ended rod chucked in it that fits inside the escutcheon recess to press the escutcheon into its hole in the forearm. Finish the job. If glass-bedding has been planned for or is required, then that job is next in line. After that the forearm can be shaped and finished.

THAT RUSTY OLD ACTION

Most single-shot rifle fans and amateur gunsmiths that I am acquainted with are constantly on the search for single-shot rifles no matter what condition the rifle may be in. If you have not already encountered that mass of rusty iron that resembles a rifle, you will sooner or later. And when you do come upon this hunk of junk you naturally will buy or swap for it and then rush home to take it apart. I know this is true for it has happened to me many times, and even as I write this there is a rusty Hopkins & Allen action in my shop soaking up penetrating oil. Knowing what I used to do in these situations and what you are most apt to do, I have some advice.

"Take it easy" are my first three words of advice. *"Lay that screwdriver down"* are four more words of advice. Instead, carefully examine the rusty hulk of parts first. Do not pry or hammer on any of the parts such as the finger lever, hammer, or trigger to get them loose. If any of these parts will move by hand pressure, fine, but don't force anything. If it already is a battered-up action and shows signs that others have tried to take it apart, then you probably can't harm it much. But if that rifle was a very good one when it was left to get rusty, you do not want to mar it up or break anything.

There is no product or other means I know of that is an instant loosener of stuck screws. I have tried them all. I have been told many times that soaking a rusty action in Coca-Cola works as well as anything, although I have not tried it.

Here is the way I generally go about getting a tightly rusted action loosened up and apart. If I have either on hand at the time, I prefer to soak the action in a can of kerosene or in furnace fuel oil. I put the can in a place where it can't be knocked over and where it won't be a fire hazard and then forget about it for two to three weeks. If I do not have the kerosene or fuel oil, then I prefer using a thin oil such as Three-in-One, keeping the action well saturated with it for a couple of weeks. Anyway, whatever liquid I use, by the end of a couple of weeks it probably has penetrated into all the crevices and joints as far as it will ever go by itself.

At the end of the soaking time I am ready to take the action apart. Often this is still not easy and it will have to be worked at. I start by cleaning out the screwdriver slots in the screw heads and finding (or filing) screwdrivers to fit. Then, holding the

action solidly on the workbench or in a vise, and with a small crescent wrench on the screwdriver to turn it, and with all the pressure I can muster on the screwdriver, I loosen and remove as many screws as I can. If while doing this I notice that the screwhead is being upset or the screwdriver slipping out, I try another tactic. If a screw can be turned ever so little I put additional oil on the ends of it and then work it back and forth until it can be entirely removed. If I can get no movement at all then I try the brass hammer trick, tapping the screw at both ends if both ends are in the open. If that fails, then I leave those screws alone for the time being.

By this time I may have removed some of the screws and other parts that hold the springs in place, so those springs are removed. Anyway, I make every effort to get the springs out undamaged. It is the flat springs you want out; you need not worry too much about the little coil wire springs that may be hidden in the action as they may already be rusted in two and are easily replaced. In some actions with flat mainsprings, the spring can be moved back and forth slightly and sometimes this is all that it takes to loosen the screw that holds it to the tang. Once the flat springs are removed from the action I can safely proceed to the next step— removing the *real* stubborn screws.

A little heat will usually do it. I use an acetylene torch and heat up the head and thread ends good and hot. That will almost always do the trick, unless the screwhead is so damaged that a screwdriver can't take hold in the slot. In this case more drastic measures must be taken.

How best to get out a stuck screw that has a chewed-out slot will depend on a number of factors. Can it be sawed in two inside the action? Or try working it loose and out by using a prickpunch on the edge of its head and tapping the punch with a hammer. Or carefully drill out at one or both ends and try an easy-out in it. Above all, do not get mad, because when you have gotten to the mad stage you are in no position to judge your actions. Whenever I reach that point I simply put the action aside for a day or two and when next I tackle it I will have the answer as to how to remove that screw and then wonder why I hadn't thought of it before.

Most pins will be easy to drift out except the very small ones such as the roller pin in the hammer. I find it best not to attempt to remove this pin or similar pins unless absolutely necessary, and then only after the action is cleaned up and de-rusted.

You will want to clean the action after you have gotten it apart. I simply dump the dirty mess in a pail, cover the parts with water, put in a handful of laundry soap, and boil the parts for fifteen or twenty minutes. I then flush the parts with hot water and place them in a jar of rust remover. The rust remover that Brownell sells is good. The parts will come out nice and grey, and clean to handle. You are then ready to do with the action what you had in mind doing with it—make some new parts for it, fit a barrel to it, stock it, and then polish and blue it.

If, after you have the action apart and cleaned up, you find that it is in much poorer condition than you hoped for or in such a shape that it cannot be restored, you still have not lost anything. Don't throw any part of it away, but put the entire works in a marked box. If you are on the single-shot make, then sooner or later you will find need for some of the parts to repair or complete another action just like it. Every year that passes makes parts for obsolete single-shot rifles ever more valuable. It can be a lowly Flobert or a No. 722 H & A rifle or a very beat-up Sharps-Borchardt—the day will come when you or another single-shot gunsmith will need those parts.

YOU DON'T HAVE A PATTERN?

Ever since my book *Single-Shot Rifles And Actions* first came out showing all the parts photos and sectional view drawings of 50 or more single-shot actions, readers seem to think that I have the actions on hand or that I have dimensional drawings of all the parts. I wish I had both, but I do not. I do not have parts for any action for sale either. The most common letter that I receive reads something like this: "I just acquired a Stevens No. 26 CrackShot but the firing pin is missing. Do you have a pattern or drawing showing its dimensions so that I can make one?" My answer is about as follow: "Sorry, but I cannot help you out. You already have

the pattern you want—the firing pin hole in the breechblock."

I just can't figure out why so many beginning gun tinkerers cannot figure this out for themselves. Of course, the firing pin hole does not give the total length of the pin but this is not hard to figure out. Anyway, for your information, here is a short, short course in making a simple .22 rimfire firing pin for most single-shot rifles other than bolt action: Make the firing pin so that its two diameters, tip and body, fit quite closely the two-diameter hole in the breechblock and long enough so both ends project. Push the firing pin in place and hold it all the way in and file the tip down so it protrudes slightly less than the depth of the cartridge rim recess in the chamber or about .035" to .040". Now file the rear end of the pin so that it is flush with the rear of the breechblock. Then notch the pin for the retainer pin or screw, notching it just enough so that the pin can move back until the tip is flush or slightly deeper than the face of the block. That is about all there is to it. You do not have to follow my order of making it, nor should the pin be a sloppy fit or made from a nail, but there you have it and every dimension you need was the breechblock and barrel.

Since I have just mentioned my book *Single-Shot Rifles And Actions*, I'd like to point out that all of the sectional view drawings in it are scaled. The book is mighty handy for the single-shot gunsmith to have around if he has to make a hammer for a Stevens or some other part for any of the rifles shown in it.

MAKING A TANG SIGHT

On this and the following pages are described and illustrated in photos and drawings two tang sights that I designed and made. Both are of rather simple design and construction with round uprights made of drill rod. On both sights the elevation slide is held in a locked position or adjustable up or down between two opposing nuts threaded on one of the upright rods. The slide on either sight can be made with or without the windage adjustment, and if the sight is made without this feature then the front sight should have it as in the windgauge target front sight described and illustrated in Chapter 9. The

Schuetzen tang sight is larger and the more rugged of the two, and it is best suited for use on a heavy Schuetzen-styled target rifle while the Hunter tang sight is best adapted for use on a hunting rifle.

Figures 12-12 and 12-13 show the F.D.H. Schuetzen tang sight in actual size with the base ⅝″ wide and the uprights made of 3/16″ diameter rods. However, this sight can be made larger and heavier than I made it, or smaller and lighter.

Make the base (1) from mild steel stock and shape it as shown if the sight is to be mounted on the tang of the action. In this case I would recommend 8×40 Weaver scope mounting screws be used and the base counterbored to accept them. Counterbores for Weaver screws are available from Brownell's.

This sight is also a good choice to mount on the heel of the buttstock if you want to do some back-position target shooting. In this case make an extra base, making it a bit deeper with rounded ends to inlet into the stock. Wood screws of adequate

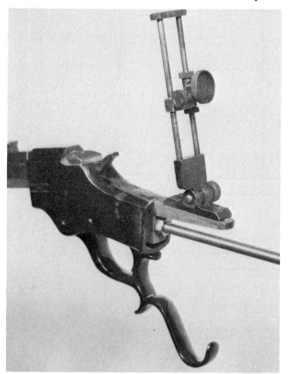

Fig. 12-12. The F.D.H. Schuetzen tang sight mounted on a Model S Falling Block Works action.

length will do for attaching this base.

The hinge screw (2) can be 3/16″ diameter or one size larger with 32 or finer pitch threads and with a large knurled and coin-slotted head.

Make the upright base (3) about as shown of mild easy-working steel. Make the hinge butt a close fit in the base and the hinge screw should be a snug fit through both parts.

Drill the twin holes for the twin sets of plungers and springs (4 and 5) into the upright base close to the sides of the hinge butt. A plunger diameter of ⅛″ or 5/32″ is adequate. The bearing end can be flat to bear against flat spots on the base, but these should not be made until their correct location is determined to match the angle of the tang and stock the sight is to be mounted on. The springs should be of heavy tension.

The elevation slide (7) should be made next and the holes for the uprights drilled through it. After the drilling has been done, the slide can then be used for a drilling guide to drill the holes in the upright base and top crossbar (11). Both holes in the upright base for the upright rods are then tapped, as well as one hole in the crossbar. The holes in the crossbar, slide, and the upright base must be accurately aligned if the slide is to move without bind on the uprights.

Make the upright rods (6) as long as you want the sight high, and if it is to be used on the stock for back-position shooting at long ranges, six inches would not be too long. Make the uprights from 3/16″ drill rod. Thread one of them at one end only; the other one can be threaded its entire length. A 32 pitch thread is okay, although a 36 or 40 pitch is better. File and polish the long threaded section down so that its diameter is no greater than the unthreaded rod. Make the two elevation adjustment nuts (8 and 9) about as shown.

There are three ways to complete the elevation slide and fit it with an aperture disc. The simplest method is merely to drill and tap a hole in its center to accept a commercial aperture sighting disc such as Redfield's. Or you can make the disc to your own liking. The result is a no windage adjustment sight. To accommodate for this limitation you can fit the rifle with a windgauge front sight. Such a

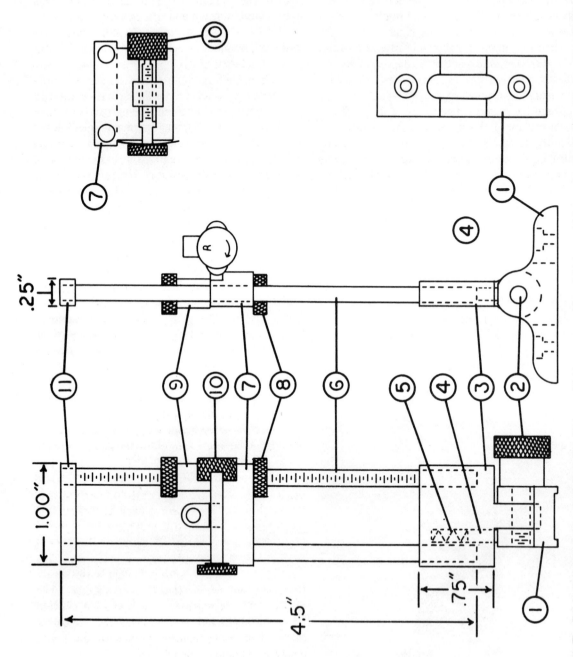

Fig. 12-13. The F.D.H. Schuetzen tang sight. Parts list: (1) base, (2) hinge screw, (3) upright base, (4) base plunger (2), (5) plunger spring (2), (6) uprights (2), (7) elevation slide, (8), (9) elevation adj. nuts, (10) brace, (11) top bar.

sight is described and illustrated in Chapter 9.

The second method is to make the elevation slide with a simple windage adjustment, the details of which are shown and described in the following part on the F.D.H. Hunter tang sight.

The third method is shown in Figs. 12-12 and 12-13. With this method, the windage arm and its parts, removed from a Lyman No. 57 or similar receiver sight (as is necessary to do when making a windgauge front sight mentioned earlier), is attached by silver-soldering to the elevation slide. If the windage arm is from a Lyman No. 57 sight it may be necessary to brace the sawed-off end with a small piece of steel (10 in the drawing). The result is a click adjustment for windage and a ready-made holder for a sighting disc.

The key in the assembly and disassembly of this sight is the unthreaded upright; it is the last part to assemble and the first part to remove when disassembling.

The F.D.H. Hunter tang sight (Figs. 12-14, 12-15) is somewhat similar to the Schuetzen tang sight just described except that it is of simplier design and construction and therefore easier to make. In making it you can get along without a milling machine but you do need an accurate drill

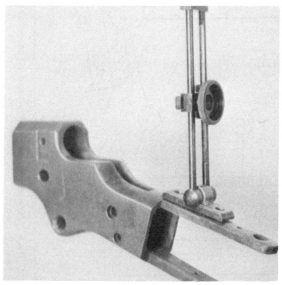

Fig. 12-14. The F.D.H. Hunter tang sight mounted on a Stevens No. 44 receiver.

press and a small lathe. It has the twin round uprights with one threaded nearly its entire length. Its base is very simple and quite easily made. This sight can be made any height and with or without windage adjustment. I wonder why someone has not made a sight like it before; maybe someone has but I've never heard of it.

Make the base (1) about as shown. The hole through it for the pivot base (2) must be square with it and preferably reamed to size for a smooth close fit. A base long enough to space the uprights ½" apart is a good choice, although the uprights can be spaced closer for small rifles. I would recommend ⅜" as the minimum diameter for the pivot base.

For this sight I would recommend 9/64" diameter drill rod uprights (5) and 40 pitch threads. The threads can be cut with an 8×40 die and tap. Use a piece of drill rod for the pivot base and drill and tap the two holes for the uprights square and true to each other and to the base. The holes must also be spaced correctly so that when the uprights are in place they fit snug against the base. An alternate method of fastening the uprights in the pivot base would be to drill the holes all the way through and drill and tap a small hole for a socket head set screw in the ends of the pivot base to hold the uprights in place.

Thread the uprights as shown. Make the top bar (10), accurately spacing the tapped holes the same as the upright holes in the pivot base. One of the holes in the top bar must be threaded. Make the two elevation adjustment nuts (9) as shown. The elevation slide (6) can be made from ⅜" square stock, wide and long enough for the properly spaced upright holes. The slide can then be drilled and tapped to accept the aperture sighting disc if you do not want an adjustment for windage. However, I would suggest doing a bit more work to provide a windage adjustment as shown. All that is needed is a horizontal slot made in the elevation slide between the two upright holes and windage slide (7) into which the sighting disc is threaded. You can elaborate on this arrangement and provide the slide with a screw adjustment for windage.

Finding a commercially-made sighting disc of large diameter will be difficult, so you may have to

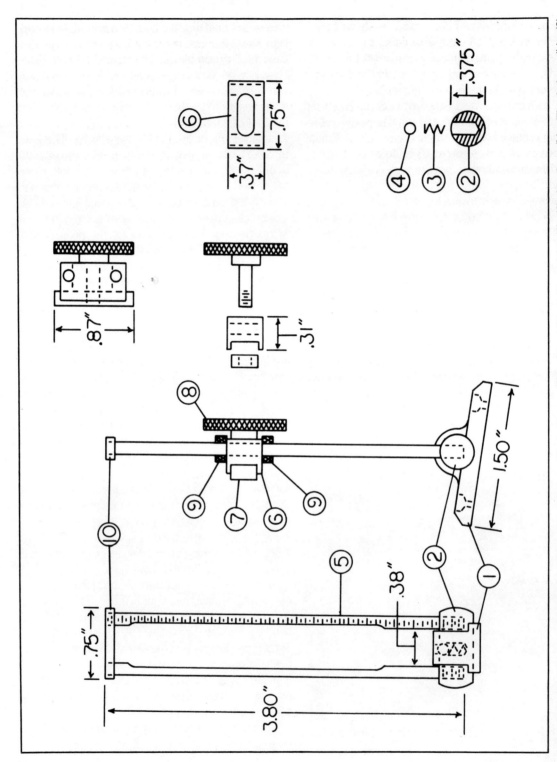

Fig. 12-15. The F.D.H. Hunter tang sight. Parts list: (1) base, (2) pivot base, (3) spring, (4) ball, (5) uprights (2), (6) elevation slide, (7) windage slide, (8) aperture disk, (9) elevation nuts (2), (10) top bar.

make one. In this case make it about as shown in the drawing with a 3/16×32 threaded stem.

A small spring (3) and plunger (4) are fitted into the pivot base of the uprights to hold the sight in the upright shooting position and at a 90 degree angle to the bore. Mount the sight on the rifle you intend to use it on and using a square, position the uprights square with the top of the receiver. Then, without moving the uprights, remove the sight from the rifle, disassemble the uprights from the piv-

ot base and drill a 3/32″ hole through the base and pivot base. Remove the pivot base and enlarge the hole to ⅛″ almost all the way through. A ball bearing can be used for the plunger. The completed sight is here shown mounted on a Stevens No. 44 receiver.

The key to disassembling this sight as well as reassembling it is the unthreaded upright. In disassembling, this part is removed first; in reassembling it, it is the last part.

Index

Edited by Steven Mesner